Conversational KOREAN GRAMMAR

Created by Katarina Pollock and Chelsea Guerra

GOOSE APPLE
BOOKS

Conversational Korean Grammar by Katarina Pollock and Chelsea Guerra

Published by Gooseapple Books, LLC
209 Archer Street
Houston, TX, 77009
www.gooseapplebooks.com

Copyright © 2022 Katarina Pollock, Chelsea Guerra

All rights reserved. No portion of this book may be reproduced in any form without permission from the publisher, except as permitted by U.S. copyright law. For permissions contact: support@gooseapple-books.com

Cover and illustrations by 김유진.
Proof-reading by 백은경

ISBN: 978-1-7376777-4-1 (print)

Printed in the United States of America

Edition 4.1

A big
thank you
to all the people who
contributed to this book.
Especially 김유진
and 백은경

정말 감사합니다

GOOSE APPLE
BOOKS

INTRODUCTION

Table of Contents
To Conversational Korean Grammar

INTRODUCTION 8
- The Korean Language 12
- Korean Grammar 14
- Korean Word Order 15
- Grammatical Particles 16
- Dropping Subjects 18
- Agglutinative Verbs 19
- Honorifics in Korean 21
- Naver Dictionary 24
- Papago 25

LEVEL ONE A 26
- ~은/는 Topic Particle 29
- ~이/가 Subject Particle 31
- ~을/를 Object Particle 33
- 제가/저는/제 35
- "You" in Korean 37
- Asking Questions in Korean 38
- N~이에요/예요 39
- N~(이/가) 아니에요 40
- Present Tense ~아/어요 42
- Present Tense ~아/어요 45
- 하다 Verbs 49
- ~이/가 + Descriptive Verbs 51
- ~을/를 + Action Verbs 53

LEVEL ONE B 55
- A/V~았/었다 Past Tense 58
- A/V~(으)ㄹ 것이다 Future Tense 60
- 안 A/V 61
- A/V~지 않다 63

- 못 V 65
- V~지 못 하다 67
- V~는 것 69
- Place~에 가다/오다 71
- Place~(으)로 73
- Time~에 V 74
- N~에 V 76
- N~에서 & N~까지 77
- N~부터 & N~까지 78
- N~에서 Particle 80
- N~들 82
- N~도 83
- N~만 85

LEVEL TWO 87
- The ㅂ Irregular 90
- V~고 싶다 93
- N~와/과, N~(이)랑, N~하고 96
- 잘 & 잘 못 V 99
- A~ㄴ/은/는 N 100
- V~고 있다 102
- 아직 104
- 누구, 무엇, 언제, 어디, 왜 & 어떻게 106
- 그리고, 그래서 & 하지만 107
- A/V~고 N~(이)고 108
- A/V~지만, N~(이)지만 112
- A/V~아/어서 N(이)라서 115
- Words of Frequency 118
- 더 & 덜 119
- N~보다 120
- N~(으)로 122

보통, 주로 & 평소에	123
A/V~(으)면	125
V~기 시작하다	127
처음(으로)	128

LEVEL THREE 129

A/V~ㄹ/을 때, N 때	132
V~(으)면서, N(이)면서	135
V~(으)며	137
V~는 동안, N 동안	139
V~거나, N(이)나	141
N~의	142
가장 & 제일	143
V~는 N	144
V~(으)ㄴ N	145
V~(으)ㄹ N	146
V~아/어 보다	147
V~(으)ㄴ 적이 있다/없다	149
N 때문에	151
A/V~기 때문에	153
V~(으)ㄹ 수 있다/없다	155
A/V~았/었으면 좋겠다	157
N~께/에게/한테	159
V~(으)세요	162
A/V~지 마세요	163
V~아/어 주다	165

LEVEL FOUR 167

Banmal (반말)	169
A/V~(스)ㅂ니다	172
A/V~ㄴ다/는다/다	175
V~(으)려고 [하다]	177
V~다가, V~았/었다가	180
V~기 전에	183
V~(으)ㄴ 후에/다음에	184
V ~(으)ㄹ 줄 알다/모르다	186

V~아/어야 하다/되다	189
N~처럼	191
N~마다	192
A/V~아/어도, N(이)라도	193
A~아/어지다	195
V~게 되다	197
V~은/는/을 것 같다	199
A/V~(ㄴ/는)다고 생각하다	204
N 중에(서)	207
A~게/이/히	209
V~기	211
N~에 대해(서)	213
V~는 대신(에), N 대신(에)	215

LEVEL FIVE 216

A/V~겠다	218
V~기 위해(서) N 위해(서)	222
A/V~(으)ㄹ까(요)	225
A/V~잖다 N(이)잖다	228
A/V~죠/지(요), N(이)죠/지요	231
A/V~네(요), N(이)네요	234
A/V~더라고(요)	236
A/V~(으)ㄴ/는 편이다	238
A/V~거든(요)	240
A/V ~(으)ㄴ/는/~(으)ㄹ지	243
A/V~ㄴ/는다면, N(이)라면	246
A/V~(으)ㄹ 정도(로)	249
V~(으)러 가다/오다	251
A/V~기도 하다, N이기도 하다	253
A/V~(으)ㄴ/는데	255
V~던 N	259
A/V~았/었던 N	261
A~구나, V~는구나, N~(이)구나	263
A~(으)ㄴ 가요? V~나요?	266
A/V~(으)니까	269
"N"~(이)라는 N	273

INTRODUCTION

APPENDIX	274
The Topic & Subject Particles	276
Clausal Verb Tenses	280
Passive & Active Verbs	282
Small Numbers in Korean	284
Large Numbers in Korean	285
Korean Counters	286
Words for Times & Dates	287
Words for People	288
Honorific Vocabulary	290
Common Expressions	291
ㄷ Irregular	292
ㅅ Irregular	293
ㅇ Irregular	294
르 Irregular	295
ㄹ Irregular	296

Want Practice Exercises?

CHECK OUT OUR WORKBOOKS

1
CONVERSATIONAL KOREAN FOR BEGINNERS
A book for beginner learners
Create sentences about yourself and your life
Understand conversational language
Reading, writing, and listening practice

2
CONVERSATIONAL KOREAN GRAMMAR WORKBOOK
The workbook to accompany Conversational Korean Grammar. Contains reading, writing, and listening exercises to accompany each lesson.

Introduction

To the Korean Language

Introduction

What we will learn

The Korean Language 12
Korean Grammar..14
Korean Word Order..15
Grammatical Particles 16
Dropping Subjects 18
Agglutinative Verbs 19
Honorifics in Korean 21
Naver Dictionary 24
Papago 25

Introduction

Welcome!

Book overview

THE AIM OF THIS BOOK
To introduce all the grammar you need in order to use the *Writing Conversational Korean* Series and beyond.

WHAT IS THE WRITING CONVERSATIONAL KOREAN SERIES?
Writing Conversational Korean is a workbook series where you practice Korean using writing prompts. Each workbook has about 250 different writing prompts collected into themed chapters, such as "food," "nature," and "travel." Each writing prompt has space allocated for you to write your own answer, with the aid of some suggested vocabulary. Each chapter also has answers written by native speakers for you to read, and YouTube videos made by native speakers for you to watch. We recommend *Writing Conversational Korean* for intermediate and advanced learners who already have a working knowledge of Korean grammar and vocabulary.

NO PRIOR KNOWLEDGE REQUIRED
This book is appropriate for complete beginners. It aims to teach **everything** you need to get you started on your Korean learning journey. However, learning to read and write is not the primary focus of this book. Although we do give a brief explanation to the Korean alphabet and writing system, if you are completely new to the Korean alphabet (한글), we recommend you also check resources online. There are lots of free resources available to give more detailed information.

WHAT THIS BOOK INCLUDES
This book includes about 110 grammar forms in total, spread over five Levels of short grammar lessons. Each grammar lesson teaches one grammar form. The grammar lessons include a short description, the grammar conjugation rules, and some example sentences. When applicable, the grammar form is also contrasted with other similar grammar forms to explain their differences.

Note: this book does **not include practice exercises**. This book is designed to be a grammar reference guide to use alongside other language learning materials, including other books in the *Writing Conversational Korean* Series.

INTRODUCTION

WHAT TO EXPECT IN THIS BOOK
This book is designed to follow and grow alongside you on your language learning journey. The first couple of chapters start with the very basics. As you progress, you slowly add in more grammar and vocabulary, taking you from a beginner level at the start of the book, to an intermediate level by the end of the book. At first, you will learn how to write very simple sentences, but as the book progresses, you will learn the various tools needed to create more developed and nuanced sentences.

HOW TO USE THIS BOOK
1 As a grammar reference guide
2 Alongside other language materials (including *Writing Conversational Korean*)
3 You do not have to read this book in chronological order (although you are welcome to)

WHAT IS THIS SYMBOL?
 463 times

This symbol appears on some grammar pages to show the number of times that the grammar form was used over all the content in *Writing Conversational Korean*.

How did we calculate this number?
We took all the content from *Writing Conversational Korean* (the writing prompts and the example answers from native speakers) and put it all into one big file. This file has over 35,000 words, all written by native Korean speakers using conversational language. In this file, we used search tools to find the number of occurrences of each specific grammar form.

What's the point of this number?
The point of this number is to add some gravity and weight to the concepts you are learning, and to emphasize their importance and usefulness in real Korean. To some extent, you can also use this number to compare and contrast similar grammar forms.

Note: we only included counts for grammar forms when we could reliably do so. Some forms are not easily isolated, and therefore their count was not included.
Note: this count **does not necessarily** represent the true frequency of these grammar forms used in the Korean language. The grammar used depended on the writing prompts that were asked, and because *Writing Conversational Korean* uses written language, the grammar count favors written forms.

Introduction

The Korean Language

An introduction to the Korean language & alphabet

Korean is the most widely spoken **language isolate** in the world, meaning that it is a language that is unrelated to any others - although it has received influences from Chinese, Japanese, and, in more recent times, English. It is spoken by approximately 80 million people, mostly in North Korea and South Korea. It is also spoken in parts of Russia, China, and south-east Asia.

THE KOREAN ALPHABET (한글)

Modern Korean is written using Hangul (한글), a simplified alphabet developed by King Sejong in the 15th century. Modern Hangul uses 24 basic letters and 27 complex letters.

Regular Consonants | Aspirated Consonants

ㄱ	ㄴ	ㄷ	ㄹ	ㅁ	ㅂ	ㅅ	ㅇ	ㅈ	ㅎ	ㅊ	ㅋ	ㅌ	ㅍ
기역	니은	디귿	리을	미음	비읍	시옷	이응	지읒	히읗	치읓	키읔	티읕	피읖
g/k	n	d	r/l	m	p/b	s	ng	j	h	ch	k	t	p

Double Consonants (Tense Consonants)

ㄲ	ㄸ	ㅃ	ㅆ	ㅉ
쌍기역	쌍디귿	쌍비읍	쌍시옷	쌍지읒
gg/kk	dd	bb/pp	ss	jj

Vertical Vowels | Horizontal Vowels

ㅏ	ㅑ	ㅓ	ㅕ	ㅣ	ㅗ	ㅛ	ㅜ	ㅠ	ㅡ
아	야	어	여	이	오	요	우	유	으
ah	ya	eo	yeo	i/ee	oh	yo	oo	yu	eu

Combination Vowels

ㅔ	ㅐ	ㅖ	ㅒ	ㅘ	ㅝ	ㅙ	ㅞ	ㅚ	ㅟ	ㅢ
eh	ae	yeh	yah	wa	weo	wah	weh	way	wii	ooe

Note: to listen to these sounds being pronounced, and for pronunciation guides, we highly recommend checking out videos online. The phonetic English equivalent is often a poor substitute.

INTRODUCTION

SYLLABLE BLOCKS

Korean symbols/letters are **not used on their own**, but combined into **blocks**. These blocks are pronounced as one **syllable**. Different symbols combine in different ways to create different syllables.

Legend

C = Regular Consonant | FC = Final Consonant* | V V = Vertical Vowel | HV = Horizontal Vowel

1
가, 다, 나, 라
거, 더, 너, 러

2
고, 도, 노, 로
구, 두, 누, 루

3
괴, 되, 뇌, 뢰
궈, 둬, 눠, 뤄

4
간, 단, 난, 란
걸, 덜, 널, 럴

5
곤, 돈, 논, 론
굴, 둘, 눌, 룰

6
괸, 된, 뇐, 뢴
궐, 될, 눨, 뤨

7
값, 잃, 읽, 잖, 많

8
곪, 굶, 뚫

9
웠, 왔, 괜

* Final consonants are consonants on the **bottom** of a syllable block. They are called 받침 (bat-chim) and they play an important role in Korean grammar. Keep this in mind for later!

Note: the top two rows of syllable blocks (1-6) are the most commonly encountered. 7, 8, and 9 are fairly uncommon. For more practice forming syllable blocks, check for activities online.

Introduction

Korean Grammar

Five things to know

Here are the **first five things** we believe are important to know about the Korean language when you're just starting out. We'll introduce them briefly in this chapter, and focus in more detail later on.

KOREAN WORD ORDER (SOV)
The sentence order for Korean is: Subject - Object - Verb (SOV)
This means when you speak Korean, the verb comes at the **end** of the sentence.
Korean (SOV): I apple eat.   English (SVO): I eat (an) apple.

KOREAN GRAMMATICAL PARTICLES
Korean uses particles to create grammatical structure. They attach to nouns and function as markers, helping identify what role the word they're attached to plays in the sentence (i.e. whether the noun is the subject, the object, etc). We go into more detail about particles in later chapters.

KOREAN DOES NOT NEED SUBJECTS
A sentence subject is who (or what) is performing some action or receiving some description. Unlike English, Korean does **not** need to include a subject to create a complete sentence. Korean people naturally and comfortably assume subjects from context, so subjects are frequently dropped from Korean sentences, while still maintaining the original meaning and remaining grammatically correct.

KOREAN HONORIFICS
Honorifics play a major role in both Korean culture and Korean language. In Korean society, it is important to show respect to one's elders and superiors by using honorific language. There are many different language formality levels in Korean.

AGGLUTINATIVE VERBS IN KOREAN
Korean is an agglutinative language, which means the verbs have a base morpheme that can be conjugated by sticking one or more grammatical suffixes onto the base morpheme.
For example: 먹다 = to eat, 먹어요 = I eat (present tense), 먹었어요 = I ate (past tense).

REFERENCE PAGES
Korean Word Order - page 15   Dropping Subjects - page 18
Grammatical Particles - page 16   Honorifics in Korean - page 21

Korean Word Order

How you should order words in a sentence

SOV SENTENCE STRUCTURE

Korean follows an SOV grammatical structure. (Subject - Object - Verb). In an SOV sentence structure, sentences are formed with the **subject** of the verb coming first, followed by the **object** of the verb, and then the **verb** itself coming last.

Note: Subjects, objects, verbs, etc. are universal concepts present in languages worldwide. Understanding the difference between sentence subjects and objects in English will help you form sentences in Korean.

메리가	사과를	먹어요.
[Subject]	[Object]	[Verb]
Mary	Apple	Eat

What is a subject?
The subject of the sentence is who or what is **performing some action** or receiving some description. In the sentence above, the **subject** is "Mary" (메리).

What is an object?
The object of the sentence is who or what is **receiving some action.** In the sentence above, the **object** is "apple" (사과).

What is a verb?
The verb of the sentence is the **action** that is being performed. In the sentence above, the **verb** is "eat" (먹어요).

What is the "가" and "를?"
These are Korean **grammatical particles**. We will learn more about them on the next page.

SENTENCE STRUCTURE RIGIDITY

In English, we have a fairly rigid sentence structure. We can't move words around in a sentence without changing the overall meaning or making it grammatically incorrect. But Korean is **not** like this - the sentence structure in Korean is fairly loose, so words can change position easily and with little to no change in meaning. This is possible thanks to Korean particles (see next page).

Note: Worldwide, the SOV grammatical structure (the one used in Korean) is actually more common in languages than the English SVO structure.

Introduction

Grammatical Particles

A quick introduction to particles

In English, we denote the subjects and objects of verbs by noticing their placement in the sentence. Because of this, the order of words in English is very important. In English, you cannot rearrange words in a sentence without changing the sentence's meaning.
However, **Korean does not work this way.** Korean uses **particles** to denote what part of the sentence a noun is - for example, which nouns are the subject and object of the verb. Because of this, as long as nouns are not separated from their designated particles, words in Korean sentences **can be written in almost any order**, and the meaning of the sentence **does not change**.

SUBJECT PARTICLE:
The subject particle is written either as **~이 or ~가**, and it follows directly after the noun.
~이 and ~가 are two halves of the same whole - they are identical in meaning.
The subject particle shows that the noun it is attached to is the **subject** of the sentence.
In the example sentence on the previous page, the particle ~가 is attached to the noun "Mary" to show that she is the subject of the sentence.
Note: like ~이/가, many grammatical concepts in Korean have two forms. The duality exists purely to make pronunciation easier. You will learn more about this in later chapters.

OBJECT PARTICLE:
The object particle is written either as **~을 or ~를**, and it follows directly after the noun.
~을 and ~를 are two halves of the same whole - they are identical in meaning.
The object particle shows that the noun is the **object** of the sentence.
In the example sentence on the previous page, the particle ~를 is attached to the noun "apple" to show that it is the object of the sentence.

{
~이/가 is the Korean **subject particle**
~을/를 is the Korean **object particle**
}

INTRODUCTION

KOREAN PARTICLES HAVE NO MEANING ON THEIR OWN
Korean particles **can't exist** as stand-alone words. They are **not** equivalent to "a/an," "the," "is," or any other word. They are a concept specific to the Korean language with no English equivalent.

KOREAN PARTICLES ARE LIKE FLAGS
A good way to think of Korean particles is this: whenever you see a particle attached to a noun, imagine that noun is holding a little flag. The noun is waving it's flag at you - the flag being the particle - and it's telling you it's role in the sentence.

KOREAN PARTICLES ARE NOT STRICTLY REQUIRED
When the subject and object are clear from context, it is common to drop the attached particle - particularly when speaking. For example, the sentence "메리가 사과를 먹어요" could be said as: "메리 사과 먹어요." The particles are clear from context and there is no ambiguity in this sentence because apples cannot eat people. However, it is still good practice to use particles, especially as a beginner.

DO NOT BE AFRAID OF PARTICLES
A common beginner trap is to drop the particle because you're afraid of using the wrong one. They might seem difficult at first, but it's important to practice using them. Particles exist to make your life easier, not harder (though it may not feel like it at first). In time, using the right particle in your sentences **will become second-nature**.

WE WILL PRACTICE USING PARTICLES SOON
Don't worry too much about the specifics of ~이/가 and ~을/를 right now, we will do more practice later! The main point for you to understand about particles right now is that they **drive the relationships between the subjects, objects, and verbs in a sentence.**

Note: Japanese, Hebrew, and Romanian also use some grammatical particles.

INTRODUCTION

Dropping Subjects
An introduction to dropping subjects

This is a topic that often confuses Korean learners. There are two main things you need to know:

1 SUBJECTS ARE NOT REQUIRED
In fact, they are often dropped from the sentence when the speaker believes the subject is clear from context. Native English speakers often find this difficult to get used to, because subjects are always required in English sentences.

English (needs subjects)	Korean (does not need subjects)
I/you/we/they eat an apple.	(optional subject) 사과를 먹어요.
He/she/it eats an apple.	(optional subject) 사과를 먹어요.

Note: as you can see, the sentence "사과를 먹어요" can imply "any subject (I/you/he/she/they... etc.) eats an apple." The subject is not required in the sentence and can be assumed from context.

2 SUBJECTS ARE OFTEN ASSUMED FROM CONTEXT
For example, imagine you're having a conversation with someone in Korean. If that person looks at you and says, "사과를 먹어요?" you know they're asking "do **you** eat apples?," even though the word "you" is not explicitly stated in the sentence. Likewise, If someone points at someone else and says to you, "사과를 먹어요?" you know it means "does **he/she/they** eat apples?" And so on. When the context of the situation is clear, it's often **more natural** to drop the subject from the sentence.

Do misunderstandings happen? Well, yes, sometimes! This is a well-used miscommunication trope in Korean dramas or stories. But it works fine most of the time.

> { *If you want to make sure the meaning of your sentence is understood, you can always include a subject if you wish to.* }

Note: Korean technically has words for "he," "she," "they," etc. (and they are frequently taught in beginner books and language apps) but they are rarely used in actual Korean.

Agglutinative Verbs

Introducing agglutinative verbs

Korean verbs have a base morpheme (also known as the **verb stem**) which can then be conjugated into different forms by attaching a wide variety of suffixes onto the end of that verb stem. These suffixes can also stack together to create longer and longer suffixes, adding nuance, and slightly changing the meaning each time. You can imagine Korean verbs like trains, where the locomotive is the base morpheme and the train cars attach one by one onto the first car to add extra meaning.

Verb Stem   Verb/Grammar Conjugations

먹다 = to eat (dictionary form)
먹 = base morpheme of the verb (the **verb stem**)
먹어요 = I eat
먹었어요 = I ate
먹고 싶어요 = I want to eat
먹고 싶었어요 = I wanted to eat
먹고 싶지 않아요 = I don't want to eat
먹고 싶지 않았어요 = I didn't want to eat

Note: don't worry about the verb conjugations going on here. We will learn how to do all of these conjugations (and many more) in the pages ahead.

The key thing to notice is that in all of the above examples, there is one base morpheme (먹) that forms the foundation of all the conjugations.
This base morpheme comes from the dictionary form of the verb 먹다 (to eat).

Note: other agglutinative languages include Hungarian, Turkish, Indonesian, Native American languages, Mongolian, and even Klingon.

INTRODUCTION

THE DICTIONARY FORM
All Korean verbs exist in a form known as **the dictionary form.** This is the form you will encounter if you look up a verb in a language dictionary. All verbs in their dictionary forms end in -다.

먹다	살다	좋다	공부하다	재미있다
To eat	To live	To be good	To study	To be fun

Verbs in their dictionary forms **are not usable** in a sentence. They have to be conjugated first. There are many different verb conjugations one can perform in Korean, but the first step of almost any verb conjugation is to find the **verb stem**.

THE VERB STEM
The verb stem is important because finding the verb stem is almost always the first step one takes when doing verb conjugations in Korean. To find the verb stem, simply remove "-다" from the dictionary form.

먹다	살다	좋다	공부하다	재미있다
먹	살	좋	공부하	재미있

Similarly to the dictionary form, the verb stems by themselves **are not useable** in a sentence. They must be conjugated using some kind of verb ending attachment.

You can imagine the verb stem of a verb being like a verb in "pairing mode." It isn't usable yet, but it's ready and waiting for a connection to take place. The verb stem of a verb is like the head of a train waiting for train cars to be attached to it.

KOREAN GRAMMAR CONJUGATIONS
Grammar conjugations in Korean **also** often end in -다. Grammar conjugations can be added and connected together by using -다 as the connecting piece for adding on another verb conjugation.

For example, let's take our verb "먹다," and add some grammar conjugations to it.
1 "-고 싶다" is a grammar form meaning "to want to do something."
   "먹고 싶다" therefore means, "to want to eat something."
2 "-지 않다" is a grammar form meaning, "to not do something."
   먹고 싶지 않다 therefore means, "to not want to eat something."
The -다 on the end of " 먹고 싶지 않다" is also waiting for another verb conjugation to be added.

INTRODUCTION

Honorifics in Korean

What honorifics are and why they are important

Honorifics play a major role in the Korean language. In English, formality is mostly coded in the vocabulary, but in Korean, it is mostly coded in the grammar. In fact, you cannot conjugate verbs (and therefore cannot create sentences) in Korean without choosing some level of formality to use. To choose the level of formality in Korean, you attach a certain ending to your verb conjugation.

There are four main formality ending types, each showing different levels of formality. You will probably use all of these forms at some point in your Korean learning journey.

ONE: ~(스)ㅂ니다 FORM - a formal ending used in formal writing, official announcements, and other formal or professional situations like job interviews, presentations, weddings, funerals, etc.

TWO: ~아/어요 FORM - a casual polite form commonly used in spoken language between people who are being polite to each other. This can be considered as the **default** level of formality in Korean interactions. You will probably use this form in most situations. It is polite, but not overly formal.

THREE: ~아/어 FORM - also called 반말, or banmal, (literally "half-speaking") - is used casually between people that have a close relationship. It is also used when talking to yourself, to people younger than you, and to animals. It is not polite at all, so if used inappropriately it can be awkward at best and offensive at worst.

FOUR: ~ㄴ/는다 FORM - also called the plain form. It is commonly used in writing where formality does not apply because there is no relationship between the writer and reader. For example: in novels, newspapers, diaries, journals, and exams.

{ *Because this book focuses on conversational language, we will predominantly use the* **~아/어요 Form** *in this book.* }

REFERENCE PAGES

A/V~(스)ㅂ니다 - page 172
Present Tense ~아/어요 - page 45

Banmal (반말) - page 169
A/V~ㄴ/는다면, N(이)라면 - page 246

INTRODUCTION

WHY THE FORMALITY RULES?
The rules behind honorifics and formality levels are complex and rooted in Korean society and culture. In Confucian, Taoist, and Chinese Buddhist ethics, filial piety is a virtue of respect for one's parents, elders, and ancestors. In Korean, you **show respect to your elders and superiors** by speaking in formal language. Speaking in casual language - while it can be a sign of closeness in some situations - can also be a sign of disrespect in others.

The basic rule is that if someone is your "social superior," you should use formal language (known as 존댓말 or 높임말), and if someone is your "social inferior" or "social equal," you can use casual language (반말). There are many factors that come into play when determining this ranking, such as: age, knowledge and experience, the closeness of the relationship, social standing, and social expectations. Not only this, but each situation is different, and different people have different preferences when it comes to formality.

WHICH FORMALITY LEVEL SHOULD I USE?
As a foreigner, it's always good to err on the side of caution. Our recommendation to you is thus: When in doubt, speak formally and politely: ~(스)ㅂ니다 ending in professional writing, and ~아/어요 or ~(스)ㅂ니다 when speaking.

WHAT IF I USE THE WRONG LEVEL OF FORMALITY?
Generally speaking, native Korean speakers are quite forgiving of language errors when it comes to Korean learners. Korean people know that English doesn't have language formality the same way that Korean does, so if you make a mistake and use the wrong level of formality, it's not the end of the world. That being said, it's always good to **aim to be respectful**.

Here is a quick list of situations where you can use casual language and formal language.

Situations where you can use casual language (반말):
1. Speaking to young children
2. Speaking to animals
3. When talking to yourself
4. When someone tells you that you can

Situations where you should use formal language (존댓말 / 높임말):
1. Talking to people on the street
2. Talking to your Korean teacher
3. When meeting someone for the first time
4. Ordering at a restaurant
(And many others)

HONORIFICS USED IN *WRITING CONVERSATIONAL KOREAN*

In the Writing Conversational Korean series, native speakers were asked to answer various writing prompts in their own words. So what level of formality did they choose to use?

To answer this, we took a random sample of 55 answers and determined their formality level. Keep in mind that these answers were collected in written form, so this count will likely have a higher proportion of written forms (~(스)ㅂ니다 and ~ㄴ/는다) compared to the spoken forms (~아/어요 and ~아/어).

Formality Level	Usage Count	Percentage
~아/어요 Casual Polite	29	53%
~(스)ㅂ니다 Honorific	14	25%
~아/어 Banmal	6	11%
~ㄴ다/는다/다 Plain Form	6	11%

We will learn all four of these formality levels in time, starting with the most common conversational form "~아/어요" in Level One A. To learn about the others, you can jump ahead to Level Four. See reference pages below.

REFERENCE PAGES

Present Tense ~아/어요 - page 45
A/V~(스)ㅂ니다 - page 172

Banmal (반말) - page 169
A/V~ㄴ/는다면, N(이)라면 - page 246

Introduction

Naver Dictionary

Recommended dictionary

A good dictionary is an essential tool for any language learner. We recommend that you use **Naver Dictionary,** a free tool provided by the Korean company, *Naver.*

We recommend Naver for these main reasons:
1 It's generally accurate and reliable
2 It's highly informative
3 It has a large bank of example sentences to refer to

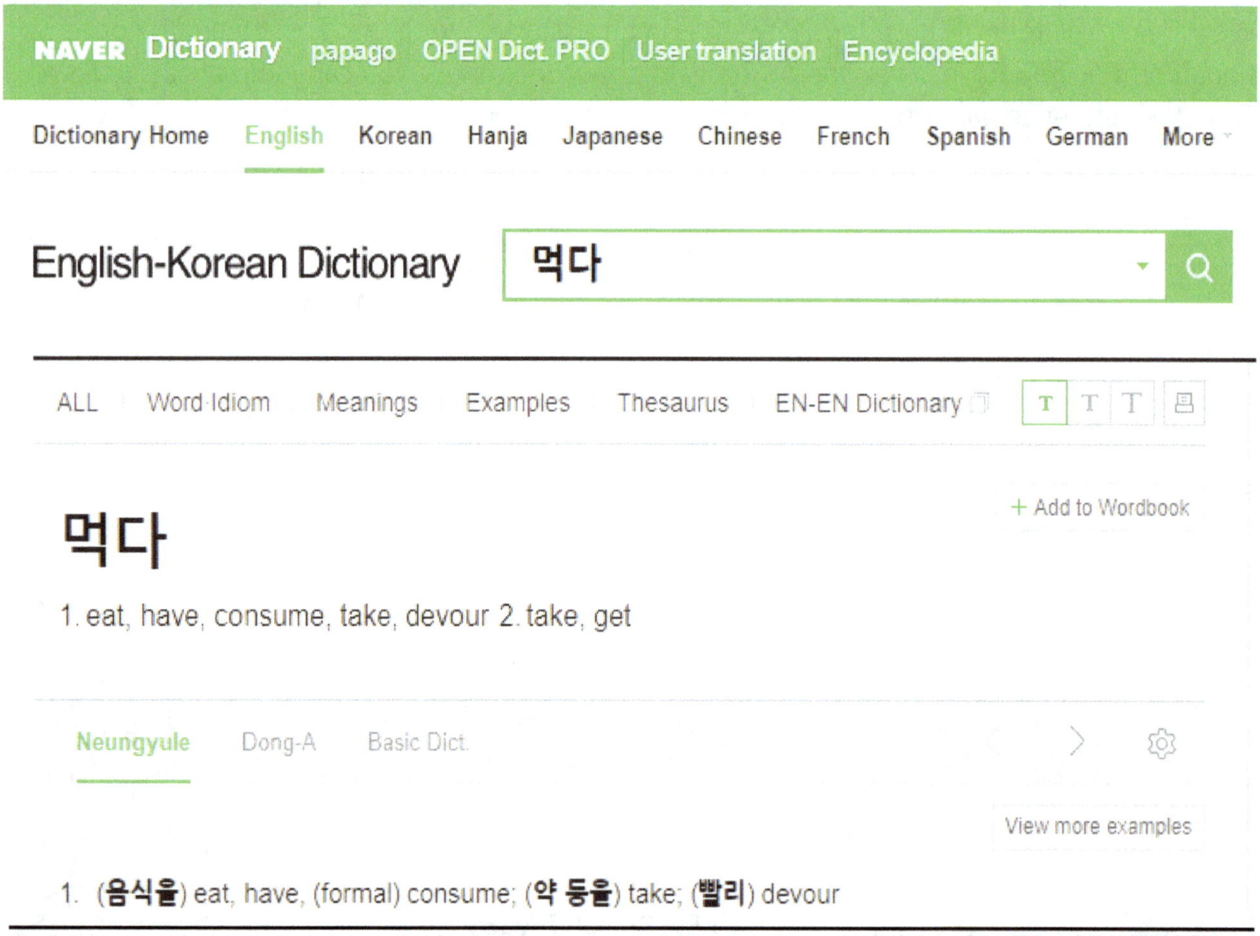

| NAVER Dictionary | papago | OPEN Dict. PRO | User translation | Encyclopedia |

Dictionary Home | **English** | Korean | Hanja | Japanese | Chinese | French | Spanish | German | More

English-Korean Dictionary   [먹다]

ALL | Word·Idiom | Meanings | Examples | Thesaurus | EN-EN Dictionary

먹다   + Add to Wordbook

1. eat, have, consume, take, devour 2. take, get

Neungyule   Dong-A   Basic Dict.

View more examples

1. (음식을) eat, have, (formal) consume; (약 등을) take; (빨리) devour

Papago

Recommended translator

If you need to translate something, we recommend *Papago*. This is also a Naver product that is free to use.

Benefits of using *Papago*:

1 Generally good translations for simple sentences
2 An option to select honorific or casual language for your translation
3 A vocabulary breakdown is included below the translation
4 The vocabulary breakdown links directly to *Naver Dictionary*

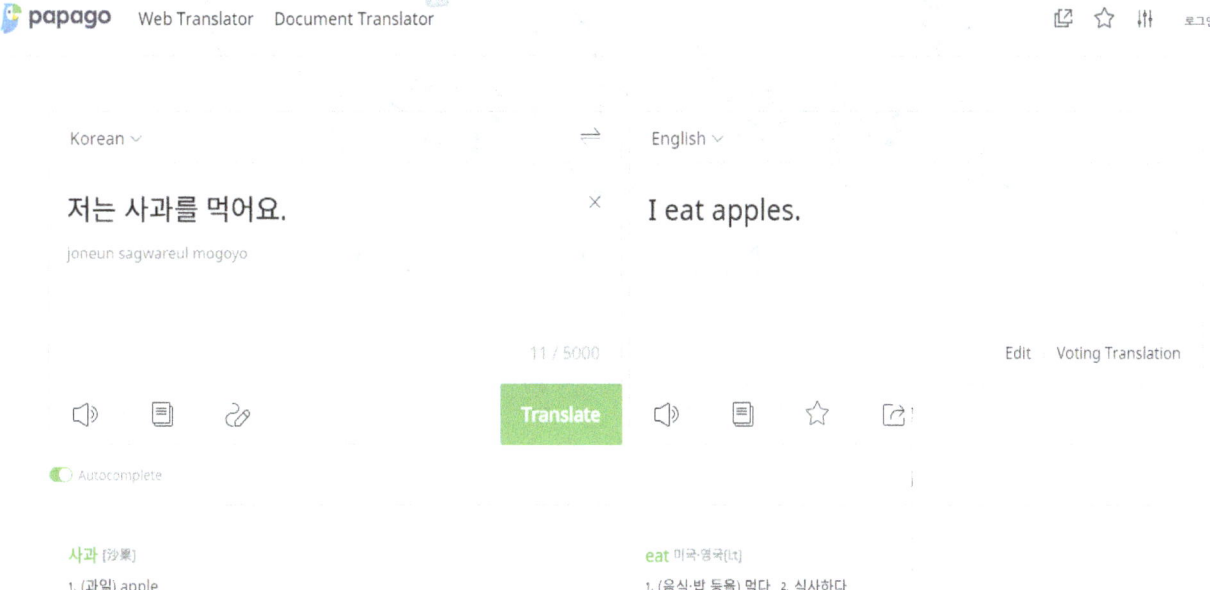

WHAT ABOUT GOOGLE TRANSLATE?

Google Translate is another good, freely available option. For short, simple sentences, both *Papago* and *Google Translate* are generally adequate. In our personal experience with longer, more complex texts, *Papago* provides slightly more natural English → Korean translations, and *Google Translate* provides slightly more natural Korean → English translations. This is not a rule, just our general personal observation.

Level One A

GETTING STARTED

DIFFICULTY LEVEL: EASY
The example sentences are written using simple grammar and vocabulary designed to help you understand the grammar concept in the most accessible way.

Level One A Grammar

What we will learn

"한국어 문법을 공부하자!"
"Let's study Korean grammar!"

~은/는 Topic Particle	29
~이/가 Subject Particle	31
~을/를 Object Particle	33
제가/저는/제	35
"You" in Korean	37
Asking Questions in Korean	38
N~이에요/예요	39
N~(이/가) 아니에요	40
Present Tense ~아/어요	42
Present Tense ~아/어요	45
하다 Verbs	49
~이/가 + Descriptive Verbs	51
~을/를 + Action Verbs	53

Note: the lessons in Level 1A cover the essential components of basic Korean grammar. **You should know all of the content in this Level** before moving on to the later Levels of the book. While any lesson in this book can be referenced at any time, we highly recommend that you go through this Level sequentially first. Once you are familiar with the content in Level 1A, please feel free to jump around the book to reference and learn additional grammar forms as you need them.

Level One A Vocab

What we will learn

한국어 어휘를 배우자!
Let's learn Korean vocabulary!

NOUNS
빵 - bread
샐러드 - salad
아이스크림 - icecream
저 - I/me/the concept of self
사과 - apple
피자 - pizza
고기 - meat
채소 - vegetables
친구 - friend
엄마 - mom
아빠 - dad
네 - yes
아니요 - no
이것 - this (thing)
그것 - that (thing)
사람 - person
음식 - food
물 - water
한국 - Korea
미국 - America

한국어 - Korean language
영어 - English language

DESCRIPTIVE VERBS
좋다 - to be good/nice; to be liked
맛있다 - to taste delicious
맛없다 - to taste disgusting
이다 - to be
아니다 - to not be

ACTION VERBS
먹다 - to eat
공부하다 - to study
요리하다 - to cook
좋아하다 - to like
운동하다 - to work out; to exercise

Use flashcards on Quizlet!

Note: This is a list of all the main vocabulary you will encounter in the upcoming chapter. Some additional vocabulary may be included. You do not have to memorize all of this vocabulary, but by the end of this chapter you should be able to recognize most if not all the vocabulary on this list. In Chapter 1B, we will introduce new vocabulary while also incorporating words from this Chapter 1A list.

~은/는 Topic Particle

For introducing sentence topics

톰은 먹어요.
Tom eats.

In the introduction, we introduced the **subject particle** and **object particle**. To refresh, check the reference page below. But there is a third grammatical particle that is used just as often (if not more) than either of them: **the topic particle**.

WHAT IS THE TOPIC PARTICLE?
The topic particle attaches to the end of a noun. It shows that the noun it is attached to is the **topic of the sentence**: the person or thing that is the main focus, or overarching theme, of the sentence.

THE TOPIC PARTICLE
To assign a noun as the topic of the sentence, attach either ~은 or ~는 to the end of the noun.

If the noun ends in a consonant sound, you attach ~은

| Tom: 톰 | → | 톰은 | ("Tom" is the topic of the sentence) |
| Bread: 빵 | → | 빵은 | ("bread" is the topic of the sentence) |

If the noun ends in a vowel sound, you attach ~는

| Sara: 사라 | → | 사라는 | ("Sara" is the topic of the sentence) |
| Sophie: 소피 | → | 소피는 | ("Sophie" is the topic of the sentence) |

> 사라는 먹어요.   Sara eats.   ("Sara" is the topic)
> 톰은 먹어요.   Tom eats.   ("Tom" is the topic)
> 소피는 공부해요.   Sophie studies.   ("Sophie" is the topic)
> 메리는 요리해요.   Mary cooks.   ("Mary" is the topic)
> 빵은 좋아요.   The bread is good. ("The bread" is the topic)
> 한국어는 좋아요.   I like Korean.   ("Korean" is the topic)

REFERENCE PAGES

Grammatical Particles - page 16

1

WHAT'S THE DIFFERENCE?

~은	~는
Attaches to nouns ending in a **consonant** sound.	Attaches to nouns ending in a **vowel** sound.
O 톰은 먹어요. Tom eats. As for Tom, he is eating. X 사라은 먹어요. Incorrect grammar. 사라 does not end in a consonant sound.	X 톰는 먹어요. Incorrect grammar. 톰 does not end in a vowel sound. O 사라는 먹어요. Sara eats. As for Sara, she is eating.

To check which letters are vowels and which letters are consonants, check the reference page below.

Note: the reason that this particle has two halves is for ease of pronunciation. When speaking, it's easier for our mouths to move between vowel sounds and consonant sounds, rather than stacking up multiple vowels or multiple consonants right after each other. Many grammar concepts in Korean make use of these "dual forms."

PRACTICE EXERCISES

Attach the ~은/는 particle to the following nouns.

1. 메리 ....
2. 톰 ....
3. 사과 ....
4. 아이스크림 ....
5. 사라 ....

6. 사람 ....
7. 음식 ....
8. 저 ....
9. 이것 ....
10. 물 ....

ANSWERS: 1. 메리는 2. 톰은 3. 사과는 4. 아이스크림은 5. 사라는 6. 사람은 7. 음식은 8. 저는 9. 이것은 10. 물은

REFERENCE PAGES

The Korean Language - page 12

~이/가 Subject Particle

For introducing sentence subjects

톰이 먹어요.
Tom eats.

We touched on the subject particle in the Introduction. To refresh, check the reference page below. In this grammar lesson, we are going to look at the subject particle in more detail.

WHAT IS THE SUBJECT PARTICLE?

The subject particle also attaches to the end of a noun. It shows that the noun it is attached to is the **subject of the sentence.** The subject is who or what is performing some action or receiving some description. Compared to the topic particle, it is much more closely linked to the verb.

THE SUBJECT PARTICLE

To assign a noun as the subject of the sentence, attach either ~이 or ~가 to the end of the noun.

If the noun ends in a consonant sound, you attach **~이**

Tom: 톰	→	톰**이**	("Tom" is the subject of the sentence)
Bread: 빵	→	빵**이**	("bread" is the subject of the sentence)

If the noun ends in a vowel sound, you attach **~가**

Sara: 사라	→	사라**가**	("Sara" is the subject of the sentence)
Sophie: 소피	→	소피**가**	("Sophie" is the subject of the sentence)

> 사라**가** 먹어요.   Sara eats.   ("Sara" is the subject)
> 톰**이** 먹어요.   Tom eats.   ("Tom" is the subject)
> 소피**가** 공부해요.   Sophie studies.   ("Sophie" is the subject)
> 빵**이** 좋아요.   The bread is good.   ("The bread" is the subject)

--- REFERENCE PAGES ---

Grammatical Particles - page 16

1

WHAT'S THE DIFFERENCE?	
~이	~가
Attached to nouns ending in a **consonant** sound.	Attached to nouns ending in a **vowel** sound.
O 톰이 먹어요. Tom eats. X 사라이 먹어요. 사라 does not end in a consonant sound.	X 톰가 먹어요. 톰 does not end in a vowel sound. O 사라가 먹어요. Sara eats.

WHAT'S THE DIFFERENCE BETWEEN ~은/는 AND ~이/가?

You may have noticed that the ~은/는 particle and ~이/가 particle appear to be playing a similar role in the previous example sentences. Indeed, ~은/는 and ~이/가 do have some overlap in their usages. However, they have some differences as well. While it's not important right now to understand all of the nuances surrounding their similarities and differences, it is something that puzzles many Korean learners.

One simple difference we will mention here is that: ~은/는 places emphasis on what comes **to the right** the particle, and ~이/가 places emphasis on what comes **to the left** of the particle. Therefore "톰이 먹어요" places emphasis on "톰" (Tom) and "톰은 먹어요" places emphasis on "먹어요" (eats/eating). We will practice this more in the "제가/저는/제" chapter referenced below.

However this is not the only difference between the particles. If you would like to learn more, we talk in detail about the differences between ~이/가 and ~은/는 in the Appendix. Check the reference page below.

Please note that this lesson in the Appendix is **not required** in order to start your Korean learning journey. In simple sentences, generally either the topic particle or the subject particle can be used without significantly changing the overall meaning of the sentence. Therefore feel free to shelve this question for now and continue with the next lesson in the book. You can always check the lesson referenced below later if you wish to.

REFERENCE PAGES

The Topic & Subject Particles - page 276

제가/저는/제 - page 35

~을/를 Object Particle

For introducing sentence objects

사라가 아이스크림을 먹어요.
Sara eats an ice cream.

In a sentence, the **object** is who or what is **receiving some action.** Whichever noun has the ~을/를 particle attached to it automatically becomes the object of the sentence. Verbs like "보다" (to see/watch) and "먹다" (to eat) usually have some "thing/object" that is receiving that action. For example, "I see a **movie**" or "I eat a **pizza**." The "thing" that we do the action to is the **object** of the sentence.

NOUNS

To assign a noun as the object of the sentence, attach either ~을 or ~를 to the end of the noun.

If the noun ends in a consonant sound, you attach **~을**

    Tom: 톰 → 톰을 ("Tom" is the object)
    Bread: 빵 → 빵을 ("bread" is the object)

If the noun ends in a vowel sound, you attach **~를**

    Sara: 사라 → 사라를 ("Sara" is the object)
    Sophie: 소피 → 소피를 ("Sophie" is the object)

> 소피가 샐러드를 먹어요.   Sophie eats a salad.   ("a salad" is the object)
> 톰이 아이스크림을 먹어요.   Tom eats an ice cream.   ("an ice cream" is the object)
> 사라가 빵을 먹어요.   Sara eats bread.   ("bread" is the object)
> 빵이 사라를 먹어요.   The bread eats Sara.   ("Sara" is the object)
>   This is a grammatically correct, yet unlikely situation.
> 소피가 톰을 먹어요.   Sophie eats Tom.   ("Tom" is the object)
>   Also a grammatically correct, yet unlikely situation.

Note: the ~은/는 particle can also be used on any of the nouns in the sentences above to establish that noun as the topic of the sentence.

REFERENCE PAGES

The Korean Language - page 12   ~이/가 Subject Particle - page 31

1

WHAT'S THE DIFFERENCE?

~을	~를
Placed on nouns that end in a **consonant** sound.	Placed on nouns that end in a **vowel** sound.
O 톰이 빵을 먹어요. Tom eats bread. X 톰이 고기을 먹어요. 고기 does not end in a consonant sound.	X 톰이 빵를 먹어요. 빵 does not end in a vowel sound. O 톰이 고기를 먹어요. Tom eats meat.

Note: the reason that this particle has two halves is for ease of pronunciation. When speaking, it's easier for our mouths to move between vowel sounds and consonant sounds, rather than stacking up multiple vowels or multiple consonants right after each other.

WHAT'S THE DIFFERENCE?

~이/가	~을/를
Placed on the **subject** of the sentence.	Placed on the **object** of the sentence.
사라가 톰을 좋아해요. Sara likes Tom. 톰이 빵을 먹어요. Tom eats bread.	톰이 사라를 좋아해요. Tom likes Sarah. 빵이 톰을 먹어요. The bread eats Tom.

WHAT'S THE DIFFERENCE?

~은/는	~을/를
Placed on the **topic** of the sentence.	Placed on the **object** of the sentence.
톰은 빵을 먹어요. As for Tom, he eats bread. 사라는 톰을 좋아해요. When it comes to Sara, she likes Tom.	빵은 톰을 먹어요. As for the bread, it eats Tom. 톰은 사라를 좋아해요. When it comes to Tom, he likes Sara.

{ Understanding the difference between **sentence subjects** and **sentence objects** in English will help you use ~이/가 and ~을/를 particles correctly. }

USED IN WCK   463 times

제가 / 저는 / 제

For talking about yourself

저는 사과를 먹어요.
I eat an apple.

In Korean, "저" refers to the concept of self, but it's rarely used on its own as it's usually combined with particles in a sentence.

저는 VS 제가

In order to understand the difference between 제가 and 저는, we'll have to use our knowledge of subjects and topics. To review, check the reference pages below.

WHAT'S THE DIFFERENCE?	
제가	**저는**
저 + ~이/가 subject particle	저 + ~은/는 topic particle
Used when you are talking about yourself as the **subject** of the sentence.	Used when you are talking about yourself as the **topic** of the sentence.
제가 사과를 먹어요. I eat an apple. The emphasis is on the subject who is performing the action - i.e. "me"	저는 **사과를 먹어요.** I **eat an apple**. The emphasis is on what comes after "me." I.e. my actions or descriptions.

The ~이/가 particle places emphasis on the noun that comes to the **left**, and the ~은/는 particle places emphasis on the information that comes to the **right**. Therefore, 제가 places emphasis on "저" (yourself) as the subject. In comparison, 저는 marks you as the topic and places emphasis on what comes next in the sentence (the information about yourself, e.g. what you are doing, etc.).

WHICH ONE SHOULD I USE?

If someone asks a question like, "**who** is eating an apple?" you would respond with "**제가** 사과를 먹어요." because you want to emphasize that **you** are the one eating the apple.

---REFERENCE PAGES---

~이/가 Subject Particle - page 31
~은/는 Topic Particle - page 29

The Topic & Subject Particles - page 276

If someone asks a question like, "**what** are you eating?" you would respond with " 저는 **사과를** 먹어요." because you want the emphasis to be on **what** you are doing (i.e. eating an apple).

제 - MY/MINE
In Korean, 제 by itself means my/mine. You can write 제 before a noun to mean "my noun." 제 is a combination of "저" with the "의" possesstive particle (see reference page below).

>	제 사과	my apple
>	제 피자	my pizza
>	제 빵	my bread
>	제 친구	my friend

우리 - WE/OUR
Korea is a "collectivist" culture, which means that some nouns are seen as inherently belonging to a group instead of belonging to an individual. When talking about these group nouns, it is more natural to use "우리" (we/our) instead of "제" (my). Although "우리" is used in Korean, it should still usually be translated to "my" in English.

>	우리 엄마	my mom
>	우리 아빠	my dad
>	우리 집	my house
>	우리 나라	my (home) country

COMMON MISTAKE: OVERUSING TOPIC PARTICLES
An important feature of the topic particle is that it establishes not only the the topic of your current sentence, but also your **future sentences** as well. Once you establish your topic using the ~은/는 topic particle, the topic of your future sentences remains fixed until you establish a new topic by placing ~은/는 on a new noun. Because of this, it becomes easy to overuse topic particles. For example:

O 저는 톰이에요. 저는 미국사람이에요. 저는 선생님이에요.
I am Tom. I am American. I am a teacher.

English requires subjects, so learners naturally want to include an "I" in every sentence. However, Korean does not require subjects, and the first "저는" establishes yourself as the topic moving forward. Therefore, repeating "저는," while not technically incorrect, is unnecessary and unnnatural in Korean.

REFERENCE PAGES
N~의 - page 142   Dropping Subjects - page 18

"You" in Korean

The different ways to say "you" in Korean

사과를 먹어요?
Do you eat apples?

While 제가/저는 ("I / me") and 우리 ("we") are commonly used in Korean, there is **no one easy way** to say "you." Korean does have a word to mean "you" but it's only used in casual language (반말) - see the reference page below - and can be quite rude depending on the situation. When speaking politely, you should refer to the other person using one of the following:

1 THEIR NAME + 씨
The simplest way to address someone is to use their name + 씨. For example, if their name was "유진," you could address them as "유진 씨."

유진**씨**, 피자를 좋아해요?   Yujin, do you like pizza?

2 A KOREAN TITLE
If you don't know their name, you can use a Korean title which can be said alone or combined with their family name. Korean has many of these "titles." See reference page below.

김**선생님**, 피자를 좋아해요?   Miss Kim, do you like pizza?

3 LEAVE IT OUT ALTOGETHER
Remember that **Korean sentences do not need subjects.** So you don't need to worry too much about how to say "you" in Korean because most of the time you don't have to say it at all. This might be difficult for native English speakers to get used to, but is **perfectly natural** in Korean.

피자를 좋아해요?   Do you like pizza?

WHAT ABOUT "당신"?
You may see 당신 used to mean "you." While it can be appropriately used in some circumstances, it is **not a word recommended** for Korean learners. In fact, when used incorrectly, 당신 can be an insult, sound aggressive, or even suggest a romantic relationship.

REFERENCE PAGES

Words for People - page 288   Banmal (반말) - page 169

Asking Questions in Korean

How to ask questions

아침식사를 먹어요?
Do you eat breakfast?

In Korean, statements and questions have the same essential structure. The only difference between a question and a statement is that, in spoken language, there is a **rising inflection** at the end. And in writing, questions use question marks.

> Q. 빵을 먹어요? ↗
> Do you eat bread? ↗
> Rising inflection (speech)

> A. 네, 빵을 먹어요. →
> Yes, I eat bread. →
> Steady inflection (speech)

"YES" AND "NO" IN KOREAN

In casual polite Korean, 네 means "yes," and 아니요 means "no."
There are other words for "yes" and "no" used with different levels of formality.

	Informal language (반말)	Casual polite langauge	Honorific language
Yes	응	**네**	예
No	아니	**아니요**	아닙니다

Because this book focuses on using casual polite language, we will use "네" and "아니요" in this book.

> 〉 고기를 먹어요? ↗ — Do you eat meat?
> 〉 네, 고기를 먹어요. → — Yes, I eat meat.
> 〉 고기를 먹어요? ↗ — Do you eat meat?
> 〉 아니요, 채소를 먹어요. → — No, I eat vegetables.

Note: this applies only to the casual polite tense (~아/어요) and informal language (반말). If you are speaking using honorific ~(스)ㅂ니다 form, there is a special ending used for questions: "~(스)ㅂ니까?" See the reference page below to learn more.

── **REFERENCE PAGES** ──

A/V~(스)ㅂ니다 - page 172

N~이에요/예요

To be - the Korean copula

한옥이에요.
It's a traditional Korean house (hanok).

This grammar form is used to say something **is** something. For example: "this is an apple" or "I am Tom." In linguistics, it is known as a copula. The English copula is the verb: "to be."

Note: there are many ways to conjugate "to be" in English, depending on the subject (I am, he is, they are, etc.) but in Korean, the ~이에요/예요 ending is used for all subjects; just choose between ~이에요 and 예요 depending on the final sound of the subject (see below).

NOUNS

If the noun ends in a consonant sound, attach **~이에요**.

빵	→	빵**이에요**.	(It is bread)
톰	→	톰**이에요**.	(I am Tom/this is Tom)

If the noun ends in a vowel sound, attach **~예요**.

사과	→	사과**예요**.	(It is an apple)
메리	→	메리**예요**.	(I am Mary/this is Mary)

>	빵**이에요**.	It is bread.
>	이것은 빵**이에요**.	This is bread.
>	저는 톰**이에요**.	I am Tom.
>	저는 메리**예요**.	I am Mary.
>	그것은 고기**예요**.	That is meat.

WHAT'S THE DIFFERENCE?

~이에요	~예요
Attaches to nouns ending on a consonant sound.	Attaches to nouns ending in a vowel sound.

Note: ~이예요 is technically incorrect, but is a common misspelling even for native speakers.

Note: the dictionary form for 이에요/예요 is "이다" (to be).

N~(이/가) 아니에요

To not be

저는 한국 사람이 아니에요.
I am not Korean.

This grammar form is the functional **opposite** of the ~이에요/예요 grammar form we just learned. It is used to say something is **not** something else. For example, "I am not Korean" or "that is not meat."

NOUNS

~(이/가) 아니에요 is the present tense conjugation of the dictionary form "~(이/가) 아니다"
If the noun ends on a vowel sound, attach **~가 아니에요**

사과 → 사과가 아니다 → 사과가 아니에요.   (It's not an apple)
메리 → 메리가 아니다 → 메리가 아니에요.   (It's not Mary)

If the noun ends on a consonant sound, attach **~이 아니에요**

빵 → 빵이 아니다 → 빵이 아니에요   (It's not bread)
톰 → 톰이 아니다 → 톰이 아니에요.   (It's not Tom)

> 저는 한국사람이 아니에요.   I am not Korean.
> 저는 사라가 아니에요.   I am not Sara.
> 그 사람은 톰이 아니에요.   That person is not Tom.
> 그 음식은 고기가 아니에요.   That food is not meat.
> 이 음식은 빵이 아니에요.   This food is not bread.
> 술이 아니에요. 물이에요.   It's not alcohol. It's water.
> 빵이 아니에요. 피자예요.   It's not bread. It's pizza.

WHERE DOES THE ~이/가 COME FROM?

The ~이/가 part of the grammar form "N~이/가 아니에요" is the **subject particle** that we learned about previously. The ~이/가 subject particle connects the noun to the verb "아니다." Check the reference page below to refresh your knowledge on subject particles.

--- REFERENCE PAGES ---

~이/가 Subject Particle - page 31

WHY DOESN'T ~이에요/예요 NEED THE SUBJECT PARTICLE?

~이에요/예요 is a very special verb ending. Unlike other verbs, the verb "이다" (to be) attaches **directly** to the noun and does not require a particle. There is no space between the noun and ~이에요/예요 (e.g. "빵**이에요**" and "사과**예요**"). Every other verb in Korean (including it's own opposite, "아니다" , meaning "to not be"), requires a particle to connect to the noun. The noun and the verb are separate pieces, and the particle is needed to connect them together. Because of this, in all other situations **except ~이에요/예요,** you can (and most often should) use particles to connect nouns and verbs.

Note: it is possible to drop the ~이/가 subject particle and just say, "사과 아니에요" or "빵 아니에요," but it's good practice to keep the subject particle, particularly in writing. But if you drop the particle, keep the space between the noun and the verb.

USAGE NOTE: SAYING YOU'RE WELCOME

If you look up "you're welcome" in Korean, you will probably find the word: "천만에요." If you use this word, everyone will understand you, however, "천만에요"is very old-fashioned and almost never used in modern Korean. Instead, one of the more natural ways to say "you're welcome" in Korean is actually: "아니에요." This is similar to saying "not at all," or "not a problem."

| 감사합니다! | Thank you! |
| **아니에요**! :) | Not at all! :) |

WHAT'S THE DIFFERENCE?	
아니요	아니에요
Means "no."	To not be: "it is not" or "I am not."
Q. 사과예요?　Is it an apple? A. **아니요**.　　No. Q. 톰이에요?　Are you Tom? A. **아니요**.　　No.	Q. 사과예요?　Is it an apple? A. **아니에요**.　It is not. Q. 톰이에요?　Are you Tom? A. **아니에요**.　I am not.
Typically comes at the start of a sentence.	*Typically comes at the end of a sentence.*
아니요. 사과가 아니에요. No. It is not an apple. **아니요**, 톰이 아니에요. No, I am not Tom.	아니요. 사과가 **아니에요**. No. It is not an apple. 아니요, 톰이 **아니에요**. No, I am not Tom.

Note: "아니예요" is technically incorrect, but is a common misspelling even for native speakers so you are likely to encounter it.

Note: the verb "아니다" (to not be) is the functional opposite of "이다" (to be).

Present Tense ~아/어요

Conjugating verbs that end on a consonant sound

벚꽃이 좋아요!
I like cherry blossoms!

The present tense form is a very fluid tense in Korean. It can be used to express the simple present ("I eat"), the present continuous ("I am eating"), and the future tense ("I will eat"). In fact, the only tense that present tense cannot refer to is the past tense ("I ate").
Note: specific conjugations for these other tenses **do exist**, but ~아/어요 is like a linguistic pocket-knife: when the context is already clear, it can be naturally used in many different situations.

PRESENT TENSE CONJUGATIONS - VERBS WITH A FINAL CONSONANT
Learning present tense comes with a steep learning curve of verb conjugation rules. It may take some time and patience to get comfortable doing these conjugations, so don't get discouraged! The good news is; once you are familiar with the present tense conjugation rules (and the occasional exceptions and irregularities) you will know how to conjugate **any** Korean verb into the present tense. To start with, we are going to look at conjugating verbs that end on a **final consonant sound.** This means they have a consonant on the **bottom** of the syllable. These are the easiest to conjugate. Some examples include:

먹다	맛있다	맛없다	살다	좋다
To eat	To be delicious	To be disgusting	To live	To be good

Note: all these verbs end in -다 because they are in their dictionary forms. Refer below.

DESCRIPTIVE VERBS & ACTION VERBS
To conjugate a verb into present tense, you attach ~아요, ~어요, or ~해요 onto the verb stem.
    1 If the last vowel sound of the verb is ㅏ or ㅗ, you attach **~아요**
    2 If the verb stem ends with 하, that 하 becomes **해요**.
    3 In all other situations, you attach **~어요**

──────────────── REFERENCE PAGES ────────────────

Agglutinative Verbs - page 19

1 If the verb stem ends in ㅏ, add "아요"

살다 → 살 → 살+아요 → 살아요
 1   2   3   4   5

1 살다 is a verb in its dictionary form meaning "to live"
2 살 is the verb stem of the verb "살다." To find the verb stem, just remove -다.
3 ㅏ is the last vowel sound of 살 (the verb stem)
4 ~아요 is what we attach to the verb stem since the last vowel sound is ㅏ
5 살아요 is the present tense conjugation of the verb 살다

1 If the verb stem ends in ㅗ, add "아요"

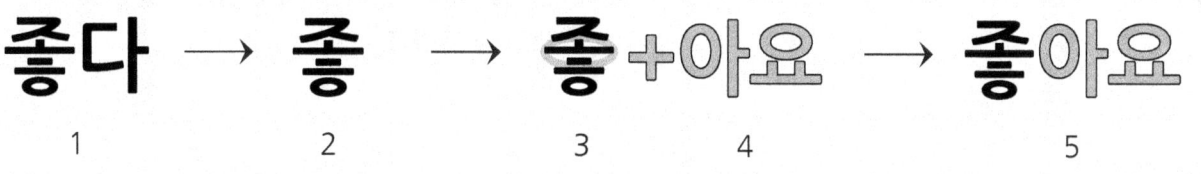

1 좋다 is a verb in its dictionary form meaning "to be good/nice"
2 좋 is the verb stem of the verb "좋다." To find the verb stem, just remove -다.
3 ㅗ is the last vowel sound of 좋 (the verb stem)
4 ~아요 is what we attach to the verb stem since the last vowel sound is ㅗ
5 좋아요 is the present tense conjugation of the verb 좋다

2 If the verb stem ends with 하, that 하 becomes 해요.

1 하다 is a verb in its dictionary form meaning "to do"
2. 하 is the verb stem of the verb "하다." To find the verb stem, just remove -다.
3. Because the verb ends in 하, technically you add '여요' and it becomes 해요. You do not need to remember this intermediate step, you can just remember that 하다 always becomes 해요.
4. 해요 is the present tense conjugation of the verb 하다.

REFERENCE PAGES

하다 Verbs - page 49

3 In all other situations, you attach ~어요

먹다 → 먹 → 먹+어요 → 먹어요
　1　　　　2　　　　3　　4　　　　　5

1 먹다 is a verb in its dictionary form meaning "to eat"
2 먹 is the verb stem of the verb "먹다." To find the verb stem, just remove -다.
3 ㅓ is the last vowel sound of 먹 (the verb stem)
4 ~어요 is what we attach to the verb stem since the last vowel sound is not ㅏ, ㅗ or 하
5 먹어요 is the present tense conjugation of the verb 먹다

{ *Notice how we have already encountered "먹어요" many times in the previous pages!*
e.g. 메리가 사과를 먹어요. ("Mary eats apples"). }

PRACTICE EXERCISES
Attach simple present tense (~아/어요) to the following verbs.

1. 살다　　..............................　　6. 받다　　..............................

2. 좋다　　..............................　　7. 싫다　　..............................

3. 먹다　　..............................　　8. 괜찮다　..............................

4. 있다　　..............................　　9. 읽다　　..............................

5. 없다　　..............................　　10. 높다　..............................

ANSWERS: 1. 살아요 2. 좋아요 3. 먹어요 4. 있어요 5. 없어요 6. 받아요 7. 싫어요 8. 괜찮아요 9. 읽어요 10. 높아요

Present Tense ~아/어요

Conjugating verbs that end on a vowel sound

메리가 가요.
Mary goes.

Until now, we've only looked at conjugating verb stems ending in a consonant sound. Now let's look at verb stems ending in a vowel sound.

COMBINING VOWEL SOUNDS
These conjugations are slightly more tricky because when you attach ~아/어요 to a verb with a verb stem ending in a vowel sound, the "~아/어" part of the present tense conjugation does not simply attach, but **combines with the existing vowel sound in the verb stem** to create a new vowel combination. However, the same essential conjugation rules still apply:

> ### DESCRIPTIVE VERBS & ACTION VERBS
> To conjugate a verb into present tense, you attach ~아/어요 onto the verb stem.
> 1 If the last vowel sound of the verb is ㅏ or ㅗ, you attach **~아요**
> 2 If the verb stem ends with 하, the 하 becomes **해요**.
> 3 In all other situations, you attach **~어요**

VOWEL BLENDS
The four vowel blends you need to know are:
1. ㅏ + ㅏ = ㅏ   (ah)   the stem ending in ㅏ and the ㅏ from ~아요 merge to make: ㅏ
2. ㅗ + ㅏ = ㅘ   (wa)   the stem ending in ㅗ and the ㅏ from ~아요 merge to make: ㅘ
3. ㅣ + ㅓ = ㅕ   (yeo)   the stem ending in ㅣ and the ㅓ from ~어요 merge to make: ㅕ
4. ㅜ + ㅓ = ㅝ   (weo)   the stem ending in ㅜ and the ㅓ from ~어요 merge to make: ㅝ

Let's look at some examples.

1. ㅏ + ㅏ = ㅏ

가다 → 가 → 가+아요 → 가요
  1   2   3   4   5

1 **가다** is a verb in its dictionary form meaning "to go"
2 **가** is the verb stem of the verb "가다"
3 **ㅏ** is the last vowel sound
4 **~아요** is what we attach to the verb stem since the last vowel sound is ㅏ. However, the extra "아" is redundant and the final conjugation always becomes "가요."
5 **가요** is the present tense conjugation of the verb 가다

Note: The same rule holds for all verb stems ending in the ㅏ vowel sound.
Other verbs include: 사다 (to buy), 자다 (to sleep), 타다 (to ride), etc.

2. ㅗ + ㅏ = ㅘ

오다 → 오 → 오+아요 → 와요
  1   2   3   4   5

1 **오다** is a verb in its dictionary form meaning "to come"
2 **오** is the verb stem of the verb "오다"
3 **ㅗ** is the last vowel sound
4 **~아요** is what we attach to the verb stem since the last vowel sound is ㅗ. These two vowels (ㅗ and ㅏ) combine neatly together to become a new vowel combination: ㅘ
5 **와요** is the present tense conjugation of the verb 오다

Note: The same rule holds for all verb stems ending in the ㅗ vowel sound.
Other verbs include: 보다 (to see), 쏘다 (to shoot), etc.

3. ㅣ + ㅓ = ㅕ

마시다 → 마시 → 마시+어요 → 마셔요
　1　　　　2　　　　3　　4　　　　5

1 **마시다** is a verb in its dictionary form meaning "to drink"
2 **마시** is the verb stem of the verb "마시다"
3 **ㅣ** is the last vowel sound
4 **~어요** is what we attach to the verb stem since the last vowel sound is not ㅏ, ㅗ or 하. These two vowels (ㅣ and ㅓ) combine together to make ㅕ
5 **마셔요** is the present tense conjugation of the verb 마시다

Note: the same rule holds for all verb stems ending in the ㅣ vowel sound.
Other verbs include: 기다리다 (to wait), 가르치다 (to teach), 생기다 (to appear), etc.

4. ㅜ + ㅓ = ㅝ

배우다 → 배우 → 배우+어요 → 배워요
　1　　　　2　　　3　　4　　　　5

1 **배우다** is a verb in its dictionary form meaning "to learn"
2 **배우** is the verb stem of the verb "배우다"
3 **ㅜ** is the last vowel sound
4 **~어요** is what we attach to the verb stem since the last vowel sound is not ㅏ, ㅗ or 하. These two vowels (ㅜ and ㅓ) combine neatly together to become a new vowel combination: ㅝ
5 **배워요** is the present tense conjugation of the verb 배우다

Note: The same rule holds for all verb stems ending in the ㅜ vowel sound.
Other verbs include: 주다 (to give), 꾸다 (to dream), 추다 (to dance), etc.

CHEAT SHEET TABLE
This table can be a quick reference for you to check whether a vowel blend occurs when conjugating the present tense forms of verbs that end in a vowel sound.

FINAL VOWEL	EXAMPLE VERB	MEANING	CONJUGATION	PRESENT TENSE
ㅏ	가다	to go	~요	가요
ㅣ	마시다	to drink	~ㅕ요	마셔요
ㅗ	보다	to see	~ㅘ요	봐요
ㅜ	배우다	to learn	~ㅝ요	배워요
ㅐ	보내다	to send	~요	보내요
ㅓ	서다	to stand	~요	서요
ㅕ	펴다	to open/spread	~요	펴요

PRACTICE EXERCISES
Attach simple present tense (~아/어요) to the following verbs.

1. 가다 ....
2. 비가 오다 ....
3. 마시다 ....
4. 배우다 ....
5. 보다 ....

6. 만나다 ....
7. 바꾸다 ....
8. 비싸다 ....
9. 다니다 ....
10. 가르치다 ....

ANSWERS: 1. 가요 2. 비가 와요 3. 마셔요 4. 배워요 5. 봐요 6. 만나요 7. 바꿔요 8. 비싸요 9. 다녀요 10. 가르쳐요

IRREGULAR VERBS
Some verbs follow their own conjugation rules separate to the ones covered above. Refer to the pages referenced below to check the irregular verb conjugation rules. Irregular verbs in this book will be marked a "(!)" symbol. The symbols will only appear when the irregular verb conjugation takes place.

REFERENCE PAGES

The ㅂ Irregular - page 90
ㄷ Irregular - page 292
ㅅ Irregular - page 293

으 Irregular - page 294
ㄹ Irregular - page 296
르 Irregular - page 295

하다 Verbs

How to use these verbs in a sentence

저는 운동해요.
I work out.

WHAT ARE 하다 VERBS?

하다 verbs are very common in Korean. The verb "하다" literally means "to do," and it is often combined with nouns to mean "to do this noun." For example: "공부" is a noun meaning "study," and "공부하다" is a verb meaning "to study." Many (but not all) nouns can combine with 하다 to make a verb.

ACTION VERBS & DESCRIPTIVE VERBS

All 하다 verbs conjugate the same way. When you attach simple present tense, 하다 becomes 해요.

공부하다	(to study)	→ 공부해요	(subj. studies)
운동하다	(to exercise)	→ 운동해요	(subj. exercises)
요리하다	(to cook)	→ 요리해요	(subj. cooks)
좋아하다	(to like)	→ 좋아해요	(subj. likes)

Note: Korean sentences don't require subjects, so we are using "subj." to represent all possible subjects (I/you/he/she/they/etc.).

> 메리가 요리**해요**.　　　　　　Mary cooks.
> 메리가 피자를 요리**해요**.　　　Mary cooks pizza.
> 톰이 공부**해요**.　　　　　　　Tom studies.
> 톰이 한국어를 공부**해요**.　　　Tom studies Korean.
> 오늘은 톰이 운동**해요**.　　　　Tom works out today.
> 톰이 사라를 좋아**해요**.　　　　Tom likes Sara.
> 사라가 아이스크림을 좋아**해요**.　Sara likes ice cream.

REFERENCE PAGES

Present Tense ~아/어요 - page 45

1

SEPARABLE & NON-SEPARABLE 하다 VERBS

하다 verbs can be distinguished into two groups: separable and non-separable 하다 verbs.
1 Separable 하다 verbs can (and sometimes must) be broken apart into their noun and 하다 parts.
2 Non-separable 하다 verbs are verbs that end in 하다, but are not made by combining a noun and a verb, and therefore cannot be split into two separate words.

Examples of Separable 하다 Verbs	Examples of Non-Separable 하다 Verbs
요리하다 - to cook (요리 + 하다)	좋아하다 - to like
공부하다 - to study (공부 + 하다)	싫어하다 - to dislike
말하다 - to speak (말 + 하다)	행복하다 - to be happy
운동하다 - to exercise (운동 + 하다)	똑똑하다 - to be smart

NOUN(을/를) 하다

Separable 하다 verbs can be written two ways: either combined into one verb (e.g. "요리하다") or split apart into their noun+하다 components and connected with the ~을/를 object particle (e.g. "요리를 하다"). 요리하다 and 요리를 하다 are equivalent expressions and mean the same thing.

The same applies for all other separable 하다 verbs. For example, "공부하다" versus "공부를 하다," and "운동하다" versus "운동을 하다." These pairs are all equivalent expressions.

But you **cannot** do this with non-separable 하다 verbs like 좋아하다 or 싫어하다. Saying "좋아를 하다" or "싫어를 하다" is not grammatically correct because the verbs are non-separable, and "좋아" and "싫어" are not nouns. These verbs always stay together as 좋아하다 and 싫어하다.

HOW TO SPOT THE DIFFERENCE?

Separable 하다 verbs and non-separable 하다 verbs look **exactly the same**, so it can be difficult to know if a 하다 verb is separable or non-separable. However, in general:
1 하다 verbs that are descriptive verbs tend to be **non-separable**.
2 하다 verbs that are pure Korean tend to be **non-separable**.
3 하다 verbs that are loanwords (e.g. from English or Chinese) tend to be **separable**.
In time and through practice, you will get a feeling for whether a 하다 verb is separable or non-separable.

WHY IS SEPARABILITY IMPORTANT?

Separability is important because separable 하다 verbs and non-separable 하다 verbs sometimes **conjugate differently in a sentence**. Keep this in mind, as it will be relevant to some grammar forms we will be learning in future chapters.

~이/가 + Descriptive Verbs

For describing nouns

사과가 맛있어요.
Apples are delicious.

WHAT IS A DESCRIPTIVE VERB?

In English, we have three main classifications of words: nouns, verbs, and adjectives. In Korean, there are only two categories: nouns and verbs. Words that we think of as adjectives in English behave just like verbs in Korean. Because of this, there are two sub-classifications of Korean verbs:

1 Action verbs (동사) - involved in carrying out some action. Most (but not all) action verbs in Korean are verbs in English, like "먹다" (to eat), and "보다" (to see).

2 Descriptive verbs (형용사) - involved in describing things. Most (but not all) descriptive verbs in Korean are adjectives in English, like "좋다" (to be good), and "맛있다" (to be delicious).

HOW TO DESCRIBE A NOUN

There are two main components used in order to create sentences using descriptive verbs:
1 The subject (a noun) + the 이/가 subject particle
2 The descriptive verb + 아/어요

Subject + 이/가 Particle	Descriptive Verb + 아/어요	Final Sentence	Meaning
아이스크림**이**	**좋아요**	아이스크림이 좋아요.	Ice cream is good.
피자**가**	맛있**어요**	피자가 맛있어요.	Pizza is delicious.
한국어**가**	재미있**어요**	한국어가 재미있어요.	Korean is interesting.

Note: by attaching ~이/가 to the subject noun, you are connecting it to the descriptive verb and saying that the state/characteristics of that noun is being described by the descriptive verb. Even if there are other nouns in the sentence, the noun that has the ~이/가 subject particle is the one associated with the descriptive verb.

REFERENCE PAGES

Present Tense ~아/어요 - page 45

1

NOUNS

If the noun ends in a consonant sound, attach **~이 + Descriptive Verb**

| 한국 | → | 한국이 좋다 | → | 한국이 좋아요 | (Korea is good) |
| 저녁 | → | 저녁이 맛있다 | → | 저녁이 맛있어요 | (Dinner is delicious) |

If the noun ends on a vowel sound, attach **~가 + Descriptive Verb**

| 학교 | → | 학교가 좋다 | → | 학교가 좋아요 | (School is good) |
| 한국어 | → | 한국어가 재미있다 | → | 한국어가 재미있어요 | (Korean is interesting) |

> 한국이 좋아요.   Korea is nice/I like Korea.
> 미국이 좋아요.   America is nice/I like America.
> 빵이 좋아요.   Bread is nice/I like bread.
> 빵이 맛있어요.   Bread is delicious/tasty.
> 아침식사가 맛있어요.   Breakfast is delicious/tasty.
> 한국어가 재미있어요.   Korean is fun/interesting.

USAGE NOTE:
Descriptive verbs **do not** use the ~을/를 object particle. If you are describing a noun (good, bad, fun, boring, etc.) you should use the ~이/가 subject particle (or the topic particle - see below).

O 빵이 맛있어요. → Bread is tasty.   X 빵을 맛있어요. → (I) tasty the bread.

COMMON MISTAKE: 좋다 AND 좋아하다
좋다 and 좋아하다 can both be translated to "liking" things - however; 좋다 describes nouns using the **~이/가 subject particle** and 좋아하다 acts upon nouns using the **~을/를 object particle**. This is because 좋다 is a **descriptive verb**, whereas 좋아하다 is an **action verb**. 좋다 and 좋아하다 are not the only verb pairs like this. Check the reference page below to learn more.

O 피자가 좋아요. → Pizza is good/I like pizza.   X 피자를 좋아요. → (I) good the bread.
O 피자를 좋아해요. → (I) like pizza.   X 피자가 좋아해요. → The pizza likes (sth)

WHAT ABOUT THE TOPIC PARTICLE?
The ~은/는 topic particle can be placed on **any** of the nouns above. This changes the nuance of the sentence slightly but doesn't significantly changing the meaning. To compare the ~이/가 subject particle and the ~은/는 topic particle, you can check the reference page below. Keep in mind this is a **high-level concept** and you don't have to fully understand their differences at this early stage.

REFERENCE PAGES

~이/가 Subject Particle - page 31   Passive & Active Verbs - page 282
~을/를 Object Particle - page 33   The Topic & Subject Particles - page 254

~을/를 + Action Verbs

For performing actions on nouns

톰이 수박을 먹어요.
Tom eats watermelon.

In the previous lesson, we looked at using descriptive verbs in a sentence. Now let's look at action verbs. Here are some action verbs that will be commonly used in Level One:

Dictionary Form	English Meaning	Present Tense Conjugation
공부하다	to study	공부해요
요리하다	to cook	요리해요
먹다	to eat	먹어요
운동하다	to exercise/work out	운동해요

HOW TO PERFORM AN ACTION ON/TO A NOUN

There are four main components used in order to create sentences using action verbs:
1 The subject (a noun) - note: the subject is optional.
2 The object (a noun)
3 The ~을/를 object particle
4 The action verb

Subject + 이/가 Particle	Object + 을/를 Particle	Action Verb + 아/어요	Complete Sentence
메리가	사과를	먹어요	메리가 사과를 먹어요.
사라가	빵을	먹어요	사라가 빵을 먹어요.
톰이	피자를	요리해요	톰이 피자를 요리해요

Note: by attaching the ~을/를 object particle to a noun (e.g. 사과), we indicate that the noun is the object of the verb. This is the noun that the action is being applied to (e.g. being eaten).

REFERENCE PAGES

Present Tense ~아/어요 - page 45

~을/를 Object Particle - page 33
~이/가 Subject Particle - page 31

1

NOUNS

If the noun ends on a consonant sound, attach ~을 + Action Verb

빵	→	빵을 먹다	→	빵을 먹어요	(subj. eats bread)
저녁	→	저녁을 먹다	→	저녁을 먹어요	(subj. eats dinner)
저녁	→	저녁을 요리하다	→	저녁을 요리해요	(subj. cooks dinner)

If the noun ends on a vowel sound, attach ~를 + Action Verb

피자	→	피자를 먹다	→	피자를 먹어요	(subj. eats pizza)
한국어	→	한국어를 공부하다	→	한국어를 공부해요	(subj. studies Korean)
영어	→	영어를 공부하다	→	영어를 공부해요	(subj. studies English)

> 메리가 사과를 먹어요.   톰이 빵을 먹어요.   사라가 한국어를 공부해요.
> Mary eats an apple.   Tom eats bread.   Sara studies Korean.
> 메리 is the subject.   톰 is the subject.   사라 is the subject.
> 사과 is the object.   빵 is the object.   한국어 is the object.
> 먹다 is the action verb.   먹다 is the action verb.   공부하다 is the action verb.

PARTICLES DETERMINE SENTENCE STRUCTURE

Remember that **particles are critical** to sentence structure in Korean. When you're learning, you may not know which particle you should use. But try to avoid randomly guessing - if you put particles on the wrong nouns, it **will** change the meaning of the sentence. Consider the following examples:

O 메리가 사과를 먹어요.   O 톰이 피자를 먹어요.   O 사라가 빵을 먹어요.
Mary eats an apple.   Tom eats pizza.   Sara eats bread.

메리를 사과가 먹어요.   톰을 피자가 먹어요.   사라를 빵이 먹어요.
The apple eats Mary.   The pizza eats Tom.   The bread eats Sara.

Note: these sentences are all grammatically correct, though the black sentences likely do not have the intended meaning.

{ *The longer you study Korean, the easier it will be to choose the right particles for your nouns. Eventually it will become second-nature.* }

Level One B

MAKING YOUR FIRST SENTENCES

DIFFICULTY LEVEL: EASY
The example sentences are written using simple
grammar and vocabulary designed to help you understand the
grammar concept in the most accessible way.

Level One B Grammar

What we will learn

한국어 문법을 공부하자!
Let's study Korean grammar!

A/V~았/었다 Past Tense...58

A/V~(으)ㄹ 것이다 Future Tense...60

안 A/V..61

A/V~지 않다...63

못 V..65

V~지 못 하다..67

V~는 것..69

Place~에 가다/오다..71

Place~(으)로...73

Time~에 V..74

N~에 V..76

N~에서 & N~까지..77

N~부터 & N~까지..78

N~에서 Particle..80

N~들...82

N~도...83

N~만...85

Note: Although you are most welcome to, you do not need to complete this list in order. From this point in the book onwards, feel free to jump around the grammar forms in **any order you wish**. Though bear in mind that the example sentences get more complex the further through the book you go.

Level One B Vocab

What we will learn

한국어 어휘를 배우자!
Let's learn Korean vocabulary!

NOUNS
오늘 - today
어제 - yesterday
내일 - tomorrow
지금 - now
차 - tea
집 - house, home
도서관 - library
헬스장 - the gym
학교 - school
주말 - weekend
남편 - husband
커피 - coffee
남자 - man
여자 - woman
책 - book(s)
많이 - many
점심 - lunch
고기 - meat
텔레비전 - television

영화 - movie(s)
드라마 - drama(s)

DESCRIPTIVE VERBS
맛없다 - to be disgusting
맛있다 - to be delicious/tasty
재미없다 - to be boring
재미있다 - to be fun
이다/아니다 - to be/not be
좋다 - to be good, nice, liked
싫다 - to be bad, disliked
괜찮다 - to be okay, fine

ACTION VERBS
먹다 - to eat
공부하다 - to study
운동하다 - to exercise
가다 - to go
오다 - to come
말하다 - to speak

보다 - to see
살다 - to live (!)
일하다 - to work
읽다 - to read
만들다 - to make (!)
마시다 - to drink
듣다 - to listen (!)

Use flashcards on Quizlet!

Note: This is a list of all the main vocabulary you will encounter in the upcoming chapter. You do not have to memorize all of this vocabulary, but by the end of this chapter you should be able to recognize most if not all the vocabulary on this list. In Chapter 2, we will introduce new vocabulary while also incorporating words from this Chapter 1B list.

Note: Verbs with a (!) symbol are irregular verbs - check the reference pages below.

REFERENCE PAGES

ㄷ Irregular - page 292   ㄹ Irregular - page 296

A/V~았/었다 Past Tense

The simple past tense

어제 팬케이크를 먹었어요.
I ate pancakes yesterday.

Up until now, we've only been using sentences with the ~아/어요 polite casual present tense ending. From here on, we're going to start using sentences with the polite casual past tense, also.

ACTION VERBS & DESCRIPTIVE VERBS

The process of conjugating a verb into the past tense is similar to that of the present tense, but this time you add ~았/었다, which conjugates to ~았/었어요 in polite casual language.

If the verb ends in ㅏ or ㅗ, attach **~았어요**.

가다	→	갔다	→	**갔어요**	(subj. went)
좋다	→	좋았다	→	**좋았어요**	(subj. was good)
살다	→	살았다	→	**살았어요**	(subj. lived)
보다	→	봤다	→	**봤어요**	(subj. saw)

If the verb ends in 하, attach **~했어요**.

공부하다	→	공부했다	→	공부**했어요**	(subj. studied)
일하다	→	일했다	→	일**했어요**	(subj. worked)
요리하다	→	요리했다	→	요리**했어요**	(subj. cooked)

If the verb ends in anything else, attach **~었어요**

읽다	→	읽었다	→	읽**었어요**	(subj. read)
만들다	→	만들었다	→	만들**었어요**	(subj. made)
마시다	→	마셨다	→	마**셨어요**	(subj. drank)
먹다	→	먹었다	→	먹**었어요**	(subj. ate)

{ *Shortcut! If you know how the verb conjugates to present tense, take off the -요 from the present tense conjugation and add +ㅆ어요.* }

>	오늘은 공부**했어요**.	I studied today.
>	오늘은 피자를 요리**했어요**.	I cooked pizza today.
>	어제는 차를 마**셨어요**.	I drank tea yesterday.

NOUNS

If you want to talk about a noun in the past tense, attach ~이었어요 or ~였어요.

If the noun ends with a consonant sound, attach **~이었어요**.

한국 사람	→	한국 사람**이었어요**	(subj. was Korean)
남편	→	남편**이었어요**	(subj. was my husband)
빵	→	빵**이었어요**	(it was bread)

If the noun ends with a vowel sound, attach **~였어요**.

친구	→	친구**였어요**	(subj. was my friend)
커피	→	커피**였어요**	(it was coffee)
어제	→	어제**였어요**	(it was yesterday)

>	그 사람은 제 친구**였어요**.	That person was my friend.
>	그 남자는 제 남편**이었어요**.	That man was my husband.
>	그 음식은 빵**이었어요**.	That food was bread.

USAGE NOTE: NO INFORMATION ABOUT THE PRESENT SITUATION

Unlike English, talking about nouns in the past tense in Korean **does not imply anything** about the current situation. It merely comments on the state of that object at some point in the past. For example, saying "그 남자는 제 친구**였어요**" just means that man and I were friends in the past. We may still be friends now, or we may not be.

THE DISCONTINUOUS PAST TENSE: ~았/었었다 (~았/었었어요)

You can add another -었 past tense marker to use the discontinuous past tense in Korean. This is used to talk about things that happened in the past **and don't happen** in the present. It is similar to saying you "**used to do**" something in English.

>	그 남자는 제 친구**였었어요**.	That man used to be my friend.
>	책을 많이 읽**었었어요**.	I used to read a lot of books.
>	그 커피가 좋**았었어요**.	That coffee used to be good.

A/V~(으)ㄹ 것이다 Future Tense

The simple future tense

내일 피자를 만들 거예요.
I will make pizza tomorrow.

In Korean, you can add ~(으)ㄹ 것이다 to your verb stem to talk about doing things in the future. This is similar to saying "I will" do something in English.
In polite casual language, ~(으)ㄹ 것이다 conjugates to ~(으)ㄹ 거예요.

ACTION VERBS & DESCRIPTIVE VERBS

~(으)ㄹ 것이다 can be attached to action verbs or descriptive verbs.
If the verb stem ends in a vowel sound, **or ㄹ**, attach **~ㄹ 거예요**

보다	→	볼 것이다	→	볼 거예요	(subj. will watch)
마시다	→	마실 것이다	→	마실 거예요	(subj. will drink)
만들다	→	만들 것이다	→	만들 거예요	(subj. will make)

If the verb stem ends in a consonant sound, attach **~을 거예요**

괜찮다	→	괜찮을 것이다	→	괜찮을 거예요	(subj. will be okay)
(!) 듣다	→	들을 것이다	→	들을 거예요	(subj. will listen)
먹다	→	먹을 것이다	→	먹을 거예요	(subj. will eat)

> 오늘 영화를 **볼 거예요**. I will watch a movie today.
> 내일 텔레비전을 **볼 거예요**. Tomorrow I will watch television.
> 오늘 차를 **마실 거예요**. Today I'll drink tea.
> 내일 피자를 **만들 거예요**. Tomorrow I'll make pizza.
> 저는 **괜찮을 거예요**. I'll be okay.
> 내일 음악을 **들을 거예요**. Tomorrow I will listen to music.
> 다음주 피자를 **먹을 거예요**. Next week I'll eat pizza.

Note: the verb "듣다" is a ㄷ irregular verb. In the present tense, it becomes "들어요," in the past tense it becomes "들었어요," and in the future tense it becomes "들을 거예요." Check the reference page below to learn more.

—— **REFERENCE PAGES** ——

ㄷ Irregular - page 292

USED IN WCK   48 times

안 A/V

For making negative verbs

저는 고기를 안 먹어요.
I don't eat meat.

To negate a verb, that is, to say that you **don't** do something (e.g. "I don't eat meat" or "I don't speak Korean") or that something **isn't** some description (e.g. "the game isn't fun," or "the food isn't tasty") place "안" before the verb.

Note: this grammar form is used differently with separable and non-separable 하다 verbs.

ACTION VERBS (AND NON-SEPARABLE 하다 VERBS)

Place 안 directly **before** the action verb to say that you don't do that action.

먹다	→	**안** 먹다	→	**안** 먹어요	(subj. doesn't eat)
보다	→	**안** 보다	→	**안** 봐요	(subj. doesn't watch)
좋아하다	→	**안** 좋아하다	→	**안** 좋아해요	(subj. doesn't like)

> 저는 고기를 **안** 먹어요.   I don't eat meat.
> 저는 빵을 **안** 먹어요.   I don't eat bread.
> 사라는 텔레비전을 **안** 봐요.   Sara doesn't watch television.
> 톰은 사과를 **안** 좋아해요.   Tom doesn't like apples.

SEPARABLE 하다 VERBS

When you use 안 with separable 하다 verbs, you have to place 안 **between** the noun and 하다. You can then connect the noun to the verb with the ~을/를 object particle, but this is optional.

공부하다→	공부(를) **안** 하다	→	공부(를) **안** 해요	(subj. doesn't study)
운동하다→	운동(을) **안** 하다	→	운동(을) **안** 해요	(subj. doesn't exercise)
요리하다→	요리(를) **안** 하다	→	요리(를) **안** 해요	(subj. doesn't cook)

> 제가 요리 **안** 해요.   I don't cook.

REFERENCE PAGES

하다 Verbs - page 49   ~을/를 + Action Verbs - page 53

> 메리가 공부 **안** 해요.   Mary doesn't study.
> 톰이 운동을 **안** 해요.   Tom doesn't exercise.
> 사라가 한국어를 공부 **안** 해요.   Sara doesn't study Korean.

Note: saying "안 공부해요" or "좋아 안 해요" are grammatically incorrect, but people will still understand what you mean.

DESCRIPTIVE VERBS

Place **안** directly before the descriptive verb to say that the subject is **not** that descriptive verb.

좋다	→ **안** 좋다	(to not be good)
맛있다	→ **안** 맛있다	(to not be delicious)
재미있다	→ **안** 재미있다	(to not be fun)

> 사과가 **안** 좋아요.   The apples aren't good.
> 빵이 **안** 맛있어요.   The bread isn't delicious.
> 한국어가 **안** 재미있어요.   Korean isn't fun.
> 오늘 점심이 **안** 좋아요.   The lunch isn't good today.

Note: descriptive 하다 verbs are almost always non-separable 하다 verbs.

PAST TENSE

To talk about situations in the past, conjugate the final verb into the past tense.

> 저는 고기를 **안** 먹었어요.   I didn't eat meat.
> 사라는 텔레비전을 **안** 봤어요.   Sara didn't watch television.
> 사과가 **안** 좋았어요.   The apples weren't good.

FUTURE TENSE

To talk about situations in the future, conjugate the final verb into the future tense.

> 오늘은 사라가 요리를 **안** 할 거예요.   Sara will not cook today.
> 내일은 제가 영화를 **안** 볼 거예요.   I will not watch a movie tomorrow.
> 오늘은 제가 술을 **안** 마실 거예요.   I won't drink alcohol today.

REFERENCE PAGES

~이/가 + Descriptive Verbs - page 51   A/V~았/었다 Past Tense - page 58
                                          A/V~(으)ㄹ 것이다 Future Tense - page 60

USED IN WCK — **284 times**

A/V~지 않다

For making negative verbs

저는 여행하지 않아요.
I don't travel.

Another way to negate verbs is using ~지 않다. ~지 않다 attaches to the verb stem of the verb. Just like "안," it means that you **don't** do something, or something **isn't** some description. Unlike 안, there is no distinction between separable and non-separable 하다 verbs when you use the ~지 않다 grammar form. You can attach ~지 않다 to all verb stems.

Grammar Form	Present Tense	Past Tense	Future Tense
A/V~지 않다	~지 않아요	~지 않았어요	~지 않을 거예요

ACTION VERBS & DESCRIPTIVE VERBS

Attach **~지 않다** to the verb stem of the verb. It does not matter if the verb stem ends on a vowel sound or a consonant sound.

먹다	→	먹지 않다	→	먹지 않아요	(subj. doesn't eat)
공부하다	→	공부하지 않다	→	공부하지 않아요	(subj. doesn't study)
요리하다	→	요리하지 않다	→	요리하지 않아요	(subj. doesn't cook)
맛있다	→	맛있지 않다	→	맛있지 않아요	(subj. isn't tasty)
재미있다	→	재미있지 않다	→	재미있지 않아요	(subj. isn't fun)

> 저는 공부하지 않아요. — I do not study.
> 사라가 운동하지 않아요. — Sara does not exercise.
> 톰이 요리하지 않아요. — Tom doesn't cook.
> 저는 빵을 먹지 않아요. — I do not eat bread.
> 학교가 좋지 않아요. — School isn't good.
> 피자는 맛있지 않아요. — Pizza is not delicious.
> 운동이 재미있지 않아요. — Working out isn't fun.

PAST TENSE

To talk about situations in the past, use the form **~지 않았어요**.

>	제가 공부하**지 않았어요**.	I didn't study.
>	사라가 운동하**지 않았어요**.	Sara didn't exercise.
>	학교가 좋**지 않았어요**.	School wasn't good.
>	운동이 재미있**지 않았어요**.	Exercise wasn't fun.

FUTURE TENSE

To talk about situations in the future, use the form **~지 않을 거예요**.

>	톰은 요리하**지 않을 거예요**.	Tom won't cook.
>	저는 빵을 먹**지 않을 거예요**.	I will not eat bread.
>	피자는 맛있**지 않을 거예요**.	Pizza won't be delicious.
>	운동은 재미있**지 않을 거예요**.	Working out won't be fun.

WHAT'S THE DIFFERENCE?

안 and ~지 않다 are very similar and are interchangeable most of the time. They can each be used in both spoken and written Korean. Native Korean speakers use both, depending on circumstance and personal preference.

안	~지 않다
Slightly less formal, used more in spoken language.	*Slightly more formal, used more in written language.*
고기를 **안** 먹어요. I don't eat meat. 저는 요리를 **안** 해요. I do not cook.	고기를 먹**지 않아요**. I don't eat meat. 저는 요리하**지 않아요**. I do not cook.
Placed before the verb.	*Attached to the verb stem.*
톰이 운동 **안** 해요. Tom doesn't exercise. 사라가 영화를 **안** 봐요. Sara doesn't watch movies.	톰이 운동하**지 않아요**. Tom doesn't exercise. 사라가 영화를 보**지 않아요**. Sara doesn't watch movies.

REFERENCE PAGES

안 A/V - page 61

A/V~았/었다 Past Tense - page 58
A/V~(으)ㄹ 것이다 Future Tense - page 60

USED IN WCK   150 times

못 V

For talking about things you can't do

오늘은 운동 못 해요.
I can't work out today.

Another way to negate verbs is to add "**못**." When you add 못 to your sentence, you are not just talking about a negative, you're also talking about a **lack of ability**. Similar to "can't" or "cannot" in English. Like "안," 못 acts differently with separable and non-separable 하다 verbs.

Note: 못 is generally not used with descriptive verbs.

ACTION VERBS (AND NON-SEPARABLE 하다 VERBS)

Place **못** before the action verb.

먹다	→	**못** 먹다	→	**못** 먹어요	(subj. cannot eat)
가다	→	**못** 가다	→	**못** 가요	(subj. cannot go)
보다	→	**못** 보다	→	**못** 봐요	(subj. cannot watch)

> 저는 글루텐을 **못** 먹어요. I can't eat gluten.
> 사라는 고기를 **못** 먹어요. Sara cannot eat meat.
> 저는 이 영화를 **못** 봐요. I cannot watch this movie.

SEPARABLE 하다 ACTION VERBS

Place **못** between the noun and the verb. You can connect the noun to the verb using the ~을/를 object particle, but this is optional.

공부하다	→	공부(를) **못** 하다	→	공부(를) **못** 해요	(subj. cannot study)
운동하다	→	운동(을) **못** 하다	→	운동(을) **못** 해요	(subj. cannot exercise)
요리하다	→	요리(를) **못** 하다	→	요리(를) **못** 해요	(subj. cannot cook)

> 저는 공부 **못** 해요. I can't study.
> 톰은 한국어를 공부 **못** 해요. Tom cannot study Korean.
> 저는 오늘 운동을 **못** 해요. I can't exercise today.

--- REFERENCE PAGES ---

하다 Verbs - page 49

> 사라는 오늘 요리를 **못** 해요.   Sara cannot cook today.

PAST TENSE
To talk about situations in the past, conjugate the final verb into the past tense.

> 저는 빵을 **못** 먹었어요.   I couldn't eat bread.
> 사라는 고기를 **못** 먹었어요.   Sara couldn't eat meat.
> 톰은 한국어를 공부 **못** 했어요.   Tom couldn't study Korean.

FUTURE TENSE
To talk about situations in the future, conjugate the final verb into the future tense.

> 저는 공부 **못** 할 거예요.   I won't be able to study.
> 저는 이 영화를 **못** 볼 거예요.   I won't be able to watch this movie.
> 저는 오늘 운동을 **못** 할 거예요.   I won't be able to exercise today.

WHAT'S THE DIFFERENCE?

안	못
Means that you don't do something. It's implied that you could do it, but choose not to.	*Means that you can't do something. Implies that there is some obstacle preventing you.*
저는 운동 **안** 해요. I don't exercise. You can, but you choose not to exercise.	저는 운동 **못** 해요. I can't exercise. Suggests illness or injury.
저는 고기를 **안** 먹어요. I don't eat meat. You can eat meat, but you choose not to.	저는 고기를 **못** 먹어요. I can't eat meat. Suggests religious reasons or allergies.
한국어를 **안** 해요. I do not speak Korean. You can speak Korean, but you choose not to.	한국어를 **못** 해요. I cannot speak Korean. You can't speak Korean, though you may wish to.

Note: If you want to say "I don't speak Korean," it's more natural to say "한국어를 못 해요" instead of "한국어를 안 해요."

REFERENCE PAGES

안 A/V - page 61
A/V~지 않다 - page 63
A/V~았/었다 Past Tense - page 58
A/V~(으)ㄹ 것이다 Future Tense - page 60

| USED IN WCK | 62 times |

V~지 못 하다
For talking about things you can't do

저는 서핑을 하지 못 해요.
I can't surf.

You can attach "~지 못 하다" to the verb stem of action verbs to talk about something you **can't** do. When you use the ~지 못 하다 grammar form, there is no distinction between separable and non-separable 하다 verbs. You can attach ~지 못 하다 to all action verb stems.

Note: ~지 못 하다 is generally not used with descriptive verbs.

Grammar Form	Present Tense	Past Tense	Future Tense
V~지 못 하다	~지 못 해요	~지 못 했어요	~지 못 할거예요

ACTION VERBS

Attach **~지 못 하다** to the verb stem of the action verb. It does not matter if the verb stem ends on a vowel sound or a consonant sound.

먹다 →	먹지 못 하다	→ 먹지 못 해요	(subj. cannot eat)
요리하다→	요리하지 못 하다	→ 요리하지 못 해요	(subj. cannot cook)
운동하다→	운동하지 못 하다	→ 운동하지 못 해요	(subj. cannot exercise)

> 사라는 고기를 먹지 못 해요. — Sara can't eat meat.
> 저는 글루텐을 먹지 못 해요. — I cannot eat gluten.
> 저는 커피를 마시지 못 해요. — I can't drink coffee.
> 저는 운동하지 못 해요. — I cannot exercise.
> 메리는 요리하지 못 해요. — Mary cannot cook.
> 오늘은 공부하지 못 해요. — I cannot study today.

REFERENCE PAGES

못 V - page 65

1

PAST TENSE
To talk about a situation in the past, use the form ~지 못 했어요.

> 사라는 고기를 먹**지 못 했어요.**   Sara couldn't eat meat.
> 저는 커피를 마시**지 못 했어요.**   I couldn't drink coffee.
> 어제 저는 운동하**지 못 했어요.**   I couldn't exercise yesterday.

FUTURE TENSE
To talk about a situation in the future, use the form ~지 못 할 거예요.

> 메리는 요리하**지 못 할 거예요.**   Mary will not be able to cook.
> 오늘은 공부하**지 못 할 거예요.**   I will not be able to study today.
> 내일은 커피를 마시**지 못 할 거예요.**   Tomorrow I won't be able to drink coffee.

WHAT'S THE DIFFERENCE?

못 and ~지 못 하다 are very similar and are interchangeable in most situations. Although 못 tends to be used in more spoken language, and 지 못 하다 tends to be used more in written language, they are both stilll commonly used in either.

못	~지 못 하다
Less formal, more common in spoken language.	More formal, used more in written language.
저는 운동 **못** 해요. I cannot exercise. (When speaking out loud)	저는 운동하**지 못** 해요. I cannot exercise. (When writing, for example in an email)
Placed before the verb, or in the middle of separable 하다 verbs.	Attaches to the verb stem.
톰이 그 영화를 **못** 봐요. Tom cannot watch that movie. 저는 글루텐을 **못** 먹어요. I can't eat gluten.	톰이 그 영화를 보**지 못** 해요. Tom cannot watch that movie. 저는 글루텐을 먹**지 못** 해요. I can't eat gluten.

REFERENCE PAGES

A/V~았/었다 Past Tense - page 58   A/V~(으)ㄹ 것이다 Future Tense - page 60

USED IN WCK   379 times

V~는 것

For changing verbs into nouns (nominalization)

한국어를 공부하는 것을 좋아해요.
I like studying Korean.

Nominalization sounds complicated, but it's an incredibly important grammar tool that is used every day. Essentially, nominalization turns a verb (e.g. "to eat") into it's noun form (i.e. the noun "eating"). These nominalized verbs act as nouns in the sentence, and can be used, described, or acted on just like any other noun. In English, nominalized verbs are called **gerunds**.
Note: ~는 것 can also be seen as ~는 거, particularly when speaking.
Note: ~는 것 is not used with descriptive verbs.

ACTION VERBS
To turn an action verb into a noun, attach **~는 것** to the verb stem of the action verb.

먹다	→	먹는 것	(the noun "eating")
가다	→	가는 것	(the noun "going")
보다	→	보는 것	(the noun "watching")

Once you add ~는 것 to a verb stem and turn the verb into a noun, you can use the resulting noun in new ways in the sentence. This means you can add ~이/가 if you want to describe the noun with a descriptive verb, or ~을/를 to act upon that noun with an action verb.

V~는 것이   A nominalized verb that you want to make the **subject** of the sentence.
V~는 것을   A nominalized verb that you want to make the **object** of the sentence.
V~는 것은   A nominalized verb that you want to make the **topic** of the sentence.

> 먹는 **것**이 재미있어요.   Eating is fun.
> 피자를 먹는 **것**을 좋아해요.   I like eating pizza.
> 고기를 먹는 **것**을 좋아해요.   I like eating meat.
> 영화를 보는 것을 좋아해요.   I like watching movies.
> 드라마를 보는 **것**이 재미있어요. Watching dramas is fun.

REFERENCE PAGES

~을/를 + Action Verbs - page 53   ~은/는 Topic Particle - page 29
~이/가 + Descriptive Verbs - page 51

1

WHY MUST I TURN VERBS INTO NOUNS?

Nominalization is not unique to Korean. In English, it's grammatically incorrect to say "I like eat." You have to say "I like eat**ing**." or "I like **to eat**." This is the role that ~는 것 plays in Korean. For example:

O 먹는 것이 좋아요.　　　　　　　　I like eating.
O 영화를 보는 것을 좋아해요.　　　　I like watching movies.

USING ~는 것 WITH SEPARABLE 하다 VERBS

It is **optional** to use ~는 것 when you are using separable 하다 action verbs, because separable 하다 verbs **already contain nouns**. You can either take out the noun and use it by itself, or use ~는 것 with the full 하다 verb. To refresh your knowledge on separable and non-separable 하다 verbs, check the reference page below.

> 공부를 좋아해요.　　공부하는 것을 좋아해요.　　I like studying.
> 요리가 싫어요.　　　요리하는 것이 싫어요.　　　I don't like cooking.

COLLOQUIALLY: ~는 게, ~는 걸, & ~는 건

It is common to shorten ~는 것, particularly in spoken language.

~는 것	→	**~는 거**	(used when dropping the particle)
~는 것+이	→	**~는 게**	(이 is the subject particle)
~는 것+을	→	**~는 걸**	(을 is the object particle)
~는 것+은	→	**~는 건**	(은 is the topic particle)

> 공부하는 거 재미있어요.　　　　　Studying is fun.
> 요리하는 게 좋아요.　　　　　　　Cooking is nice.
> 한국어를 공부하는 걸 좋아해요.　　I like studying Korean.
> 고기를 먹는 건 안 좋아해요.　　　As for eating meat, I don't like it.

ENDING A SENTENCE: ~는 거예요

You can end a sentence with ~는 것, which in simple present tense becomes ~는 거예요.

> Q. 뭘 하는 거예요?　　　　　What are you doing?
> A. 저는 공부하는 거예요.　　I am studying.
> A. 저는 먹는 거예요.　　　　I am eating.

_____ REFERENCE PAGES _____

하다 Verbs - page 49

Place~에 가다/오다

To talk about the destination of movement

저는 해변에 가요.
I'm going to the beach.

Now we are going to introduce a new particle: the ~에 particle. This particle is used many different ways in Korean. First, we are going to look at how it is used to indicate a **direction of movement** to or from some place. We will look at how it is used with the verbs "가다" (to go) and "오다" (to come).

Note: the ~에 particle is used with many other movement-related verbs in Korean as well, such as "도착하다" (to arrive), "돌아가다" (to return, come back), "나오다" (to come out), etc.

Grammar Form	Present Tense	Past Tense	Future Tense
N~에 가다	~에 가요	~에 갔어요	~에 갈 거예요
N~에 오다	~에 와요	~에 왔어요	~에 올 거예요

PLACE~에 가다

One verb commonly seen with the ~에 particle is "가다," which means "to go." When you attach "~에 가다" to a place noun, it means: "to go to that place."

집 →	집에 가다 →	집에 가요	(subj. goes home)
학교 →	학교에 가다 →	학교에 가요	(subj. goes to school)
도서관 →	도서관에 가다 →	도서관에 가요	(subj. goes to the library)

> 저는 집에 가요. — I go home.
> 저는 학교에 가요. — I go to school.
> 메리는 도서관에 가요. — Mary goes to school.
> 톰은 집에 가요. — Tom goes home.
> 사라가 학교에 갔어요. — Sara went to school.
> 제 친구가 도서관에 갈 거예요. — My friend will go to the library.

--- REFERENCE PAGES ---

A/V~았/었다 Past Tense - page 58   A/V~(으)ㄹ 것이다 Future Tense - page 60

1

PLACE~에 오다

The second verb commonly seen with the ~에 particle is "오다," which means "to come."

집	→	집에 오다	→	집에 와요 (to come home)
학교	→	학교에 오다	→	학교에 와요 (to come to your school)
도서관	→	도서관에 오다	→	도서관에 와요 (to come to the library)

> 오늘 학교에 와요?　　　Coming to school today?　　(the speaker is at school)
> 오늘 도서관에 와요?　　Coming to the library today? (the speaker is at the library)
> 지금 집에 와요.　　　　Come home now.　　　　　(the speaker is at home)
> 한국에 와요.　　　　　Come to Korea.　　　　　 (the speaker is in Korea)
> 저는 집에 왔어요.　　　I came home.　　　　　　(the speaker is at home)
> 사라가 학교에 올 거예요. Sara will come to school.　(the speaker is at school)

USAGE NOTE: 오다 & 가다

You cannot use "오다" and "가다" in all the same places you use "to come" and "to go" in English. This is because "가다" and "오다" in Korean are always based on the **speaker's** current position. All the things coming towards your position always use "오다" and all the things (including yourself) going away from your position always use "가다."

For example: imagine you're home and your friend is texting you from school. They say:

　　Q. 학교에 **와요**?　　　Are you coming to school?
　　A1. 네, **가요**.　　　　Yes, I'm coming/going.
　　A2. 아니요, 안 **가요**.　No, I'm not coming/going.

In English, you can use either "coming" or "going" in your answer. But in Korean, the **only** possible answer is "가요" (or "안 가요") because it is always in reference to your location as the speaker. You are not currently at school, so you must say that you are **going** (or not going) there. However, the person asking you can use "와요?" because they **are** at school, so from their position, you are coming towards them.

Note: for more explanation and clarification on this point, check out videos online.

MORE THAN ONE PLACE?

If you are talking about going to more than one place, you can join the places together with the "and" particle, see the reference page below. (e.g. "I'm going to Korea and Japan" or "I'm going to school and the library.")

REFERENCE PAGES

N~와/과, N~(이)랑, N~하고 - page 96

Place~(으) 로

To talk about a direction of movement

지금 집으로 가요.
I'm going home.

We just saw that we can use the ~에 particle to talk about direction (to some place), but there is another particle that can be used in a very similar way, which is ~(으)로. First let's look at how ~(으)로 is conjugated onto nouns.

Place~(으) 로

If the noun ends on a vowel sound or ㄹ, you attach ~로.

| 학교 | → | 학교로 | (towards the school) |
| 거실 | → | 거실로 | (towards the living room) |

If the noun ends on a consonant sound you attach ~으로.

| 집 | → | 집으로 | (towards home) |
| 헬스장 | → | 헬스장으로 | (towards the gym) |

> 집으로 가요.   I'm going home.
> 학교로 가요.   I'm going to school.
> 한국으로 갈 거예요.   I will go to Korea.
> 미국으로 갔어요.   I went to America.
> 일본으로 이사했어요.   I moved to Japan.

WHAT'S THE DIFFERENCE?

These two particles are very similar and are frequently interchangeable, although there is a nuanced difference.

N~에	N~(으)로
Focuses on the final location.	Focuses on the direction of movement.
집에 가요. I'm going **home**. (Home is the location to where I am going)	집으로 가요. I'm **going** home. (I'm aiming in that general direction)

Time~에 V

The time particle

저는 아침에 운동해요.
I work out in the morning.

The ~에 particle is also used with nouns related to time to indicate that something happens on/at a certain time.

TIME NOUNS

The ~에 particle is also attached to nouns relating to time to indicate something happens at/on a certain time. Simply attach the ~에 particle after a time-related noun.

아침	→	아침에	(in the morning)
저녁	→	저녁에	(in the evening)
3시	→	3시에	(at 3 o'clock)
일요일	→	일요일에	(on Sunday)

> 저녁에 먹어요. — I eat in the evening.
> 내년에 한국에 가요. — I go to Korea next year.
> 5시에 운동해요. — I work out at 5 o'clock.
> 1시에 점심을 먹어요. — At 1 o'clock, I eat lunch.
> 일요일에 운동하지 않아요. — I don't work out on Sunday.
> 토요일에 학교에 안 가요. — On Saturday I don't go to school.
> 금요일에 요리를 안 해요. — I don't cook on Friday.

Note: for more information on numbers (and their pronunciations) check the reference page below.

MORE THAN ONE ~에 PARTICLE?

When a sentence uses **both** a location and a time, there can be more than one ~에 particle used in the sentence. For example:

──────────────── REFERENCE PAGES ────────────────

Words for Times & Dates - page 287

O 6시에 집에 가요.　　　　　I go home at 6 o'clock.
O 월요일에 학교에 있어요.　　On Monday I'm at school.

Even though the same particle is used, they have a slightly different purpose. When ~에 is used on place nouns, it indicates movement to or from that place. When ~에 is used on time nouns, it indiciates an action occuring at that time.

MORE THAN ONE TIME?
If listing more than one time, the ~에 particle is placed on the **last** word in the list.
Also, times should be ordered from largest to smallest. For example:

O 아침 7시에...　　　　　　　　At 7 o'clock in the morning...
X 아침에 7시에　　　　　　　　Incorrect grammar
O 내년 1월 1일 오전 10시에...　　on January 1st next year at 10am...
X 1일 1월 내년에 오전 10시에　Incorrect grammar

TIME NOUNS THAT DON'T USE ~에
Most time nouns use the ~에 particle in Korean. However, some time words in Korean **do not** use the ~에 particle. This is similar to how we don't say "on today" or "on yesterday" in English. Instead of using the ~에 particle, these words appear **alone or with the ~은/는 topic particle**.

오늘	어제	지금	내일	올해	요즘
today	yesterday	now	tomorrow	this year	these days

O 오늘(은) 학교에 가요.　　　　I go to school today.
X 오늘에 학교에 가요.　　　　　I go to school on today.
O 지금(은) 한국어를 공부해요.　Now I study Korean.
X 지금에 한국어를 공부해요.　　On now I study Korean.
O 내일(은) 운동해요.　　　　　Tomorrow I work out.
X 내일에 운동해요.　　　　　　On tomorrow, I work out.

{ *Generally, but not always, if the time noun doesn't use a preposition (in/at/on/etc.) in English, it doesn't use one in Korean.* }

───────────── REFERENCE PAGES ─────────────

Place~에 가다/오다 - page 71

N~에 V

The prepositional particle

지금 집에 있어요.
I'm at home right now.

Previously we looked at how the ~에 particle is used with verbs relating to movement, and with nouns relating to times. But ~에 has a wide variety of usages beyond that. You can think of ~에 being a general prepositional particle, taking the role of common prepositions in English like "in," "at," "on," etc.

N~에 V

Here are some more examples of ways the ~에 particle can connect nouns and verbs.

N~에 있다 →	N~에 있어요	(subj. is at N)
N~에 앉다 →	N~에 앉아요	(subj. sits on N)
N~에 도착하다 →	N~에 도착해요	(subj. arrives at N)
N~에 참여하다 →	N~에 참여해요	(subj. participates in N)
N~에 관심이 있다 →	N~에 관심이 있어요	(subj. has interest in N)

> 오늘 집에 있어요. — I'm at home today.
> 지금 학교에 있어요. — I'm at school right now.
> 메리가 의자에 앉아요. — Mary sits on a chair.
> 학교에 사람이 많아요. — There are many people at school.
> 도서관에 도착해요. — I'm arriving at the library.
> 대회에 참여해요. — I'm particpating in a contest.
> 저는 한국에 관심이 있어요. — I am interested in Korea.
> 주제에 집중해요. — I concentrate on the topic.

Note: we do not expect you to know or remember all of this vocabulary. The important take-away is to remember that ~에 is often used as a preposition, like "at," "in" or "on."

N~에서 & N~까지

For talking about going between places

샌프란시스코에서 서울까지 가요.
We go from San Francisco to Seoul.

If you want to say you are moving between two places, use "**~에서**" on the noun you are leaving from, and "**~까지**" on the place you are going to. It's used with verbs about movement (e.g. 가다, 오다).

PLACE NOUNS: ~에서
Add ~에서 to a place noun to say that you're going from that place. Simply attach ~에서 after the noun. It does not matter if the noun ends on a vowel sound or a consonant sound.

학교	→ 학교**에서**	(from school)
헬스장	→ 헬스장**에서**	(from the gym)
집	→ 집**에서**	(from home)

PLACE NOUNS: ~까지
Add ~까지 to a place noun to say you're going to that place (from another). Simply attach ~까지 after the noun. It does not matter if the noun ends on a vowel sound or a consonant sound.

학교	→ 학교**까지**	(to school)
헬스장	→ 헬스장**까지**	(to the gym)
집	→ 집**까지**	(to home)

> 집**에서** 학교**까지** 가요. — I go from home to school.
> 학교**에서** 도서관**까지** 가요. — I go from school to the library.
> 4시에 도서관**에서** 헬스장**까지** 가요. — At 4 o'clock I go from the library to the gym.
> 사라가 한국**에서** 미국**까지** 가요. — Sara goes from Korea to America.
> 톰이 미국**에서** 한국**까지** 가요. — Tom goes from America to Korea.

Note: it's common to drop the beginning movement (i.e. place~에서) and just state your final destination (place~까지). E.g. 집까지 가요 means "I go home" (from somewhere else).

N~부터 & N~까지

For talking about spans of time

아침부터 저녁까지 일해요.
I work from morning until night.

You can use the ~부터 and ~까지 particles to talk about a span from one time to another. When talking about time, ~부터 is the **from** particle, and ~까지 is the **to** particle.

NOUNS: ~부터

To add ~부터 to a time noun, simply place it after the noun. It does not matter if the noun ends on a vowel sound or a consonant sound.

아침	→	아침**부터**	(from morning)
월요일	→	월요일**부터**	(from Monday)
8시	→	8시**부터**	(from 8 o'clock)
2019년	→	2019년**부터**	(from the year 2019)
지난주	→	지난주**부터**	(from last week)

NOUNS: ~까지

To add ~까지 to a time noun, simply place it after the noun. It does not matter if the noun ends on a vowel sound or a consonant sound.

아침	→	아침**까지**	(until morning)
저녁	→	저녁**까지**	(until evening)
3시	→	3시**까지**	(until 8 o'clock)
2021년	→	2021년**까지**	(until the year 2021)
7월	→	7월**까지**	(until July)

CREATING SENTENCES

You can follow this formula to construct simple sentences using ~부터 and ~까지

Subject + Time~부터 + Time~까지 + Action Performed

> 저는 아침**부터** 저녁**까지** 공부해요.   I study from morning until night.

─── **REFERENCE PAGES** ───

Words for Times & Dates - page 287

> 톰은 아침**부터** 저녁**까지** 요리해요.
> 사라가 8시**부터** 9시**까지** 운동해요.
> 메리가 1시**부터** 2시**까지** 점심을 먹어요.
> 여름은 6월**부터** 9월**까지**예요.

Tom cooks from morning until night.
Sara exercises from 8 o'clock until 9 o'clock.
I eat lunch from 1 o'clock until 2 o'clock.
Summer is from June until September.

WHAT'S THE DIFFERENCE?

~부터	~에서
Used when talking about time.	Used when talking about places.
X 한국부터 미국까지 가요. (한국 is not a time)	O 한국에서 미국까지 가요. I go from Korea to America.
O 8시부터 3시까지 학교에 있어요. I am at school from 8 o'clock until 3 o'clock.	X 8시에서 3시까지 학교에 있어요. (8시 is not a place)

Note: times & places use different particles for "from," but use the same particle for "to" (까지).

USAGE NOTE: USING ON THEIR OWN

While frequently used in pairs to show a range, these paricles (~에서, ~부터, and ~까지), can also appear alone. For example:

> 지금**부터** 공부해요.
> 2시**까지** 공부할 거예요.
> 서울**까지** 갔어요.
> 미국**에서** 왔어요.
> 내일**까지** 끝낼 거예요.

I'm studying from now onwards.
I will study until 2 o'clock.
I went to Seoul.
I came from America.
I will finish it by tomorrow.

PRACTICE EXERCISES

Given the following English sentences, write an equivalent Korean expression.

1. I study from 6 o'clock until 7 o'clock.

2. I will work until six.

3. I go to school from Monday to Friday.

4. Tomorrow I go from Busan to Seoul.

ANSWERS: 1. (저는) 6시부터 7시까지 공부해요. 2. (저는) 6시까지 일할 거예요. 3. (저는) 월요일부터 금요일까지 학교에 가요. 4. (저는) 내일 부산에서 서울까지 가요.

USED IN WCK — 324 times

N~에서 Particle

The location of action particle

저는 집에서 한국어를 공부해요.
I study Korean at home.

The particle **~에서** attaches to a place noun to say that you're **doing some action in that location.**

NOUNS

When attaching to place nouns, simply add **~에서** after the noun. It does not matter if the noun ends on a vowel sound or a consonant sound.

집	→	집에서	(at home)
헬스장	→	헬스장에서	(at the gym)
도서관	→	도서관에서	(at the library)

> 집에서 요리해요. — I cook at home.
> 집에서 공부해요. — I study at home.
> 집에서 운동해요. — I work out at home.
> 헬스장에서 운동해요. — I work out at the gym.
> 도서관에서 공부해요. — I study at the library.

SPECIAL CASE: "살다"

살다, the verb meaning "to live" is a special case. It can use either ~에 or ~에서. Both are correct and natural. When using the verb "살다," placing ~에 on the noun just specifies that it's **the place** where you live. Using ~에서 puts more thought towards the **action of living** that you do in that location.

> 미국에 살아요.   I live in America.   (America is the place where I live)
> 미국에서 살아요.   I live in America.   (I **live** in America. I eat, sleep, work, here)

Note: this is a nuanced difference. When talking about living places, you can use either ~에 or ~에서.

USAGE NOTE: NOT NECESSARILY A PHYSICAL PLACE

The 'place' that you are talking about actions occuring in may be figurative. For example:

> 웹사이트에서 다운받아요. — Download it on our website.
> 반지의 제왕에서 호빗이 모르도르에 가요. — In The Lord of the Rings, the hobbits go to Mordor.
> 꿈에서 저는 날고 있었어요. — In my dream I was flying.

WHAT'S THE DIFFERENCE?

~에	~에서
~에 is used to talk about a direction of movement, to indicate times, and with some other verbs like 있다/없다.	~에서 is used to talk about doing an action in, or at, some location.
X 집에 사과를 먹어요. I eat an apple to home. O 집에 가요. I go home. X 한국에 한국어를 공부해요. I study Korean to Korea. O 3시에 집에서 공부해요. At 3 o'clock I study in my house.	O 집에서 사과를 먹어요. I eat an apple at home. X 집에서 가요. I'm going at home. O 한국에서 한국어를 공부해요. I study Korean in Korea. X 3시에서 집에 공부해요. In 3 o'clock, I study to my house.

WHAT'S THE DIFFERENCE?

~에서 ("IN/AT")	~에서 ("FROM")
~에서 is the location of action particle used to show that an action is performed in a place.	~에서 is also used to mean "from" when talking about going between two places.
집에서 먹어요. I eat at home. Because the verb is the action verb "먹다" (to eat), ~에서 is the "location of action" particle here.	집에서 학교까지 가요. I go from home to school. Because the verb is the motion verb "가다" (to go), ~에서 is the "from" particle here.

REFERENCE PAGES

Place~에 가다/오다 - page 71   N~에서 & N~까지 - page 77

> USED IN WCK   64 times

N~들

The plural particle

제 친구들이 농구를 해요.
My friends play basketball.

The ~들 particle attaches to nouns to indicate that there is more than one of that noun. After adding ~들, add the appropriate particle given it's role in the sentence: i.e. whether the noun is the subject (~이/가), object (~을/를), or topic (~은/는).

NOUNS

When attaching to place nouns, simply add **~들** after the noun. It does not matter if the noun ends on a vowel sound or a consonant sound.

친구 →	친구들	Friends
사람 →	사람들	People
가족 →	가족들	Families/family members

> 제 친구들이 공부해요. — My friends study.
> 그 사람들이 고기를 먹어요. — Those people eat meat.
> 우리 가족들은 집에 살아요. — My family members live in a house.

USAGE NOTE: NOT REQUIRED

In English, we always have to specify if something is plural. However, this is **not the case** in Korean. In Korean, nouns **do not need** ~들 even if you are talking about more than one.

> 사과를 먹어요. I eat apple(s). (could mean one apple or multiple apples)
> 당근을 요리해요. I cook carrot(s). (could mean one carrot or multiple carrots)
> 영화를 봐요.   I see movie(s). (could mean one movie or multiple movies).

The one place ~들 is most commonly used is on **people nouns.**

N~도

The "too" particle

제 친구도 요가를 해요.
My friend does yoga, too.

If you want to say something like: "this thing as well" or "I also do this," you can use the ~도 particle.

NOUNS
You can attach **~도** to all nouns regardless if the noun ends on a vowel sound or a consonant sound.

저	→	저**도**	(me too)
친구	→	친구**도**	(a friend, too)
한국어	→	한국어**도**	(Korean, too)

> 저**도** 미국에 살아요. — I, too, live in America.
> 제 친구**도** 한국어를 공부해요. — My friend also studies Korean.
> 저는 한국어**도** 공부해요. — I study Korean as well.
> 아침에 물**도** 마셨어요. — In the morning I also drank water.

COMBINING WITH OTHER PARTICLES
The ~도 particle **takes the place** of subject, object, and topic particles. For example:
O 김치도 먹어요.   I also eat kimchi.
X 김치를도 먹어요.   Incorrect grammar

The ~도 particle is placed **after** other particles (like ~에 and ~에서 particles).
O 카페에도 가요.   I'm also going to a cafe.
O 카페에서도 먹어요. I also eat at cafes.

PLACEMENT ON DIFFERENT NOUNS IN A SENTENCE
You can place ~도 on any noun in the sentence, and the meaning of the sentence will chance slightly depending on where you place ~도. The noun that you place ~도 on is the noun that

gets the meaning of "also." In English, the words "also/as well/too" are all somewhat ambiguous in their meaning. They are not tied to specific nouns like ~도 is. For example, if someone says: "I also drink coffee in the morning," it can mean any of:

1 "I drink **coffee** (as well as other things) in the morning."
2 "I drink coffee in the **morning** (as well as at other times)."
3 "**I** (as well as other people) drink coffee in the morning."

In English, **we rely on intonation**. We put emphasis on the word in the sentence we are referring to. However, in Korean, you just mark that word clearly with ~도.

1 저는 아침에**도** 커피를 마셔요.
I also drink coffee in the **morning**.
(As well as at other times)

2 저는 아침에 커피**도** 마셔요.
I also drink **coffee** in the morning.
(As well as other drinks)

3 저**도** 아침에 커피를 마셔요.
I also drink coffee in the morning.
(As well as other people)

1 저는 오늘**도** 영화를 봐요.
Today I'm also watching a movie.
(As well as on previous days)

2 저는 오늘 영화**도** 봐요.
Today I'm also watching a **movie**.
(As well as watching other things)

3 저**도** 오늘 영화를 봐요.
Today **I'm** also watching a movie.
(As well as other people)

1 저는 헬스장에서**도** 운동을 해요.
I also work out at the **gym**.
(As well as at other places)

2 저는 헬스장에서 운동**도** 해요.
I also **work out** at the gym.
(As well as doing other things there)

3 저**도** 헬스장에서 운동을 해요
I also work out at the gym.
(As well as other people)

PRACTICE EXERCISES

Given the following Korean sentences, write an equivalent English expression.

1. 저도 한국어를 공부해요.

2. 저는 빵도 먹어요.

3. 저는 헬스장에서도 운동해요.

4. 저는 먹는 것도 좋아해요.

5. 고기를 먹는 것도 좋아하지 않아요.

ANSWERS: 1. I also study Korean.   2. I also eat bread.   3. I also work out at the gym.   4. I also like eating.   5. I also don't like eating meat.

USED IN WCK   88 times

N~만

The "only" particle

아침에 사과만 먹어요.
In the morning I only eat an apple.

If you want to say that you "only" use/do something, you can attach ~만 to any noun.

NOUNS
Attach **~만** to all nouns regardless of whether the noun ends on a vowel sound or a consonant sound.

커피 →	커피**만**	(only coffee)
차 →	차**만**	(only tea)
드라마 →	드라마**만**	(only dramas)

> 저는 아침에 커피**만** 마셔요.   In the morning, I only drink coffee.
> 저는 저녁에 차**만** 마셔요.   I only drink tea in the evening.
> 저는 한국 드라마**만** 봐요.   I only watch Korean dramas.
> 어제 한국어**만** 공부했어요.   Yesterday I only studied Korean.

COMBINING WITH PARTICLES
~만 **replaces** the subject, object, and topic particles. For example:
O 고기만 먹어요.   I only eat meat.
X 고기를만 먹어요.   Incorrect grammar

~만 is placed **after** other particles (like ~에 and ~에서 particles).
O 한국에만 가요.   I'm only going to Korea.
O 한국에서만 여행해요.   I'm only traveling in Korea.

COMBINING WITH "그냥" (JUST)
~만 is often combined with "그냥" in a sentence to emphasize "just" this thing.

1

> 아침에 그냥 사과**만** 먹어요.   In the morning, I just only eat an apple.
> 그냥 카페에**만** 가요.   I'm just only going to a cafe.
> 그냥 친구**만** 만나요.   I'm just only meeting a friend.

PLACEMENT ON DIFFERENT NOUNS IN A SENTENCE

You can place ~만 on any noun in the sentence to say that you're talking about "only" that noun. Moving ~만 to different nouns in the sentence will change the meaning of the sentence slightly.

> 오늘**만** 영화를 봐요.   Today is the only day I'm watching a movie.
> 오늘 영화**만** 봐요.   Today I am only watching movies.
> 아침에**만** 커피를 마셔요.   The only time I drink coffee is in the morning.
> 아침에 커피**만** 마셔요.   In the morning, the only thing I drink is coffee.

저는 아침에**만** 커피를 마셔요.   저는 아침에 커피**만** 마셔요.   저**만** 아침에 커피를 마셔요.
I only drink coffee in the **morning**.   I only drink **coffee** in the morning.   **I** only drink coffee in the morning.
(Not at any other times)   (No other drinks, only coffee)   (I'm the only one)

PRACTICE EXERCISES

Given the following Korean sentences, write an equivalent English expression.

1. 저는 도서관에서만 한국어를 공부해요.

2. 내일은 물만 마실 거예요.

3. 어제는 차만 마셨어요.

4. 돼지고기만 못 먹어요.

5. 여름에는 아이스커피만 마셔요.

6. 집에서 영어만 말해요.

ANSWERS: 1. I only study Korean at the library. 2. Tomorrow I'll only drink water. 3. Yesterday I only drank tea. 4. I only can't eat pork. 5. I only drink iced coffee in the summer. 6. I only speak English at home.

Level Two

Expanding your Sentences

DIFFICULTY LEVEL: EASY
The example sentences are written using simple grammar and vocabulary designed to help you understand the grammar concept in the most accessible way.

Level Two Grammar

What we will learn

한국어 문법을 공부하자!
Let's study Korean grammar!

The ㅂ Irregular	90
V~고 싶다	93
N~와/과, N~(이)랑, N~하고	96
잘 & 잘 못 V	99
A~ㄴ/은/는 N	100
V~고 있다	102
아직	104
누구, 무엇, 언제, 어디, 왜 & 어떻게	106
그리고, 그래서 & 하지만	107
A/V~고 N~(이)고	108
A/V~지만, N~(이)지만	112
A/V~아/어서 N(이)라서	115
Words of Frequency	118
더 & 덜	119
N~보다	120
N~(으)로	122
보통, 주로 & 평소에	123
A/V~(으)면	125
V~기 시작하다	127
처음(으로)	128

Level Two Vocab

What we will learn

한국어 어휘을 배우자!
Let's learn Korean vocabulary!

NOUNS
People:
친구 - friend
엄마 - mom
아빠 - dad
Places:
카페 - cafe
식당 - restaurant
서점 - bookstore
콘서트 - concert
영화관 - movie theater
직장 - work/the office
Miscellaneous:
책 - a book
음악 - music
노래 - song
물 - water
커피 - coffee
차 - tea
김치 - kimchi
자주 - often
날씨 - weather
영화 - movie

드라마 - dramas/tv-series
음식 - food
돈 - money
비행기 - plane
어제 - yesterday
여행 - vacation

DESCRIPTIVE VERBS
춥다 - to be cold (!)
덥다 - to be hot (!)
맵다 - to be spicy (!)
어렵다 - to be difficult (!)
쉽다 - to be easy (!)
비싸다 - to be expensive
싸다 - to be cheap
있다 - to have
없다 - to not have
많다 - to be many

ACTION VERBS
사다 - to buy
읽다 - to read
듣다 - to listen (!)
쓰다 - to write (!)
마시다 - to drink
비가 오다/내리다 - to rain
보다 - to see/watch
일하다 - to work
눈이 오다 - to snow
만나다 - to meet
만들다 - to make (!)

Use flashcards on Quizlet!

Note: in this Level you will find the vocabulary above plus the vocabulary used in Level One.
Note: verbs with a (!) symbol are irregular verbs. Check the reference pages below to learn more.

REFERENCE PAGES

The ㅂ Irregular - page 90
ㄷ Irregular - page 292

으 Irregular - page 294
ㄹ Irregular - page 296

The ㅂ Irregular

Conjugating these irregular verbs

더워요.
It's hot.

ㅂ irregular verbs are very common among Korean descriptive verbs. Some examples include:

덥다	춥다	어렵다	쉽다
to be hot	to be cold	to be hard/difficult	to be easy

To conjugate these verbs into the present tense, follow these steps:
1 Find the verb in its dictionary form
2 Remove -다 to find the verb stem
3 Take away the ㅂ
4 Add an 우 after what remains
5 Conjugate the 우 into present tense by adding ~어요, hence becoming ~워요.
Let's look at four examples: 덥다, 춥다, 쉽다 and 돕다.

1 덥다 is a verb in its dictionary form meaning "to be hot"
2 덥 is the verb stem of the verb 덥다
3 Take away the ㅂ and you're left with 더
4 Add an 우 and you have 더우
5 To conjugate to the present tense, add ~어요 because the last vowel sound is not ㅏ, ㅗ or 하
6 더워요 is the present tense conjugation of the verb 덥다. "더워요." means; "It is hot," in casual polite formality.

In this book we will mark ㅂ irregular verbs with a (!) symbol.

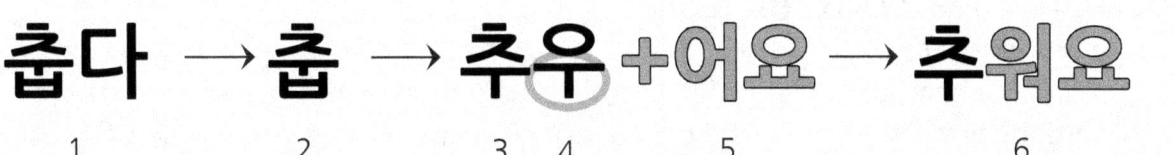

1 춥다 is a verb in its dictionary form meaning "to be cold"
2 춥 is the verb stem of the verb 춥다
3 Take away the ㅂ and you're left with 추
4 Add an 우 and you have 추우
5 To conjugate to the present tense, add ~어요 because the last vowel sound is not ㅏ, ㅗ or 하. 우 combines with 어 to make 워.
6 추워요 is the present tense conjugation of the verb 춥다. "추워요." means; "It is cold," in casual polite formality.

쉽다 → 쉽 → 쉬우 +어요 → 쉬워요
  1   2   3 4   5   6

1 쉽다 is a verb in its dictionary form meaning "to be easy"
2 쉽 is the verb stem of the verb 쉽다
3 Take away the ㅂ and you're left with 쉬
4 Add an 우 and you have 쉬우
5 To conjugate to the present tense, add ~어요 because the last vowel sound is not ㅏ, ㅗ or 하. 우 combines with 어 to make 워.
6 쉬워요 is the present tense conjugation of the verb 쉽다. "쉬워요." means; "It is easy," in casual polite formality.

EXCEPTIONS: REGULAR ㅂ VERBS
There are some exceptions to the ㅂ irregular. These verbs end in ㅂ but conjugate the regular way.
씹다 (to chew) → 씹어요
입다 (to wear) → 입어요
잡다 (to catch) → 잡아요

Note: you will have to memorize which verbs are regular and irregular.

TWO SPECIAL ㅂ IRREGULARS: "돕다 & 곱다"

There are two exceptions to the ㅂ irregular conjugation rules: 돕다 (to help) and 곱다 (to be pretty - less commonly used than 예쁘다). They are still irregular verbs, but when you're conjugating into the present tense, instead of adding "우" after the verb stem, you add "오." After that, you add ~아요 and the two vowels merge to become "와요."

돕다 → 돕 → 도오 + 아요 → 도와요
  1   2   3   4   5   6

1 돕다 is a verb in its dictionary form meaning "to help"
2 돕 is the verb stem of the verb 돕다
3 Take away the ㅂ and you're left with 도
4 Add an 오 and you have 도오
5 To conjugate to the present tense, add **~아요** because the last vowel sound is ㅗ. 오 combines with 아 to make 와.
6 **도와요** is the present tense conjugation of the verb 돕다. "도와요." means; "subj. helps," in casual polite formality.

PAST TENSE

To conjugate ㅂ irregular verbs in the past tense, the -워요 ending becomes -**웠어요**.

>	날씨가 더**웠어요**.	The weather was hot.
>	어제는 추**웠어요**.	It was cold yesterday.
>	시험이 어려**웠어요**.	The test was hard.
>	제 친구가 **고왔어요**.*	My friend was pretty. (*See above for special case)

FUTURE TENSE

To conjugate ㅂ irregular verbs into the future tense, the -워요 ending becomes **-울 거예요**.

>	날씨가 더**울 거예요**.	The weather will be hot.
>	내일은 추**울 거예요**.	Tomorrow will be cold.
>	시험이 어려**울 거예요**.	The test will be difficult.
>	제 친구가 저를 도**울 거예요**.	My friend will help me.

Note: 돕다 and 곱다 only use "아" when "아" is an option in the conjugation. If a different vowel sound is being conjugated on, (e.g. "으"), then 우 is added like other ㅂ irregular verbs.

USED IN WCK — 249 times

V~고 싶다

For things you want to do

저는 여행하고 싶어요.
I want to travel.

Attach ~고 싶다 to the verb stem of action verbs to say that you want to do that verb.

Note: ~고 싶다 is only used to talk about things **you** want to do. If you want to talk about things other people want to do, you have to attach ~고 싶어하다 instead (see next).

Grammar Form	Present Tense	Past Tense	Future Tense
~고 싶다	~고 싶어요	~고 싶었어요	~고 싶을 거예요

Note: from now on, the conjugation boxes (like below) will only have the dictionary form conjugation of the grammar. Final conjugations can be seen in the example sentences.

ACTION VERBS

~고 싶다 can be attached to action verbs. Attach ~고 싶다 to the verb stem of the action verb regardless of whether it ends on a vowel sound or a consonant sound.

읽다 →	읽고 싶다	(to want to read)
듣다 →	듣고 싶다	(to want to listen)
만들다 →	만들고 싶다	(to want to make)
만나다 →	만나고 싶다	(to want to meet)

> 저는 책을 읽고 **싶**어요. I want to read a book.
> 저는 음악을 듣고 **싶**어요. I want to listen to music.
> 피자를 만들고 **싶**었어요. I wanted to make pizza.
> 친구를 만나고 **싶**어요. I want to meet a friend.

REFERENCE PAGES

A~아/어지다 - page 195

USAGE NOTE: DESCRIPTIVE VERBS

In order to attach ~고 싶다 to descriptive verbs, you have to attach the ~아/어지다 grammar form first. This is similar to how you can't say "I want smart" or "I want tall" in English. You will learn this grammar form in the chapter referenced below.

NOUNS

If you want to talk about becoming something (e.g. "I want to become a teacher," or "I want to become a doctor"), you can use **~이/가 되고 싶다**.

선생님	→	선생님**이 되고 싶다**	(to want to become a teacher)
의사	→	의사**가 되고 싶다**	(to want to become a doctor)

> 저는 선생님**이 되고 싶어요**. — I want to become a teacher.
> 저는 의사**가 되고 싶어요**. — I want to become a doctor.
> 저는 부자**가 되고 싶어요**. — I want to become rich (a rich person).
> 저는 모델**이 되고 싶어요**. — I want to become a model.

TO MISS SOMEONE: N~이/가 보고 싶다

When you attach ~이/가 보고 싶다 to a noun, it has the idiomatic meaning of: "to miss someone." Note that it uses the 이/가 subject particle. In all other usages, the verb 보다 uses the ~을/를 object particle (i.e. "~을/를 보고 싶다" means "to want to watch").

> 엄마**가 보고 싶어요**. — I miss my mom.
> 제 친구**가 보고 싶어요**. — I miss my friend.
> 우리 강아지**가 보고 싶어요**. — I miss our dog.
> 저는 형**이 보고 싶어요**. — I miss my older brother.
> 영화를 보고 싶어요.* — I want to watch a movie.

Note: this is most commonly used for people, or things that are living. If you want to say you miss something (e.g. an object or place), you use the verb "그립다," (to miss), instead. e.g. "한국이 그리워요." (I miss Korea). If you say "한국이 보고 싶어요," it's understandable but unnatural.

TO TALK ABOUT THINGS YOU DON'T WANT TO DO

If you want to say you don't want to do something, either attach ~고 싶지 않다 to the verb stem, or use 안. Remember that with separable 하다 verbs, 안 goes between the noun and 하다.

---

* This example sentence uses the ~을/를 particle so it does not have to idiomatic meaning of "missing" something, but keeps the standard meaning of "보다" (to see/watch).

>	수학을 공부하고 **싶지 않**아요.	I don't want to study math.
>	운동하고 **싶지 않**아요.	I don't want to exercise.
>	김치를 먹고 **싶지 않**아요.	I don't want to eat kimchi.
>	영어를 공부 **안** 하고 싶어요.	I don't want to study English.
>	집에서 운동 **안** 하고 싶어요.	I don't want to exercise at home.
>	가지를 **안** 먹고 싶어요.	I don't want to eat eggplant.

TO TALK ABOUT THINGS OTHER PEOPLE WANT TO DO (V~고 싶어하다)

Attach **~고 싶어하다** to the verb stem to say that **someone else wants to do** that verb.

>	아빠가 요리하고 **싶어해**요.	Dad wants to cook.
>	엄마가 운동하고 **싶어해**요.	Mom wants to work out.
>	형이 의사가 되고 **싶어해**요.	My older brother wants to become a doctor.
>	언니가 가수가 되고 **싶어하지 않**아요.	My older sister doesn't want to become a singer.

PRACTICE EXERCISES

Given the English sentences, write an equivalent Korean expression.

Note: you can use 안 for the negative expressions, but the answers use ~지 않다.

1. I want to learn Korean.

2. I want to watch a movie.

3. I want to become a mom.

4. I don't want to become a doctor.

5. I miss my dad.

6. I don't want to work at home.

7. I don't want to go to school.

8. My mom doesn't want to cook.

ANSWERS: 1. (저는) 한국어를 배우고 싶어요. 2. (저는) 영화를 보고 싶어요. 3. (저는) 엄마가 되고 싶어요. 4. (저는) 의사가 되고 싶지 않아요. 5. 아빠가 보고 싶어요. 6. 집에서 일하고 싶지 않아요. 7. 학교에 가고 싶지 않아요. 8. (우리) 엄마는 요리하고 싶어하지 않아요.

REFERENCE PAGES

A/V ~지 않다 - page 63   안 A/V - page 61

USED IN WCK   430 times*

N~와/과, N~(이)랑, N~하고
For listing multiple nouns

남자와 여자예요.
It's a man and a woman.

There are three ways to connect nouns with "and" in Korean. They involve the following particles: ~와/과, ~(이)랑, and ~하고. All of these particles are commonly used.

NOUNS: ~와/과

~와 and ~과 are two sides of the same particle. They mean the same thing.
If the noun ends in a vowel sound, attach **~와**

영화	→ 영화**와**	(a movie and)
엄마	→ 엄마**와**	(mom and)

If the noun ends in a consonant sound, add **~과**

책	→ 책**과**	(a book and)
음식	→ 음식**과**	(food and)

> 김치**와** 밥을 먹어요.   I eat kimchi and rice.
> 영화**와** 드라마를 봐요.   I watch movies and dramas.
> 책**과** 만화를 읽어요.   I read books and manga.

NOUNS: ~(이)랑

If the noun ends in a vowel sound, attach **~랑**

영화	→ 영화**랑**	(a movie and)
엄마	→ 엄마**랑**	(mom and)

If the noun ends in a consonant sound, add **~이랑**

책	→ 책**이랑**	(a book and)
음식	→ 음식**이랑**	(food and)

> 김치**랑** 밥을 먹어요.   I eat kimchi and rice.
> 영화**랑** 드라마를 봐요.   I watch movies and dramas.

* This count does not include ~하고 because of the overlap with another grammar form.

> 책**이랑** 만화를 읽어요.   I read books and manga/comics.

NOUNS: ~하고

Unlike the other two particle sets, ~하고 can be used on any noun. It does not matter if the first noun ends on a vowel sound or a consonant sound.

영화 → 영화**하고**   (a movie and)
음식 → 음식**하고**   (food and)

> 김치**하고** 밥을 먹어요.   I eat kimchi and rice.
> 영화**하고** 드라마를 봐요.   I watch movies and dramas.
> 책**하고** 만화를 읽어요.   I read books and manga/comics.

ACTION VERBS

~와/과, ~(이)랑, and ~하고 can **only** be used between nouns. However, remember that using **~는 것 turns a verb into a noun**. So you can use ~와/과, ~(이)랑, and ~하고 on verbs that have had ~는 것 added to their verb stems (because in doing so, they become nouns).

요리하다 → 요리하는 것**과/이랑/하고**   (cooking and)
먹다   → 먹는 것**과/이랑/하고**   (eating and)

> 요리하는 것**과** 먹는 것을 좋아해요.   I like cooking and eating.
> 공부하는 거**랑*** 운동하는 게* 재미있어요.   Studying and exercising is fun.

* Because ~(이)랑 is a form used most often in speaking, it is more natural to **also** use the speaking form of ~는 것. "~는 것" is used in writing, but in conversation, it is shortened to ~는 거, ~는 걸, or ~는게. Check the reference page below to learn more.

WHAT'S THE DIFFERENCE?

Native speakers commonly use all three forms. Which form they use mostly comes down to circumstance and personal preference.

~와/과	~(이)랑	~하고
Mostly used in writing and formal speech.	Mostly used in casual speech.	Used in both.

Note: this is not a strict rule. You can use ~와/과 in speaking and ~랑/이랑 in writing if you wish. However, ~와/과 has a more formal, bookish feeling (either spoken or written), while ~(이)랑 has a more casual feeling (either spoken or written). ~하고 is fairly neutral.

REFERENCE PAGES

V~는 것 - page 69

2

TO TALK ABOUT DOING THINGS WITH OTHERS

~와/과, ~(이)랑, and ~하고 are commonly used in a sentence to talk about **doing things with other people**. When ~와/과, ~(이)랑, or ~하고 is attached to a "person" noun, it means "with" that person.

> 아빠가 엄마**와** 요리해요.   My dad cooks with my mom.
> 저**랑** 제 친구가 한국어를 공부해요.   My friend studies Korean with me.
> 한국사람**하고** 말하고 싶어요.   I want to talk with a Korean person.

ADDING 같이/함께

You will commonly see the words "같이" or "함께" (which both mean "together"), added into these sentences. Because 함께 is most commonly used in writing, and is slightly more formal, it pairs naturally with ~와/과.

> 엄마**와** 아빠가 **함께** 요리해요.   My mom and dad cook together.
> 제가 제 친구**랑 같이** 한국어를 공부해요.   My friend and I study Korean together.
> 한국사람**하고 같이** 말하고 싶어요.   I want to talk together with a Korean person.

TALKING ABOUT MULTIPLE PEOPLE: 들

To talk about doing things with multiple people, use the ~들 plural marker. Check the reference page below for usage notes.

USING MORE THAN ONE "AND"

If you're listing multiple things, you have the option to place the "and" particle on the final noun.
For example, "(I) eat cheese and bread" can be any of the following:

| 치즈랑 빵이랑 먹어요. | 치즈하고 빵하고 먹어요. | X 치즈와 빵과 먹어요. |
| 치즈랑 빵을 먹어요. | 치즈하고 빵을 먹어요. | O 치즈와 빵을 먹어요. |

Note: ~와/과 cannot be placed on final nouns. See how the object particle should be used instead.
As a final note, you cannot mix-and-match particles in the same sentence.

> X 치즈와 포도랑 빵하고 먹어요.

REFERENCE PAGES

N~들 - page 82

USED IN WCK — 223 times

잘 & 잘 못 V

For talking about your proficiency at things

저는 공부를 잘 해요.
I do well in my studies.

Add these adverbs to your sentence to talk about **proficiency**. Place these adverbs right before or close to the verb.

잘	잘 못
well	not well

ACTION VERBS

Place either 잘 or 잘 못 before the verb. If the verb is separable (see "하다 Verbs" chapter referenced below), place 잘 or 잘 못 between the noun and the verb.

먹다	→	**잘 / 잘 못 먹다**	(to eat well/not well)
공부하다	→	공부 **잘 / 잘 못** 하다	(to study well/not well)
노래하다	→	노래 **잘 / 잘 못** 하다	(to sing well/not well)

> 김치를 **잘** 먹어요.   I eat kimchi well / I'm good with eating kimchi
> 김치를 **잘 못** 먹어요.   I don't eat kimchi well / I don't really like to eat kimchi
> 노래를 **잘** 해요.   I sing well/I'm a good singer
> 노래를 **잘 못** 해요.   I don't sing well/I'm not a good singer.
> 공부를 **잘** 해요.   I study well /I do well at school
> 공부를 잘 못 해요.   I don't study well/I don't do well at school

PRACTICE EXERCISES

Given the English sentences, write an equivalent Korean expression.

1. I'm not a good cook.   ....

2. I work well at home.   ....

ANSWERS: 1. (저는) 요리(를) 잘 못 해요.   2. (저는) 집에서 일(을) 잘 해요.

REFERENCE PAGES

못 V - page 65   하다 Verbs - page 49

A~ㄴ/은/는 N

For making adjectives

맛있는 버거를 먹어요.
I eat a delicious burger.

In the first chapter we learned that Korean doesn't really have adjectives - at least not in the same way that English does. But there is a way to turn a descriptive verb into an adjective to describe a noun. You use this rule when you want to say things like "a delicious pizza" or "good bread."

DESCRIPTIVE VERBS

In order to turn a descriptive verb into an adjective, you need to attach either ~ㄴ, ~은, or ~는 to the verb stem of the descriptive verb.

If the verb stem ends in a consonant sound, attach ~은

좋다	→ 좋은 N	(good N)
많다	→ 많은 N	(many N)

If the verb stem ends in a vowel sound, attach ~ㄴ

비싸다	→ 비싼 N	(expensive N)
싸다	→ 싼 N	(cheap N)
(!) 어렵다	→ 어려운 N	(difficult N)
(!) 맵다	→ 매운 N	(spicy N)
(!) 힘들다	→ 힘든 N	(difficult/tiring N)

If the verb stem ends in 있 or 없, attach ~는

맛있다	→ 맛있는 N	(delicious N)
재미있다	→ 재미있는 N	(funny/interesting N)

> 톰은 **좋은** 친구예요. — Tom is a good friend.
> **비싼** 음식을 좋아하지 않아요. — I don't like expensive food.
> **싼** 여행을 하고 싶어요. — I want to have a cheap vacation.
> 우리가 맛있**는** 저녁을 먹었어요. — We ate a delicious dinner.
> 오늘은 **힘든** 날이에요. — Today is a difficult day.
> **매운** 음식을 잘 못 먹어요. — I'm not very good with spicy food.

REFERENCE PAGES

~이/가 + Descriptive Verbs - page 51

> 맛있는 식당을 알아요. I know a delicious restaurant.
> 우리는 재미있는 영화를 봐요. We are watching an interesting movie.

YOU CAN USE DESCRIPTIVE VERBS TWO WAYS
Just like English, you can phrase things two ways:
  1 It is a(n) _____ N.
  2 The N is _____.
The two are essentially equivalent in meaning. This is the same in Korean.

> 피자가 맛있어요. The pizza is delicious.
> 맛있는 피자예요. It is a delicious pizza.

> 날씨가 더워요. The weather is hot.
> 더운 날씨예요. It's hot weather.

{ A~ㄴ/은/는 N is not to be confused with the ~은/는 topic particle.
Remember that the topic particle only attaches to nouns and A~ㄴ/은/는 N attaches to descriptive verbs. }

PRACTICE EXERCISES
Given the English sentences, write an equivalent sentence in Korean.

1. I like expensive coffee.

2. I don't like hot weather.

3. I like eating spicy food.

4. I want to meet good people.

5. I want to drink cheap wine.

6. I can't drink cheap coffee.

ANSWERS: 1. (저는) 비싼 커피를 좋아해요. 2. (저는) 더운 날씨를 안 좋아해요. 3. (저는) 매운 음식 먹는 것을 좋아해요. 4. (저는) 좋은 사람들을 만나고 싶어요. 5. (저는) 싼 와인을 마시고 싶어요. 6. (저는) 싼 커피를 못 마셔요.

USED IN WCK   128 times

V~고 있다
The present progressive tense

샐러드를 먹고 있어요.
I am eating salad.

This grammar form is used to talk about actions that are currently in progress. This is also known as the **present progressive tense**. It can be used to talk about situations that are currently happening right at this moment, or events that are generally happening in the present time.

Grammar Form	Present Tense	Past Tense	Future Tense
~고 있다	~고 있어요	~고 있었어요	~고 있을 거예요

ACTION VERBS

~고 있다 can only be attached to action verbs. Simply attach ~고 있다 to the verb stem of the action verb regardless of whether the verb stem ends in a vowel sound or a consonant sound.

읽다	→	읽고 있다	(to be reading)
마시다	→	마시고 있다	(to be drinking)
가다	→	가고 있다	(to be going)
공부하다	→	공부하고 있다	(to be studying)

> 저는 책을 읽고 있어요.   I am reading a book.
> 저는 커피를 마시고 있어요.   I am drinking coffee.
> 저는 학교에 가고 있어요.   I am going to school.
> 저는 도서관에서 공부하고 있어요. I am studying at the library.

ADDING 지금 OR 요즘

It is common to add either 지금 or 요즘 to sentences using the ~고 있다 grammar form to specify the time frame. "지금" means "now" and "요즘" means nowadays/these days.

지금 공부하고 있어요.   I am studying right now.
요즘 공부하고 있어요.   I am studying these days.

PAST TENSE: ~고 있었다

You can add "~고 있었어요" to the verb stem of an action verb to use the past continuous tense in Korean (e.g. "I was studying" or "I was working").

› 한국어를 공부하고 있었어요.	I was studying Korean.
› 회사에서 일하고 있었어요.	I was working at an office.
› 미국에서 살고 있었어요.	I was living in America.
› 좋은 책을 읽고 있었어요.	I was reading a good book.

FUTURE TENSE: ~고 있을 것이다

You can add ~고 있을 거예요 to use the ~고 있다 form in the future tense (e.g. "I will be studying" or "I will be living").

› 내년에 한국에서 공부하고 있을 거예요.	Next year I'll be studying in Korea.
› 내년에 일본에서 일하고 있을 거예요.	Next year I'll be working in Japan.
› 주말에 책을 읽고 있을 거예요.	On the weekend I'll be reading a book.

WHAT'S THE DIFFERENCE?

~아/어요	~고 있어요
Can mean simple present tense, present progressive tense, or simple future tense.	The present progressive tense.
저는 공부해요. I study/I am studying/I will study. 커피를 마셔요. I drink coffee/I am drinking coffee/I will drink coffee.	저는 공부하고 있어요. I am studying. 커피를 마시고 있어요. I am drinking coffee.

Note: you may be wondering why ~고 있다 exists when ~아/어요 can already mean the present progressive tense. Because ~아/어요 can be used in the multiple ways shown above, there are situations where the tense of the sentence could be unclear. You can use ~고 있다 when you want to clearly state that the tense is present progressive, without any possible confusion for the listener.

REFERENCE PAGES

A/V~았/었다 Past Tense - page 58
A/V~(으)ㄹ 것이다 Future Tense - page 60

Present Tense ~아/어요 - page 45

USED IN WCK   **64 times**

아직
Still

저는 한국이 아직 그리워요.
I still miss Korea.

아직 is an adverb that can be added to sentences to mean "yet" or "still." Place 아직 before the verb. It is commonly used with the ~고 있다 form to show that you are still in the process of doing something. A similar word is 여전히, check the next page for a comparison between these two words.

DESCRIPTIVE VERBS & ACTION VERBS

아직 can be placed before descriptive verbs or action verbs.

공부하다 →	**아직** 공부하다	(to still study)
먹다 →	**아직** 먹다	(to still eat)
어렵다 →	**아직** 어렵다	(to still be difficult)
그립다 →	**아직** 그립다	(to still miss)

> 한국어를 **아직** 공부하고 있어요.   I'm still studying Korean.
> 피자를 **아직** 먹고 있어요.   I'm still eating the pizza.
> 한국어가 **아직** 어려워요.   Korean is still difficult.
> 지금도 한국이 **아직** 그리워요.   Even now, I still miss Korea.
> 숙제를 **아직** 안 했어요.   I haven't done my homework yet.

NOUNS

아직 can also be placed before nouns to say something is still that noun.

학생 →	**아직** 학생이다	(to still be a student)
백수 →	**아직** 백수다	(to still be unemployed)
미성년자 →	**아직** 미성년자다	(to still be underage)

> 저는 **아직** 학생이에요.   I'm still a student.

> 저는 **아직** 백수예요.   I'm still unemployed.
> **아직** 미성년자라서 술을 못 마셔요.   I'm still underage so I can't drink alcohol.

ADDING EMPHASIS - 아직도

You can add emphasis to your statement by using "아직도" instead of just "아직." This makes your sentence feel stronger and more emphatic. Using 아직도 will likely add the impression that you are discontent or unsatisfied with the current situation.

> 저는 **아직도** 백수예요.   I'm STILL unemployed.
> 저는 **아직도** 숙제를 하고 있어요.   I'm STILL doing my homework.
> 한국어가 **아직도** 어려워요.   Korean is STILL difficult.
> 저는 **아직도** 설거지를 안 했어요.   I STILL haven't done the dishes yet.

Note: "아직도" is a combination of the noun, 아직, with the ~도 particle.

WHAT'S THE DIFFERENCE?

There is another word that is used to mean "yet/still" and that's 여전히.

아직	여전히
Means something is still in progress and yet to be completed. When you use 아직 (or 아직도) it gives the slight feeling of "despite other things" or "even though X."	Means that something is still in the same state as it was before.
그 여자는 **아직도** 예뻐요. That girl is still pretty. (Even though she's old) 저는 **아직도** 한국어를 배워요. I'm still learning Korean. (Even though I live in the U.S. now)	그 여자는 **여전히** 예뻐요. That girl is still pretty. (Like she was before/as always) 저는 **여전히** 한국어를 배워요 I'm still learning Korean. (Like I was before/as always)
Used much more frequently in everyday Korean.	More formal and poetic. It's the sort of flowery language used in poems and songs.

Note: in Writing Conversational Korean, 아직 was used 64 times and 여전히 was used only 7 times.

REFERENCE PAGES

N~도 - page 83

누구, 무엇, 언제, 어디, 왜 & 어떻게
Who, what, when, where, why, how

언제 한국에 왔어요?
When did you come to Korea?

In English, we have WWWWWH. In Korean, they have the same concept, called: "육하원칙."

누구	무엇	언제	어디	왜	어떻게
Who	What	When	Where	Why	How

Note: when said on their own, these words are in informal language (반말) and can be rude. To create polite questions with the words on their own, combine with ~아/어요 informal polite form.

누구예요?	뭐예요?	언제예요?	어디에요?	왜요?	어떻게요?
Who is it?	What is it?	When is it?	Where is it?	Why?	How?

> **누가*** 샀어요? Who bought it?   **무엇**을 샀어요? What did you buy?
> **언제** 샀어요? When did you buy it?   **어디**에서 샀어요? Where did you buy it?
> **왜** 샀어요? Why did you buy it?   **어떻게** 샀어요? How did you buy it?

USAGE NOTE: 왜 VS 어떻게
"왜" can be rude in some situations because it feels quite direct. Sometimes 어떻게 is used instead. For example, one of the most common questions you will be asked if you go to Korea is something like: "한국에 **어떻게** 왔어요?" Even though this uses the word 어떻게, it does **not** mean "**how** did you come to Korea?" It actually means, "**why** did you come to Korea?" By using 어떻게 instead, you are saying something like: "**how did you end up** coming to Korea?" This makes the question feel softer and more polite.

Q. 한국에 **어떻게** 왔어요?   How did you end up coming to Korea?
O 한국어를 배우고 싶어서 한국에 왔어요.   I came to Korea because I wanted to learn Korean.
X 한국에 비행기로 왔어요.   I came to Korea by plane.

Note: the sentence above is grammatically correct, it's just not the appropriate response to the question.

---

* Anytime "누구" is the subject of a sentence (e.g. "who did it?") we must add the ~가 subject particle. But it is never written as "누구가." It is always contracted to "누가."

USED IN WCK   224 times*

그리고, 그래서 & 하지만
For starting sentences with "And," "So," or "But"

날씨가 더워요. 그래서 수영을 하고 싶어요.
The weather is hot. So I want to swim.

그리고, 그래서 and 하지만 are linking words that create connections between separate sentences. They can only be used to start sentences. To link clauses together, see the next few pages.

그리고	그래서	하지만
And	So, since, therefore	But, however

그리고
> 한국에 가요. **그리고** 일본에 가요. — I go to Korea. And I go to Japan.
> 저는 미국 사람이에요. **그리고** 한국에 살아요. — I'm American. And I live in Korea.
> 사과가 좋아요. **그리고** 사과가 맛있어요. — Apples are good. And apples are delicious.
> 한국사람이에요. **그리고** 영어를 공부해요. — I'm Korean. And I study English.

그래서
> 한국에 가고 싶어요.
  그래서 한국어를 공부하고 있어요. — I want to go to Korea. So I'm studying Korean.
> 한국 음식을 좋아해요.
  그래서 한국에 가고 싶어요. — I like Korean food. So I want to go to Korea.
> 날씨가 더워요. **그래서** 수영을 하고 싶어요. — The weather is hot. So I want to swim.

하지만
> 한국어를 공부해요. **하지만** 잘 못 해요. — I study Korean. But I'm not very good.
> 아침식사를 싫어하지 않아요.
  하지만 자주 먹지 않아요. — I don't dislike breakfast. But I don't eat it often.
> 한국어를 공부하는 것을 좋아해요.
  하지만 쉽지 않아요. — I like studying Korean. But it's not easy.

Note: there are many more linking words in Korean, these three are common ones to start with.

* 그리고 - 67 times | 그래서 - 55 times | 하지만 - 102 times

2

A/V~고 N~(이)고

For connecting clauses with "and" or "and then"

미국 사람이고 한국어를 공부해요.
I'm American and I study Korean.

Instead of finishing a sentence and starting a new one with "그리고," you can also join the two sentences together by attaching ~고 to the verb stem of the first sentence. This allows you to link two clauses within on sentence, and build longer sentences.

Grammar Form	Present Tense	Past Tense	Future Tense
~고	~고	~았/었고	~(으)ㄹ 거고

ACTION VERBS & DESCRIPTIVE VERBS

You can attach ~고 to action verbs and descriptive verbs. Attach ~고 regardless of whether the verb stem ends on a vowel sound or a consonant sound.

읽다	→	읽고	(to read and...)
듣다	→	듣고	(to listen and...)
비싸다	→	비싸고	(to be expensive and...)

> 책을 읽고 음악을 들어요. I read a book and I listen to music.
> 음악을 듣고 점심을 먹어요. I listen to music and I eat lunch.
> 날씨가 춥고 비가 와요. The weather is cold and it's raining.

NOUNS

When attaching to a noun, attach ~(이)고.
If the noun ends on a consonant sound, attach ~이고

미국 사람	→	미국 사람이고	(to be American and...)
학생	→	학생이고	(to be a student and...)

If the noun ends on a vowel sound, attach ~고

여자	→	여자고	(to be a woman and...)
남자	→	남자고	(to be a man and...)

Note: ~(이)고 comes from the combination of the verb "이다," which means "to be," and ~고.

> 저는 미국사람**이고** 한국어를 공부해요. I am American and I study Korean.
> 저는 학생**이고** 영어를 공부하고 있어요. I'm a student and I'm studying English.
> 저는 여자**고** 20살이에요. I am a woman and I'm 20 years old.

JOINING TWO CLAUSES TOGETHER

You can use ~고 to join clauses together and make longer, more natural sentences. For example, instead of saying: You can say:

> 저는 미국 사람이에요. 한국어를 공부해요. → 저는 미국 사람**이고** 한국어를 공부해요.
> I am American. I study Korean. I'm American and I study Korean.
> 친구를 만나요. 영화관에 가요. → 친구를 만나**고** 영화관에 가요.
> I meet a friend. We go to the movies. I meet a friend and go to the movies.
> 한국에 가요. 그리고 일본에 가요. → 한국에 가**고** 일본에 가요.
> I go to Korea. And I go to Japan. I go to Korea and Japan.

DROPPING SUBJECTS

If the subject of both sentences is the same, it's natural to drop the subject from the second clause so that you're not giving repeated information. For example:

> 사과가 좋**고** 사과가 맛있어요. → 사과가 좋**고** 맛있어요.
> Apples are good and apples are delicious. Apples are good and delicious.

The subject (사과) can be dropped because it has already been established by the first clause. The second 사과 is not necessary, so it is natural to drop it from the second clause.

> 한국어를 공부하**고** 한국어가 재미있어요. → 한국어를 공부하**고** 재미있어요.
> I study Korean and Korean is interesting. I study Korean and **it's** interesting.

Even though "한국어" is the **object** of the first clause and the **subject** of the second clause, it is still more natural to drop the second "한국어" because it's already established by the first clause.

Notice above that we do something similar in English by replacing previous nouns or noun phrases with "it/they." In Korean, instead of using pronouns (like "it/they"), the unnecessary subject is simply dropped.

TALKING ABOUT A SERIES OF EVENTS

Another useful way to use ~고 is to talk about a series of events. In this case, the order of events follows the order of the clauses in the sentence. When used like this, ~고 means "and then."

———————— REFERENCE PAGES ————————

Dropping Subjects - page 18

> 커피를 마시고 직장에 가요.	I drink coffee and then go to my workplace.
> 피자를 먹고 집에 가요.	I eat pizza and then I go home.
> 공부하고 도서관에 가요.	I study and then I go to the library.
> 직장에 가고 커피를 마셔요.	I go to my workplace and then I drink coffee.
> 식당에 가서 피자를 먹어요.*	I go to a restaurant and eat pizza.
> 도서관에 가서 공부해요.*	I go to the library and study.

* When talking about a sequence of events, it's sometimes more natural to use the ~아/어서 grammar form (see reference below), particularly when using 가다 to say, "I go and do..."

YOU CAN ADD AS MANY CLAUSES AS YOU WISH

You can keep adding clauses with ~고 to talk about more actions that you do. For example:
아침식사를 먹고 학교에 가고 점심을 먹고 도서관에 가고... (etc.)
I eat breakfast and then I go to school and then I eat lunch and the then I go to the library...

PAST TENSE: ~고 OR ~았/었고

To use ~고 in a past tense sentence, just conjugate the **final verb** into the past tense.

> 커피를 마시고 직장에 **갔어요**.	I drank coffee and went to my workplace.
> 친구를 만나고 피자를 먹**었어요**.	I met a friend and ate pizza.

A past tense form of ~고 does exist (~았/었고), although it is completely optional and these two conjugations (~고 versus ~았/었고) are roughly equivalent in meaning. To learn more, you can check the "Clausal Verb Tenses" chapter in the Appendix.

> 책을 읽었고 음악을 **들었어요**.	I read a book and listened to music.
> 날씨가 추웠고 비가 **왔어요**.	It was cold and it rained.

FUTURE TENSE: ~고 OR ~(으)ㄹ 거고

The use ~고 in a future tense sentence, just conjugate the **final verb** into the future tense.

> 친구를 만나고 피자를 먹**을 거예요**.	I'll meet a friend and eat pizza.
> 커피를 마시고 직장에 **갈 거예요**.	I will drink coffee and go to my workplace.

A future tense form of ~고 does exist (~(으)ㄹ 거고), although it is optional and these two con-

---

REFERENCE PAGES

A/V~아/어서 N(이)라서 - page 115
Clausal Verb Tenses - page 280

A/V~았/었다 Past Tense - page 58
A/V~(으)ㄹ 것이다 Future Tense - page 60

jugations (~고 and ~(으)ㄹ 거고) are essentially the same in meaning when talking about the future.

> 책을 읽을 거고 음악을 들을 거예요.   I will read a book and listen to music.
> 날씨가 추울 거고 비가 올 거예요.   The weather will be cold and it will rain.

SENTENCE ENDING: ~고요

You can also end a sentence using the ~고 grammar form. This is very common, especially in conversation. To use, just attach ~고 to the verb stem and then add "~요" to add casual polite formality. It has multiple uses:

1 To give an afterthought (to add something on to whatever you spoke about previously).
   요리를 했어요. 설거지도 했**고요**.   I cooked. And I also washed the dishes.
   프랑스어도 배우고 싶**구요**.*   I also want to learn French.

2 To suggest that you're going to talk some more about a subject.
   그때는 제가 한국에서 살았**고요**.   At that time, I lived in Korea. (and...)
   어제 친구를 만났**구요**.*   Yesterday I met a friend. (and...)

3 To indicate to the listener that you are open to talking about a topic and encouraging them to ask you more about it.
   저는 한국어를 공부하**고요**!   I study Korean! (I'm happy to talk about it!)
   저는 학생**이구요**!*   I'm a student! (I'm happy to explain more!)

4 To generally make a sentence sound softer and more conversational.

* SENTENCE ENDING: ~구(요)

"~구요" is a commonly used alternative to "~고요." While not technically correct, it's very common particularly with the younger generation. "~구요" is easier to pronounce and is also thought to sound cuter or more friendly than "~고요," but they both mean the same thing.

Note: In Writing Conversational Korean, "~고요" and "~구요" were used about equally.

REFERENCE PAGES

N~도 - page 83

USED IN WCK   343 times

A/V~지만, N~(이)지만

For connecting clauses with "but," or "however"

저는 뉴욕에서 살지만 캘리포니아에 살고 싶어요.
I live in New York but I want to live in California.

Instead of stopping one sentence and starting another one with 하지만, you can join the two sentences together by attaching ~지만 to the verb stem of the first sentence. This will help you build longer sentences.

Grammar Form	Present Tense	Past Tense	Future Tense
Descrip. & Action V	~지만	~았/었지만	~겠지만 or ~(으)ㄹ 거지만
Nouns	~(이)지만	~이었지만/였지만	~(이)겠지만 or ~일 거지만

Note: when using ~지만, the two sentences must be contrasting sentences.

ACTION VERBS & DESCRIPTIVE VERBS

Attach **~지만** to the verb stem at the end of the first clause. ~지만 can be attached to action verbs or descriptive verbs. Attach ~지만 regardless of whether the verb ends on a vowel sound or a consonant sound.

가다	→	가**지만**	(subj. goes, but…)
춥다	→	춥**지만**	(it's cold, but…)
마시다	→	마시**지만**	(subj. drinks, but…)

> 저는 운동하**지만** 좀 재미없어요.   I work out, but I don't really like it.
> 날씨가 춥**지만** 맑아요.   The weather is cold, but sunny.
> 커피는 마시**지만** 아메리카노는 마시지 않아요. I drink coffee but not americano (black).

NOUNS

If the noun ends on a consonant sound, attach **~이지만**.

미국 사람	→	미국 사람**이지만**	(subj. is American, but…)
학생	→	학생**이지만**	(subj. is a student, but…)

If it ends on a vowel sound, attach **~지만**.

Note: ~이지만 is a combination of the verb "이다" (to be) and ~지만

백수	→	백수**지만**	(subj. is unemployed, but...)
남자	→	남자**지만**	(subj. is a man, but...)

> 미국 사람**이지만** 한국에 살고 싶어요. — I'm American, but I want to live in Korea.
> 한국 사람**이지만** 김치를 잘 못 먹어요. — I'm Korean, but I can't handle kimchi.
> 백수**지만** 부자예요. — He's unemployed, but he's rich.

JOINING CLAUSES TOGETHER

You can use ~지만 to join two clauses together and make longer sentences.

> 한국어 공부가 재미있어요. 하지만 어려워요. → 한국어 공부가 재미있**지만** 어려워요.
> Korean study is fun. But it's difficult. → Korean study is fun, but it's difficult.

> 드라마를 보고 싶어요. 하지만 시간이 없어요. → 한국 드라마를 보고 싶**지만** 시간이 없어요.
> I want to watch dramas. But I don't have time. → I want to watch dramas, but I don't have time.

DROPPING SUBJECTS

If the subject is the same on both sides of ~지만, you can drop the second subject. For example:

그 피자는 맛있**지만** 그 피자는 비싸요. → 그 피자는 맛있**지만** 비싸요.
That pizza is delicious but that pizza is pricey. → That pizza is delicious but it's pricey.

USAGE NOTE: DIFFERENT SUBJECTS MUST USE THE ~은/는 TOPIC PARTICLE

If the **subject is different** in the second clause, you should attach ~은/는 to the subject on each side of the ~지만 grammar form. This is because you are contrasting these two subjects, and ~은/는 is the particle that provides contrast.

> 날씨는 덥**지만** 물은 추워요. — The weather is hot, but the water is cold.
> 식당은 비싸**지만** 카페는 싸요. — Restaurants are expensive, but cafes are cheap.
> 차는 마시**지만** 커피는 마시지 않아요. — I drink tea, but I don't drink coffee.
> 돈은 없**지만** 시간은 있어요. — I don't have money, but I do have time.
> 운동은 좋**지만** 밖에서 운동하는 건 싫어요. — Working out is good, but I don't like doing it outside.

REFERENCE PAGES

~은/는 Topic Particle - page 29

PAST TENSE: ~았/었지만

Unlike with the ~고 grammar form we learned previously, where you can place tense on **just** the final verb in the sentence and have it apply to both clauses, sentences with ~지만 are being contrasted (and not a series of events), so usually the tense is required on both clauses to make the meaning of your sentence clear.

> 운동**했**지만 좀 재미없**었어요**. I worked out, but I didn't really like it.
> 날씨가 **추웠**지만 맑**았어요**. The weather was cold, but sunny.
> 한국어 공부가 재미있**었**지만 어려**웠어요**. Studying Korean was fun, but difficult.
> 작년은 힘들**었**지만 포기하지 않**았어요**. Last year was hard, but I didn't give up.

FUTURE TENSE: ~겠지만 OR ~(으)ㄹ 거지만

Like with past tense, when using ~지만 in future tense sentences, you should conjugate tense in both clauses. In the case of future tense, you have two options: ~겠지만 or ~(으)ㄹ 거지만. They have essentially the same meaning.

> 저는 운동**하겠**지만 좀 재미없**을 거예요**. I will work out, but it won't be much fun.
> 날씨가 **추울 거지만** 맑**을 거예요**. The weather will be cold, but it'll be sunny.
> 한국어 공부가 재미있**겠**지만 어려**울 거예요**. Studying Korean will be fun, but difficult.
> 내년은 힘들**겠**지만 포기하지 않**을 거예요**. Next year will be hard, but I won't give up.

MIXED TENSE SENTENCES

If the two clauses are happening in different time periods, which is common in contrasting sentences, conjugate the tenses in both clauses accordingly.

> 어제는 **추웠**지만 내일은 더**울 거예요**. Yesterday was cold, but tomorrow will be hot.
> 오늘 한국어를 공부하**지만** 내일은 안 **할 거예요**. Today I study Korean, but tomorrow I don't.
> 지금은 미국에 살**지만** 작년에 일본에 **살았어요**. Now I live in the US, but last year I lived in Japan.

REFERENCE PAGES

Clausal Verb Tenses - page 280
A/V~겠다 - page 218
A/V~았/었다 Past Tense - page 58
A/V~(으)ㄹ 것이다 Future Tense - page 60

USED IN WCK 504 times

A/V~아/어서 N(이)라서

For connecting clauses with "so" or "because"

날씨가 좋아서 캠핑을 가고 싶어요.
The weather is good so I want to go camping.

Instead of finishing one sentence and starting a new one with 그래서 ("therefore" or "so"), you can connect the two sentences together by attaching ~아/어서 to the verb stem at the end of the first sentence.

ACTION VERBS & DESCRIPTIVE VERBS

~아/어서 can be attached to the verb stems of action verbs and descriptive verbs.
If the verb stem of the verb ends in ㅏ or ㅗ, attach ~아서

비싸다	→	비**싸서**	(to be expensive, so...)
많다	→	많**아서**	(to be many, so...)
보다	→	**봐서**	(to watch, so...)

If the verb stem of the verb ends in 하, it becomes ~해서

일하다	→	일**해서**	(to work, so...)
공부하다	→	공부**해서**	(to study, so...)
요리하다	→	요리**해서**	(to cook, so...)

If the verb stem of the verb ends in anything else, attach ~어서

없다	→	없**어서**	(to not have any, so...)
읽다	→	읽**어서**	(to read, so...)
마시다	→	마**셔서**	(to drink, so...)
(!) 듣다	→	들**어서**	(to listen, so...)
(!) 덥다	→	더**워서**	(to be hot, so...)

> 음식이 비**싸서** 다른 식당에 가고 싶어요. The food is expensive, so I want to go to a different restaurant.
> 돈이 없**어서** 여행 못 해요. I have no money, so I can't travel.
> 음식이 매**워서** 물을 많이 마시고 있어요. The food is spicy, so I'm drinking a lot of water.

REFERENCE PAGES

그리고, 그래서 & 하지만 - page 107

> 날씨가 너무 더**워서** 집에 갔어요.   The weather was too hot, so I went home.

NOUNS

If the noun ends in a vowel sound, attach **~라서**

| 고양이 | → | 고양이**라서** | (it's a cat, so...) |
| 강아지 | → | 강아지**라서** | (it's a dog, so...) |

If the verb ends in a consonant sound, attach **~이라서**

| 생일 | → | 생일**이라서** | (it's subj.'s birthday, so...) |
| 16살 | → | 16살**이라서** | (subj. is 16 years old, so...) |

> 고양이**라서** 하루종일 잠을 자요.   He's a cat, so he sleeps all day.
> 제 생일**이라서** 케이크를 먹고 싶어요.   It's my birthday, so I want to eat cake.
> 저는 16살**이라서** 술을 못 마셔요.   I'm 16, so I can't drink alcohol.

USAGE NOTE: NOT FOR IMPERATIVE SENTENCES

~아/어서 cannot be used in imperative sentences (i.e. for commands or requests). If you want to use "so" in an imperative sentence, you need to use the ~(으)니까 grammar form instead.

X 날씨가 추워서 재킷을 입으세요.   This sentence is grammatically incorrect.
O 날씨가 추우니까 재킷을 입으세요.   The weather is cold, so please wear a jacket.

USAGE NOTE: NO PAST OR FUTURE TENSE CONJUGATION

In the previous chapters, we learned that ~고 and ~지만 have past tense and future tense forms. However, ~아/어서 **does not have a past or future tense form.** ~아/어서 stays in the present tense form, and the overall tense of the sentence is placed on the final verb.

X 날씨가 추웠어서 공원에 안 갔어요.   This sentence is grammatically incorrect.
O 날씨가 추워서 공원에 안 갔어요.   The weather was cold, so we didn't go to the park.

Note: you might hear people use ~았/었어서, particularly in speaking. However it is **technically incorrect** and not recommended for learners to use.

SENTENCE ENDING: ~아/어서요

You can also end a sentence using the ~아/어서 grammar form. This is commonly used when you've already completed a sentence, but then you want to give a reason or explanation for it retroactively.

To use, attach ~아/어서 to the verb stem and then add "요" to provide casual polite formality.

REFERENCE PAGES

V~(으)세요 - page 162   A/V~(으)니까 - page 269

>	다른 식당에 가고 싶어요. 음식이 너무 비**싸서요**.	I want to go to a different restaurant. Because the food is too expensive.
>	여행 못 해요. 돈이 없**어서요**.	I can't travel. Since I have no money.
>	물이 많이 마셔요. 음식이 매**워서요**.	I'm drinking a lot of water. 'Cause the food's spicy.

USAGE NOTE: A SEQUENCE OF EVENTS

~아/어서 has another common usage which is to talk about a series of events. You can use ~아/어서 to talk about one action happening after another one. This is similar to how ~고 can be used, with one important difference (see below). Like ~고, ~아/어서 can carry the meaning of "and then."

>	식당에 **가서** 먹어요.	I go to the restaurant and then eat.
>	도서관에 **가서** 공부해요.	I go to the library and then study.
>	운동**해서** 샤워해요.	I work out and then shower.

WHAT'S THE DIFFERENCE?

A feature of the ~고 grammar form is that the two clauses may not necessarily have any relation to each other. However, the ~아/어서 grammar form implies a dependent relationship.

~아/어서 (Sequence of Events)	~고 (Sequence of Events)
Always dependent clauses.	*Can be independent clauses.*
친구를 만**나서** 카페에 갔어요. I met a friend and **we** went to a cafe. When using ~아/어서, the two events are strongly connected. "Going to a cafe" is strongly linked to "meeting a friend." Therefore, it is implied that you went to the cafe **together**.	친구를 만**나고** 카페에 갔어요. I met a friend and then **I/we** went to a cafe. When using ~고, the two clauses can be unrelated. "Going to a cafe" is not strongly linked to "meeting a friend," so you may have gone together, or alone. They might just be activities you did that you are listing.
카페에 **가서** 커피를 마셨어요. I went to a cafe and drank coffee (there). Using ~아/어서, the clauses are strongly linked. You drank coffee at the cafe that you went to. **This sentence is more natural.**	카페에 **가고** 커피를 마셨어요. I went to a cafe and drank coffee. Using ~고, the clauses are not strongly linked. You went to a cafe, and maybe you drank coffee there, but it could've been two separate events.

REFERENCE PAGES

A/V~고 N~(이)고 - page 108

USED IN WCK   130 times*

Words of Frequency

Never, rarely, sometimes, often, always

저는 책을 가끔 읽어요.
I sometimes read books.

Some common frequency words in Korean include:

절대	별로	가끔	자주	항상
never	rarely	sometimes	often	always

Note: it's most natural to place the frequency word right before (or as close as possible) to the action verb.

> 저는 운동을 **절대** 안 해요.   I never exercise.
> 저는 요리를 **별로** 안 해요.   I rarely cook/ I don't really cook.
> 저는 책을 **자주** 읽어요.   I often read books.
> 저는 책을 **가끔** 사요.   I sometimes buy books.
> 저는 **항상** 일해요.   I always work.

USAGE NOTE: 별로 AND 절대 (RARELY AND NEVER)

Negative words of frequency (like 별로 and 절대) always go in **negative sentences.** This means you have to add a negative form (e.g. 안 / ~지 않다 / 못) into your sentences when you use 별로 or 절대.

O 저는 음악을 별로 안 들어요.   I don't really listen to music.
O 저는 콘서트에 절대 안 가요.   I never go to concerts.
O 커피를 절대 안 마셔요.   I never drink coffee.
X 저는 음악을 별로 들어요.   This sentence is awkward.
X 저는 콘서트에 절대 가요.   This sentence is awkward.

You can use 항상 and 자주 in negative sentences to mean "not always" or "not often."
저는 **항상** 일하지 않아요.   I don't always work.
저는 책을 **자주** 안 읽어요.   I don't often read books.

118* 절대 - 14 times | 별로 - 30 times | 가끔 - 13 times | 자주 - 40 times | 항상 - 33 times

더 & 덜
More & Less

USED IN WCK — 87 times

운동을 더 하고 싶어요.
I want to exercise more.

Add these adverbs to your sentences to mean "more" and "less." Place them before the verb.

더	덜
more	less

ACTION VERBS

Place 더 or 덜 before the action verb.

| 먹다 | → | **더/덜** 먹다 | (to eat more/less) |
| 마시다 | → | **더/덜** 마시다 | (to drink more/less) |

> 저는 설탕을 **덜** 먹고 싶어요. — I want to eat less sugar.
> 어제는 비가 **더** 많이 왔어요. — It rained more yesterday.
> 저는 물을 **더** 마시고 있어요. — I am drinking more water.
> 요즘은 커피를 **덜** 마시고 있어요. — I am drinking less coffee these days.

DESCRIPTIVE VERBS

Place 더 or 덜 before the descriptive verb.

(!) 어렵다	→	**더/덜** 어렵다	(to be more/less difficult)
(!) 덥다	→	**더/덜** 덥다	(to be more/less hot)
재미있다	→	**더/덜** 재미있다	(to be more/less fun)

> 한국어는 **더** 어려워요. — Korean is more difficult.
> 그 영화는 **덜** 재미있어요. — That movie is less interesting.
> 오늘은 **더** 더워요. — Today is hotter.

Note: notice how the ~은/는 topic particle is used in the sentences above due to the implied contrast.

USED IN WCK   **89 times**

N~보다
For comparing things

추운 날씨보다 더운 날씨가 더 좋아요.
I like hot weather more than cold weather.

~보다 is used to compare two things. It is similar to "-er than" in English. It is often combined with 더 (more) and 덜 (less), however, these adverbs (더 and 덜) are not required if the meaning is clear from context. There are two main ways to translate sentences using "보다." Both are fine, but one might be easier for you to remember than the other.

    1 A보다 B = Compared to A, B is...
    2 A보다 B = B is more/less than A

NOUNS

Attach ~보다 to the noun regardless of whether it ends with a vowel sound or a consonant sound.

차 → 차보다		(more/less than tea...)
책 → 책보다		(more/less than books...)

> 차보다 커피를 더 좋아해요.   Compared to tea, I like coffee more.
> 책보다 영화를 더 봐요.   Compared to books, I watch movies more.
> 강아지보다 고양이가 더 좋아요.   Compared to dogs, cats are better.
> 고양이보다 강아지가 더 좋아요.   Compared to cats, dogs are better.
> 맥주보다 와인을 덜 마셔요.   I drink wine less than beer.
> 와인보다 맥주를 덜 마셔요.   I drink beer less than wine.

USAGE NOTE

As long you keep the appropriate particles attached to their nouns, you can rearrange A & B in the sentence and the meaning does not change. For example:

차보다 커피를 더 좋아해요. = 커피를 차보다 더 좋아해요.   → I like coffee more than tea.
드라마보다 영화를 더 봐요. = 드라마를 영화보다 더 봐요.   → I watch movies more than dramas.
와인보다 맥주를 덜 마셔요. = 와인보다 맥주를 덜 마셔요.   → I drink beer less than wine.

MUCH MORE/MUCH LESS: 훨씬 더/덜

You can add "훨씬" to emphasize that something is **much** more/less than something else. As shown below, it should come right before 더 or 덜, and close to the verb.

> 차**보다** 커피를 **훨씬** 더 좋아해요.　　I like coffee much more than tea.
> 어제**보다** 오늘이 **훨씬** 덜 더워요.　　Today is way less hot than it was yesterday.
> 그 사람은 저**보다 훨씬** 더 나이가 많아요.　That person is much older than me.
> 그 사람은 저**보다 훨씬** 더 키가 작아요.　That person is much shorter than me.

ACTION VERBS

Remember that you can turn a verb into a noun by adding ~는 것 to the verb stem.

공부하다	→	공부하는 것**보다**	(more/less than studying...)
운동하다	→	운동하는 것**보다**	(more/less than exercising...)
먹다	→	먹는 것**보다**	(more/less than eating...)

> 운동하는 것**보다** 잠을 자는 것을 더 좋아해요.　I like sleeping more than exercising.
> 공부하는 것**보다** 운동하는 것이 더 재미있어요.　Working out is more fun than studying.
> 먹는 것**보다** 요리하는 것을 덜 좋아해요.　I like cooking less than eating.
> 요리하는 것**보다** 먹는 것을 더 좋아해요.　I like eating more than cooking.

PRACTICE EXERCISES

Given the English sentences, write an equivalent Korean expression.

1. I like dogs more than cats.

2. I like coffee more than tea.

3. I drink tea more than coffee.

4. I watch dramas more than movies.

5. Sleeping is better than working.

ANSWERS: 1. (저는) 고양이보다 강아지를 더 좋아해요.　2. (저는) 차보다 커피를 더 좋아해요.　3. (저는) 커피보다 차를 더 마셔요.　4. (저는) 영화보다 드라마를 더 봐요.　5. 일하는 것보다 자는 것이 더 좋아요.

USED IN WCK **540 times**

N~(으)로

For things you use

신용카드로 사고 싶어요.
I want to buy it with my credit card.

You can attach **~(으)로** to a noun to say that the noun is being used to perform some action. In English, it's usually translated to "with," "by," or "using," some means or method.

NOUNS

If the noun ends on a vowel sound, or ends with ㄹ, attach **~로**

비행기	→	비행기**로**	(by plane)
(!) 지하철	→	지하철**로**	(by subway)
드라마	→	드라마**로**	(using dramas)
포크	→	포크**로**	(with a fork)

If the noun ends on a consonant sound, attach **~으로**

책	→	책**으로**	(with a book)
돈	→	돈**으로**	(with money)
컵	→	컵**으로**	(with a cup)
휴대폰	→	휴대폰**으로**	(by cellphone)

> 컵**으로** 물을 마셔요. — I drink water with a cup.
> 포크**로** 음식을 먹어요. — I eat food with a fork.
> 제 휴대폰**으로** 음악을 들어요. — I listen to music with my phone.
> 저는 한국어 책**으로** 공부해요. — I study with a Korean book.
> 저는 지하철**로** 출근해요. — I go to work by subway.
> 학교에서 한국말**로** 말해요. — At school I speak in Korean.
> 집에서 영어**로** 말해요. — At home I speak in English.
> 저는 드라마**로** 한국어를 자주 공부해요. — I often study Korean using dramas.

USED IN WCK 61 times

보통, 주로 & 평소에
Usually, mainly, ordinarily

아침에 보통 커피를 마셔요.
I usually drink coffee in the morning.

보통, 주로, and 평소에 can be placed in sentences to mean "usually." These words are highly interchangeable, but can have slight differences in meaning.

보통	주로	평소에
Usually/normally	Mostly/mainly	Ordinarily/on a regular day

보통

› 보통 도서관에서 공부해요.	I usually study at the library.
› 보통 매운 음식을 안 먹어요.	I don't normally eat spicy food.
› 토요일에 보통 외식해요.	I usually eat out on Saturday.

주로

› 주로 도서관에서 공부해요.	I mostly study at the library.
› 아침에 주로 커피를 마셔요.	I mainly drink coffee in the morning.
› 비가 오는 날에 주로 책을 읽어요.	I mostly read books on rainy days.

평소에

› 평소에 도서관에서 공부해요.	Ordinarily, I study at the library.
› 평소에 직장에서 일해요.	On a normal day, I work at the office.
› 평소에 개를 산책 시켜요.	On a regular day, I walk the dog.

PLACEMENT IN A SENTENCE

보통, 주로 & 평소에 can be placed anywhere, but you should place it in front of the noun that you wish to emphasize. For example, consider the difference between these sentences:

› 보통 도서관에서 한국어를 공부해요.	I usually study Korean at the **library**.
	The place where I usually study Korean is the library.
› 도서관에서 보통 한국어를 공부해요.	I usually study **Korean** at the library.

> In the library, the subject that I usually study is Korean.

These sentences are both grammatically correct, but notice how the different placement of 보통 in the sentence changes the meaning slightly. The same is also true for 주로 and 평소에.

>	아침에 **주로** 커피를 마셔요.	In the morning, I mostly drink **coffee.** The main beverage I drink in the morning is coffee.
>	**주로** 아침에 커피를 마셔요.	In the **morning**, I mostly drink coffee. The morning is the main time that I drink coffee.

>	**평소에** 직장에서 일해요.	I ordinarily work at my workplace. The place I work on an ordinary day is my workplace.
>	직장에서 **평소에** 일해요.	On a normal day at the office, I work. What I ordinarily do when I'm at work is work.

TALKING ABOUT THINGS YOU TEND TO DO: ~(으)ㄴ/는 편이다

There is also a specific grammar form you can use to talk about things you usually do, or tend to do. E.g. "I tend to study at the library," or "I tend to drink coffee in the morning." This grammar form is: ~(으)ㄴ/는 편이다. You can learn about this by checking the page referenced below.

PRACTICE EXERCISES

Given the Korean sentences, write an equivalent English expression.

1. 저는 보통 집에서 요리해요. ....

2. 저는 보통 주말에 친구를 만나요. ....

3. 저는 저녁에 주로 영화를 봐요. ....

4. 저는 주로 책 읽는 것을 좋아해요. ....

5. 평소에는 학교에 가요. ....

ANSWERS: 1. I usually cook at home. 2. I usually meet friends on the weekend. 3. I mainly watch movies in the evening. 4. I mainly like reading books. 5. On a regular day, I go to school.

REFERENCE PAGES

A/V~(으)ㄴ/는 편이다 - page 238

USED IN WCK   608 times

A/V~(으)면

To connect clauses with "if" or "when"

비가 오면 가고 싶지 않아요.
I don't want to go if it rains.

A/V~(으)면 is a very useful grammar form used to talk about hypothetical situations. ~(으)면 is usually translated to "if" or "when." It is used to join two clauses together to say something like, "If/when something happens, then this result occurs." In English, "if" and "when" are used in similar ways. I.e. "when it's expensive, I don't buy it" and "if it's expensive I don't buy it" are very similar in meaning.

Grammar Form	Present Tense	Past Tense	Future Tense
~(으)면	~(으)면	~았/었으면	~(으)ㄹ 거라면

Note: see the next page for information on the past tense and future tense usage.

ACTION VERBS & DESCRIPTIVE VERBS

~(으)면 can be attached to action verbs or descriptive verbs.

If the verb ends in a vowel sound, or ends in ㄹ, attach **~면**

가다	→	가**면**	(if/when subj. goes)
비싸다	→	비싸**면**	(if/when it's expensive)
(!) 만들다	→	만들**면**	(if/when subj. makes)

If the verb ends in a consonant sound, attach **~으면**

있다	→	있**으면**	(if/when subj. has)
많다	→	많**으면**	(if/when they're many)
(!) 듣다	→	들**으면**	(if/when subj. listens)
(!) 돕다*	→	도우**면**	(if/when subj. helps)

> 날씨가 더우**면** 물을 많이 마셔요.   When it's hot I drink a lot of water.
> 비가 오**면** 영화를 보고 싶어요.   When it rains I want to watch a movie.
> 사람이 너무 많**으면** 안 좋아요.   I don't like it if there's too many people.

>	옷이 너무 비**싸면** 사고 싶지 않아요.	If clothes are too pricey, I don't want to buy them.
>	시장에 **가면** 생선을 사요.	When I go to the market, I buy fish.

NOUNS

If you want to attach this grammar form to a noun, you use N(이)라면, which comes from the form: A/V~ㄴ/는다면. These usages have their own detailed explanations, so check the reference page below to learn more.

PAST TENSE

Attach **~았/었으면** to talk about situations in the past tense.

비싸다	→	비쌌**으면**	(if/when it was expensive)
(!) 쓰다	→	썼**으면**	(if/when it was used)
(!) 맵다	→	매웠**으면**	(if/when it was spicy)

>	책을 다 썼**으면** 읽어 보고 싶어요.	If you finished writing your book, I'd like to read it.
>	김치가 너무 매웠**으면** 왜 먹었어요?	If the kimchi was too spicy, why did you eat it?
>	표가 너무 비쌌**으면** 왜 샀어요?	If the ticket was too expensive, why did you buy it?

FUTURE TENSE: ~(으)면 OR ~(으)ㄹ 거라면

The ~(으)면 grammar form has an **optional** future tense form: ~(으)ㄹ 거라면. If the verb stem ends on a vowel sound, attach ~ㄹ 거라면. If the verb stem ends on a consonant sound, attach ~을 거라면. You do not have to use this form - you can also just use ~(으)면 and conjugate the **final** verb into the future tense.

>	시장에 **갈 거라면** 생선을 사요.	If you're going to the market, buy fish.
>	너무 비**싸면** 다른 곳에 갈 거예요.	If it's too expensive, we'll go to a different place.
>	비가 **오면** 가지 않을 거예요.	If it's raining, I'm not going.

* Note: 돕다 and 곱다 are unusual ㅂ verbs that follow slightly different conjugation rules. When they meet an ~아/어 grammar form (e.g. ~아/어요 or ~아/어서) 오 is added instead of 우. However, when it is NOT an ~아/어 conjugation, but a different vowel sound (like ~으), 돕다 and 곱다 use 우 (like all other ㅂ irregular verbs). Refer to the page below to check the ㅂ irregular conjugation rules.

REFERENCE PAGES

A/V~ㄴ/는다면, N(이)라면 - page 246
The ㅂ Irregular - page 90

A/V~았/었다 Past Tense - page 58
A/V~(으)ㄹ 것이다 Future Tense - page 60

USED IN WCK 47 times

V~기 시작하다
For things you start doing

저는 작년에 한국어를 공부하기 시작했어요.
I started learning Korean last year.

The verb "시작하다" means "to start." You can attach ~기 시작하다 to the verb stem of an action verb to talk about starting some action.

Grammar Form	Present Tense	Past Tense	Future Tense
~기 시작하다	~기 시작해요	~기 시작했어요	~기 시작할 거예요

ACTION VERBS

~기 시작하다 can only be attached to action verbs. Simply attach ~기 시작하다 to the verb stem of the action verb. It does not matter if it ends on a vowel sound or a consonant sound.

가르치다	→	가르치**기 시작하다**	(to start teaching)
기다리다	→	기다리**기 시작하다**	(to start waiting)
먹다	→	먹**기 시작하다**	(to start eating)
받다	→	받**기 시작하다**	(to start receiving)

> 저는 버스를 기다리**기 시작해요**. — I start waiting for the bus.
> 저는 수업을 가르치**기 시작해요**. — I start teaching the class.
> 7시에 저녁을 먹**기 시작해요**. — At 7 o'clock I start eating dinner.
> 저는 2019년에 한국에서 가르치**기 시작했어요**. — In 2019 I started teaching in Korea.
> 오늘은 이메일을 많이 받**기 시작했어요**. — I started getting a lot of emails today.
> 저는 작년에 한국어를 배우**기 시작했어요**. — I started learning Korean last year.
> 저는 2020년에 한국어를 공부하**기 시작했어요**. — I started studying Korean in 2020.
> 우리는 올해부터 강아지를 키우**기 시작할 거예요**. — We will start raising a dog this year.
> 이번 주부터 더 일찍 일어나**기 시작할 거예요**. — From this week on, I'll start getting up earlier.

USED IN WCK   33 times

처음(으로)

For talking about the first time

어제 처음으로 한국어 수업을 들었어요.
Yesterday I had Korean class for the first time.

처음으로 is an adverb that can be added to a sentence to mean you are doing something for the first time. It is commonly written as just "처음" (where the ~(으)로 particle is dropped). It is also commonly seen in it's noun form "처음에" or "처음에는" which means; "at first..." or "as for in the beginning..."

ACTION VERBS

Place 처음(으로) before the verb you are doing for the first time.

말하다	→	**처음(으로)** 말하다	(to speak for the first time)
타다	→	**처음(으로)** 타다	(to ride for the first time)
시작하다	→	**처음(으로)** 시작하다	(to start for the first time)
만나다	→	**처음(으로)** 만나다	(to meet for the first time)

> 어제 한국어를 **처음으로** 말했어요.   I spoke Korean for the first time yesterday.
> 비행기를 **처음으로** 타고 있어요.   I am riding an airplane for the first time.
> **처음에는** 한국어가 어려웠어요.   At first, Korean was difficult.
> 우리가 오늘 **처음** 만났어요.   We met for the first time today.
> **처음에는** 한글을 배웠어요.   At first, I learned the Korean alphabet.
> 2020년에 **처음으로** 배우기 시작했어요.   I started learning for the first time in 2020.

WHAT'S THE DIFFERENCE?

처음	처음으로	처음에는
A noun meaning "the first time"	An adverb meaning "for the first time." 처음 + ~(으)로 particle.	처음에는 means "at first..." or "as for in the beginning..." 처음 + ~에 time particle + ~은/는 topic particle.

Level Three

DEVELOPING YOUR SENTENCES

DIFFICULTY LEVEL: MEDIUM!
The example sentences are adapted from conversational sentences made by real Korean people. You can expect the difficulty to be increase compared to Level Two.

Level Three Grammar

What we will learn

"한국어 문법을 공부하자!"
"Let's study Korean grammar!"

A/V~ㄹ/을 때, N 때 132
V~(으)면서, N(이)면서 135
V~(으)며 137
V~는 동안, N 동안 139
V~거나, N(이)나 141
N~의 142
가장 & 제일 143
V~는 N 144
V~(으)ㄴ N 145
V~(으)ㄹ N 146
V~아/어 보다 147
V~(으)ㄴ 적이 있다/없다 149
N 때문에 151
A/V~기 때문에 153
V~(으)ㄹ 수 있다/없다 155
A/V~았/었으면 좋겠다 157
N~께/에게/한테 159
V~(으)세요 162
A/V~지 마세요 163
V~아/어 주다 165

Level Three Vocab

What we will learn

한국어 어휘를 배우자!
Let's learn Korean vocabulary!

NOUNS
수업 - class, lesson
대학교 - university
해변 - thse beach
회사 - office
공항 - airport
버스 - bus
이메일 - email
비행기 - plane
지하철 - subway
시험 - test/exam
스트레스 - stress
선물 - present/gift
생일 - birthday
강아지 - dog/puppy
고양이 - kitten
코로나 - Coronavirus
뉴스 - the news
시간 - time
일 - work/thing

DESCRIPTIVE VERBS
힘들다 - to be difficult (!)
나쁘다 - to be bad (!)
편하다 - to be easy, comfortable
불편하다 - to be uncomfortable, inconvenient
편리하다 - to be convenient
바쁘다 - to be busy (!)
멀다 - to be far (!)
가깝다 - to be close, near (!)
괜찮다 - to be okay, fine
아프다 - to be sick/hurt (!)
예쁘다 - to be pretty (!)
아름답다 - to be beautiful (!)
다르다 - to be different (!)

ACTION VERBS
알다 - to know (!)
모르다 - to not know (!)
자다 - to sleep
일어나다 - to get up/wake up
보내다 - to send
받다 - to receive/get
타다 - to ride
쉬다 - to rest
가르치다 - to teach
기다리다 - to wait
여행하다 - to travel
시작하다 - to start
키우다 - to raise
청소하다 - to clean
이사하다 - to move (house)

Use flashcards on Quizlet!

Note: This is a list of some of the vocabulary you will encounter in the upcoming chapter. Additional vocabulary is included.
Note: verbs marked with a (!) symbol are irregular verbs. Check the reference pages below to learn more.

REFERENCE PAGES

The ㅂ Irregular - page 90
으 Irregular - page 294
ㄹ Irregular - page 296
르 Irregular - page 295

USED IN WCK 418 times

A/V ~ㄹ/을 때, N 때

For talking about the times that you do things

저녁을 먹을 때 가족이랑 같이 이야기해요.
My family and I chat when we eat dinner.

You can attach ~ㄹ/을 때 to verbs to talk about the time some action occurs. In English, this is often translated to "when" something happens.

ACTION VERBS & DESCRIPTIVE VERBS

~ㄹ/을 때 is attached to verbs to mean "when you do that verb." It can be attached to descriptive verbs and action verbs.

If the verb ends in a consonant sound, attach ~을 때

먹다	→	먹을 때	(when subj. eats)
받다	→	받을 때	(when subj. receives)
듣다 (!)	→	들을 때	(when subj. listens)

If the verb ends in a vowel sound or ㄹ, attach ~ㄹ 때

타다	→	탈 때	(when subj. rides)
모르다	→	모를 때	(when subj. doesn't know)
힘들다 (!)	→	힘들 때	(when it's hard)

> 힘들 때 쉬어요. When it's hard, I take a break.
> 단어를 **모를 때** 찾아봐요. When I don't know a word, I look it up.
> 버스를 **탈 때** 음악을 들어요. When I ride the bus, I listen to music.
> 음악을 **들을 때** 춤을 춰요. When I listen to music, I dance.
> 저는 너무 **바쁠 때** 스트레스를 받아요. When I'm too busy I get stressed.
> 시간이 **있을 때** 책을 읽는 것이 좋아요. When I have time I like to read.

NOUNS

Simply place 때 after the noun you wish to use it with. Leave a space between the noun and 때.

| 방학 | → | 방학 때 | (during vacation) |

| 시험 | → | 시험 **때** | (during the exam) |
| 점심 | → | 점심 **때** | (during lunch) |

> 시험 **때** 도서관에 자주 가요. — During exam time, I often go to the library.
> 방학 **때** 해변에서 자주 수영해요. — During vacation I often swim at the beach.
> 점심 **때** 된장찌개를 먹어요. — During lunch I eat doenjangjjigae (a soup).
> 저녁 **때** 책을 읽어요. — During the evening, I read a book.

Note: 때 is not used with: 오전 (noon), 오후 (afternoon), 아침 (morning), seasons, or days of the week. For these, you use the ~에 particle instead. However, 때 can be used with 저녁 (evening) and 점심 (lunch).

PAST TENSE - 았/었을 때

A/V~ㄹ/을 때 has a past tense form: "~았/었을 때." If the verb stem ends on ㅏ or ㅗ, attach ~았을 때. If the verb stem ends on 하, it becomes 했을 때, and if the verb stem ends on something else, attach ~었을 때.

> 한국에 살**았을 때** 영어를 가르쳤어요. — When I lived in Korea, I taught English.
> 대학교에 다**녔을 때** 한국어를 공부했어요. — When I attended college, I studied Korean.
> 한국에서 여행**했을 때** 힘들었어요. — When I traveled in Korea, I had a hard time.
> 한국에서 여행**했을 때** 정말 좋은 시간을 보냈어요. — When I traveled in Korea, I had a really good time.
> **아팠을 때** 잠을 많이 잤어요. — When I was sick, I slept a lot.

FUTURE TENSE

The ~ㄹ/을 때 grammar form can be used for future tense sentences, but the future tense is usually just carried by the final verb in the sentence.

> 한국에 **살 때** 한국어를 공부**할 거예요.** — When I live in Korea, I will study Korean.
> 한국에서 여행**할 때** 서울에 **갈 거예요.** — When I travel in Korea, I will go to Seoul.
> 대학교에 **다닐 때** 영어를 공부**할 거예요.** — When I go to college, I'll study English.
> 여름 방학 **때** 스페인에 **갈 거예요.** — During summer vacation, I'll go to Spain.

COMMON USE: "WHEN I WAS YOUNG" - 어렸을 때

Many of the writing prompts in "*Writing Conversational Korean*" involve talking about your

---

REFERENCE PAGES

A/V~았/었다 Past Tense - page 58   A/V~(으)ㄹ 것이다 Future Tense - page 60

childhood experiences. You can use "어렸을 때" to mean "when I was young." It is a conjugation of ~았/었을 때 with the verb "어리다" which means "to be young."

> **어렸을 때** 학교에 가는 것을 좋아했어요.   I liked going to school when I was young.
> **어렸을 때** 한국에 갔어요.   I went to Korea when I was young.
> **어렸을 때** 야채를 못 먹었어요.   I couldn't eat vegetables when I was young.
> 엄마가 **어렸을 때** 멕시코에서 살았어요.   When my mom was young, she lived in Mexico.

WHAT'S THE DIFFERENCE?

Both ~(으)면 and ~ㄹ/을 때 can mean "when" in a sentence and are easily interchangeable.

~ㄹ/을 때	~(으)면
~ㄹ/을 때 focuses on the time something occurs.	~(으)면 focuses on the hypothetical situation.
시간이 있을 때 책을 읽어요. When I have time I read a book. (Specifically at that time is when I read)	시간이 있으면 책을 읽어요. If I have time I read a book. (Hypothetically speaking)
The more specific the situation is, the more natural it is to use ~ㄹ/을 때.	The more vague the situation is, the more natural it is to use ~(으)면.
일 때문에 스트레스를 많이 받을 때 잘 자지 못해요. When I'm really stressed because of work, I can't sleep very well. (More specific situation)	스트레스를 받으면 잘 자지 못해요. If I'm stressed (in general), I can't sleep well. (Less specific situation)

PRACTICE EXERCISES

Given the English sentences, write an equivalent Korean expression.

1. When I cook I listen to music. _____

2. During lunch I go to the gym. _____

3. When I was young, I didn't like veggies. _____

ANSWERS: 1. (저는) 요리를 할 때 음악을 들어요. 2. 점심 때 헬스장에 가요. 3. (저는) 어렸을 때 야채를 안 좋아했어요. / 좋아하지 않았어요.

REFERENCE PAGES

A/V~(으)면 - page 125

USED IN WCK — 105 times

V~(으)면서, N(이)면서
For talking about simultaneous actions

저는 운동하면서 음악을 들어요.
I listen to music while I work out.

This grammar form can be attached to action verbs and nouns. It is used to talk about two things occuring at the **same time**. In English it is often translated to "during" or "while." It can only be used when the **same subject** is performing both actions. If subjects in both clauses are different, you have to use the "~는 동안" grammar form instead (see next).

ACTION VERBS

If the verb ends in a consonant, attach **~으면서**

| 먹다 | → | 먹**으면서** | (while eating) |
| (!) 듣다 | → | 들**으면서** | (while listening) |

If the verb ends in a vowel, or ㄹ, attach **~면서**

기다리다	→	기다리**면서**	(while waiting)
가르치다	→	가르치**면서**	(while teaching)
(!) 살다	→	살**면서**	(while living)

> 기다리**면서** 음악을 들어요. — While I wait, I listen to music.
> 지하철을 타**면서** 이메일을 확인해요. — While I ride the subway, I check my emails.
> 먹**으면서** 넷플릭스를 봐요. — While I eat, I watch Netflix.
> 한국에 살**면서** 한국어를 공부해요. — I study Korean while living in Korea.

NOUNS

If the noun ends on a consonant, attach **~이면서**

| 학생 | → | 학생**이면서** | (while being a student) |
| 축복 | → | 축복**이면서** | (while being a blessing) |

If the noun ends on a vowel sound, attach **~면서**

| 엄마 | → | 엄마**면서** | (while being a mom) |
| 의사 | → | 의사**면서** | (while being a doctor) |

REFERENCE PAGES

V~는 동안, N 동안 - page 139

3

> 저는 학생**이면서** 엄마예요. I'm a mom while being a student.
> 그 사람은 의사**면서** 교수예요. That person is a doctor and a professor.
> **축복이면서** 동시에 부담이에요. It's a blessing while also being a burden.

USAGE NOTE: YET/THOUGH

In contrasting sentences, ~(으)면서 can mean "yet" or "though." Sometimes ~도 is added for emphasis (i.e. ~(으)면서도). This is similar to English, where "while" can mean either: "during some action" or it can mean "doing X while also doing Y." For example:

> 돈이 없**으면서** 돈을 많이 써요. They spend a lot, yet they don't have money.
> 아무것도 모르**면서도** 다 아는 척해요. They know nothing, while pretending to know it all.
> 요리는 안 하**면서도** 먹기만 해요. They only eat, though they don't cook.

WHAT'S THE DIFFERENCE?

~(으)면서 and ~ㄹ/을 때 are very similar, and when used with verbs, are mostly interchangeable.

~(으)면서	~ㄹ/을 때
"While" or "during"	"When"
기다리**면서** 음악을 들어요. While I wait, I listen to music.	기다**릴 때** 음악을 들어요. When I wait, I listen to music.
Used with many nouns to mean: "while being N"	Used with time nouns to mean: "when it's N"
저는 학생**이면서** 엄마예요. I'm a mom while being a student.	저는 학창 시절 **때** 엄마가 되었어요. I became a mom during my student days.

PRACTICE EXERCISES

Given the English sentences, write an equivalent Korean expression.

1. I listen to music while I study. _____

2. I drink tea while I read a book. _____

3. I worked at a school while living in Korea. _____

ANSWERS: 1. 공부하면서 음악을 들어요. 2. 책을 읽으면서 차를 마셔요. 3. 한국에 살면서 학교에서 일했어요.

REFERENCE PAGES

A/V~ㄹ/을 때, N 때 - page 132   N~도 - page 83

USED IN WCK   93 times

V~(으)며
1. Formal "and"   2. Formal "during"

축하드리며 항상 행복 하시기를 기원합니다.
Congratulations and best wishes for the future.

~(으)며 is only attached to action verbs. It overlaps somewhat with both the ~(으)면서 grammar form and the ~고 grammar form. It has two main usages:
1 A formal/written way to link clauses with "while/during" - similar to ~(으)면서
2 A formal/written way to link clauses with "and" - similar to ~고

1 ACTION VERBS - WHILE/DURING

If the action verb ends in a consonant sound, attach **~으며**

| 웃다 | → | 웃**으며** | (while smiling) |
| ! 듣다 | → | 들**으며** | (while listening) |

If the action verb ends in a vowel sound, or ㄹ, attach **~며**

쉬다	→	쉬**며**	(while resting)
! 울다	→	울**며**	(while crying)
! 돕다	→	도우**며**	(while helping)

그가 크게 씨익 웃**으며** 돌아섰어요.	He turned around wearing a big grin.
잡지를 읽**으며** 쿠키를 먹었어요.	I ate a cookie while reading a magazine.
나는 조용히 쉬**며** 몇 시간을 보냈어요.	I spent a few hours quietly relaxing.
여자가 울**며** 자신의 머리털을 쥐어 뜯었어요.	The woman wept while pulling out her hair.
더 많은 사람들이 서로 도우**며** 살아야 해요.	More people need to live while helping others.
코 고는 소리를 들**으며** 누워 있었어요.	I laid (in bed) listening to the sound of snoring.

WHAT'S THE DIFFERENCE?

~(으)며	~(으)면서
More formal and primarily used in written language.	A standard way to say "while/during." Used often in spoken and written Korean.

---- REFERENCE PAGES ----

V~(으)면서, N(이)면서 - page 135   A/V~고 N~(이)고 - page 108

~(으)며	~(으)면서
음악을 들으며 운동을 하고 있어요. I work out while listening to music. 채팅하며 커피를 마셔요. While chatting I drink coffee.	음악을 들으면서 운동을 하고 있어요. I work out while listening to music. 채팅하면서 커피를 마셔요. While chatting I drink coffee.

2 ACTION VERBS - "AND"

If the action verb ends in a consonant sound, attach ~으며

    받다 → 받으며   (to receive, and...)

If the action verb ends on a vowel sound, attach ~며

    축하드리다 → 축하드리며   (to give congratulations, and...)
    전달하다 → 전달하며   (to notify, and...)

› 축하드리며 항상 행복 하시기를 기원합니다.	Congratulations and best wishes for the future.
› 상을 받았으며 악수했습니다.	He received the award and shook hands.
› 회사에 그 소식을 전달했으며 고객 분들께도 사과의 말씀을 드렸습니다.	We notified the company and also apologized to the customers.

WHAT'S THE DIFFERENCE?

~(으)며	~고
Most commonly seen in formal writing. Implies the two actions happened consecutively.	Used as a standard way to say "and." Used often in both spoken and written Korean.
상을 받았으며 악수했습니다. He received an award and shook hands. For example, written in a biography, article, or announcement.	상을 받았고 악수했습니다. He received an award and shook hands. Standard sentence and could be used in most contexts.

{ This is an advanced grammar form. We are including it because it relates to the previous grammar form and you'll encounter it often. It's good to recognize it, but you do not have to use it. }

USED IN WCK **22 times**

V~는 동안, N 동안
For talking about durations of time

저는 한국에서 2년 동안 살았어요.
I lived in Korea for two years.

동안 can be used with both nouns and action verbs. With nouns, it is used to talk about a span of time. With action verbs, it means "during" or "while."

ACTION VERBS

You can attach ~는 동안 to the verb stem of action verbs to mean "while" or "during" this action.
Always attach ~는 동안 regardless of whether the verb ends in a consonant or vowel sound.

자다	→	자는 **동안**	(while sleeping)
먹다	→	먹는 **동안**	(while eating)
기다리다	→	기다리는 **동안**	(while waiting)
(!) 살다	→	사는 **동안**	(while living)

> 자는 **동안** 꿈을 꿔요. — I dream while I sleep.
> 자는 **동안** 코를 골아요. — I snore while I sleep.
> 공부하는 **동안** 커피를 마셔요. — While I study, I drink coffee.
> 공부하는 **동안** 음악을 들어요. — While I study, I listen to music.

NOUNS

동안 is commonly placed after time nouns to indicate that you did something **for** a period of time.

6시간	→	6시간 **동안**	(for six hours)
6개월	→	6개월 **동안**	(for six months)
1년	→	1년 **동안**	(for one year)

> 1년 **동안** 한국에 살았어요. — I lived in Korea for one year.
> 6개월 **동안** 한국어를 공부했어요. — I studied Korean for six months.

> 2시간 **동안** 운동했어요.   I worked out for two hours.
> 3주 **동안** 미국에 갔어요.   I went to America for three weeks.
> 방학 **동안** 영국에서 여행했어요.   I traveled in England during the school break.

Note: because 동안 literally translates to "during," you might hear native Korean speakers say "I have lived in America during two years." This is because they are literally translating "동안."

WHAT'S THE DIFFERENCE?

~는 동안	~(으)면서
Can be used when the subjects of the two clauses are different (i.e. when talking about the simultaneous actions of two different people).	Cannot be used when the subjects of the two clauses are different. (i.e. the same person has to be doing both actions).
O 제가 공부하는 동안 언니가 요리해요. I study while my older sister cooks.	X 제가 공부하면서 언니가 요리해요. Incorrect because there are two different subjects with ~(으)면서: ("제" and "언니")
O 저는 공부하는 동안 커피를 마셔요. I drink coffee while I study. If the subject in both clauses is the same, either grammar form can be used.	O 저는 공부하면서 커피를 마셔요. I drink coffee while I study. If the subject in both clauses is the same, either grammar form can be used.
Can be used with time nouns.	Not used with time nouns.
O 저는 6개월 동안 한국어를 공부했어요. I studied Korean for six months.	X 저는 6개월이면서 한국어를 공부했어요. Incorrect expression.

PRACTICE EXERCISES

Given the English sentences, write an equivalent Korean expression.

1. I listen to music while I work out. _____

2. I will live in Korea for two years. _____

3. I went to Korea during school break. _____

4. I work while my older sister sleeps. _____

ANSWERS: 1. (저는) 운동하면서 음악을 들어요. 2. (저는) 2년 동안 한국에서(서) 살 거예요. 3. (저는) 방학 동안 한국에 갔어요. 4. (저는) 언니가 자는 동안 일을 해요.

REFERENCE PAGES

Small Numbers in Korean - page 284
Korean Counters - page 286

V~(으)면서, N(이)면서 - page 135

USED IN WCK   86 times*

V~거나, N(이)나
Or

저녁에 드라마를 보거나 영화를 봐요.
In the evening I watch a drama or a movie.

This grammar form is commonly used when someone asks you a question, and you want to give several different options as a response; "I do this, or that, or this other thing..."

ACTION VERBS & DESCRIPTIVE VERBS

To connect verbs (either descriptive verbs or action verbs), attach **~거나** to the verb stem. Attach ~거나 regardless of whether the verb ends in a vowel or a consonant.

산책하다	→	산책하**거나**	(to walk or...)
시작하다	→	시작하**거나**	(to start or...)
일어나다	→	일어나**거나**	(to get up or...)

> 날씨가 좋으면 산책하**거나** 수영해요.   When the weather's good, I take a walk or I swim.
> 저녁에 주로 게임하**거나** 영화를 봐요.   In the evening, I'm mostly gaming or watching movies.
> 일요일에 청소하**거나** 세탁해요.   On Sundays I clean or do laundry.

NOUNS

If the noun ends with a consonant sound, attach **~이나**

선생님	→	선생님**이나**	(a teacher or...)
지하철	→	지하철**이나**	(a subway or...)

If the noun ends with a vowel sound, attach **~나**

뉴스	→	뉴스**나**	(news or...)
스트레스	→	스트레스**나**	(stress or...)

> 먹으면서 드라마**나** 영화를 봐요.   While I eat, I watch a drama or a movie.
> 책**이나** 인터넷으로 한국어를 공부해요.   I study Korean with books or the internet.
> 음식이 너무 매우면 물**이나** 우유를 마셔요.   When my food is too spicy, I drink water or milk.

---

* Only includes ~거나, does not include ~(이)나 because of overlap with other grammar forms

USED IN WCK   797 times

N~의

The possessive particle

사라의 샌드위치예요.
It's Sara's sandwich.

~의 is a particle used to show possession, similar to how we use "**'s**" (e.g. "Sara**'s** food") or "the noun **of** something" (e.g. "the representative **of** our team").

Note: We've already encountered ~의 several times, because "제" ("my") is a contraction of "저의" (저 + ~의 particle). "제" is more commonly used, but you may still see the long form, "저의," used in writing.

> 사라**의** 음식이에요.   It's Sara's food.
> 소피**의** 돈을 썼어요.   I spent Sophie's money.
> 우리는 반지**의** 제왕을 봤어요.   We watched The Lord of the Rings.
> 우리 팀**의** 대표예요.   He is the representative of our team.

PRONUNCIATION OF 의

"의" is tricky because it is pronounced three different ways depending on how it's used.
1 If it's at the start of a noun it's pronounced as it's written: [의]
      의사 - doctor   [의사]
      의자 - chair   [의자]
2 If it's in the middle or end, but **not being used** as the possessive particle, it's pronounced: [이]
      거의 - almost   [거이]
      문의 - inquiry   [문이]
      여의도 - Yeouido   [여이도]   (Yeouido is an island in Korea)
3 If it's being used as the possessive particle "**의**," it's pronounced as [에]
      친구**의** - my friend's (thing)   [친구에]
      사라**의** - Sara's (thing)   [사라에]
      소피**의** - Sophie's (thing)   [소피에]

USED IN WCK — 358 times*

가장 & 제일
Most & Best

초밥을 가장 좋아해요.
I like sushi the most.

가장 and 제일 are adverbs you can place in front of descriptive verbs to mean "most" or "best." If you want to use with action verbs, use "가장/제일 많이" before the action verb.

DESCRIPTIVE VERBS

가장 and 제일 can be used with descriptive verbs and **some** action verbs (like 좋아하다 and 싫어하다). Place 가장 or 제일 before the verb.

좋아하다	→	가장/제일 좋아하다	(to like most, to be one's favorite)
예쁘다	→	가장/제일 예쁘다	(to be the prettiest)
춥다	→	가장/제일 춥다	(to be the coldest)

> 한국어를 **제일** 좋아해요. — I like Korean the most.
> 메리가 **가장** 예뻐요. — Mary is the prettiest.
> 남극대륙이 **가장** 추워요. — Antarctica is the coldest.
> 아프리카가 **제일** 더워요. — Africa is the hottest.
> 저는 크리스마스 때 **가장 많이*** 먹어요. — I eat the most at Christmas time.

WHAT'S THE DIFFERENCE?

가장 and 제일 are almost identical and are interchangeable in almost all situations.

가장	제일
가장 derives from pure Korean.	제일 derives from Chinese characters.
가장 can only be used as an adverb.	제일 can be used as either a noun or an adverb.
X 아이스크림이 가장이에요. This sentence is incorrect because 가장 cannot be used as a noun.	O 아이스크림이 제일이에요. Ice cream is the best.

가장 - 268 | 제일 - 90

3

V~는 N
Present tense noun-modifying form

보는 영화가 재미있어요.
The movie I'm watching is interesting.

You can use ~는 N to an action verb stem to say "the noun that I am verb-ing." For example, "the book I am reading," or "the friend I am meeting."

ACTION VERBS

Attach ~는 to the verb stem and place it before the noun. Attach ~는 regardless of whether the verb ends on a vowel sound or a consonant sound.

모르다	→	모르는 N	(the N I don't know)
사랑하다	→	사랑하는 N	(the N I love)
(!) 알다	→	아는 N	(the N I know)

> 모르는 사람이 많아요.　　　　There are lots of people I don't know.
> 사랑하는 사람이 중요해요.　　The people you love are important.
> 보는 영화를 좋아해요.　　　　I like the movie I'm watching.
> 요즘 읽는 책이 신기해요.　　　The book I'm reading lately is fascinating.

COMMON USAGE: "MY FAVORITE N" - 가장/제일 좋아하는 N

"가장 좋아하다" or "제일 좋아하다" literally mean "to like most/best," but are more naturally thought of as meaning "(my) favorite." When used in the form **V~는 N**, "가장/제일 좋아하**는** N" means: "my favorite noun." For example: "제일 좋아하는 책" (my favorite book).

> 가장 좋아하는 나라가 한국이에요.　　　My favorite country is Korea.
> 가장 좋아하는 음식은 피자예요.　　　　My favorite food is pizza.
> 제일 좋아하는 커피는 아메리카노예요.　　My favorite coffee is americano (black coffee).

Note: V~는 is not to be confused with the N~은/는 topic particle. The topic particle "는" is only attached to nouns. The "는" in "V~는" is only attached to verbs.

REFERENCE PAGES

가장 & 제일 - page 143

V~(으)ㄴ N

Past tense noun-modifying form

먹은 초밥이 비쌌어요.
The sushi I ate was expensive.

You can add V~(으)ㄴ to an action verb stem to talk about a noun that you interacted with **in the past**. It means: "the noun that I verb-ed." For example, "the book I read," or, "the friend I met."

ACTION VERBS

If the verb stem ends in a vowel sound, or ㄹ, add ~ㄴ

사다	→	산 N	(the N I bought)
보내다	→	보낸 N	(the N I sent)
돕다	→	도운 N	(the N I helped)
만들다	→	만든 N	(the N I made)

If the verb stem ends in a consonant sound, add ~은

받다	→	받은 N	(the N I received)
먹다	→	먹은 N	(the N I ate)
듣다	→	들은 N	(the N I listened to)

> 읽은 책이 재미있었어요. — The book I read was interesting.
> 간 파티가 어색했어요. — The party I went to was awkward.
> 저를 도운 사람이 많아요. — There are many people who helped me.
> 탄 버스가 편했어요. — The bus I rode was comfortable.
> 보낸 이메일이 중요해요. — The email I sent is important.
> 받은 선물이 무거웠어요. — The present I received was heavy.
> 어제 들은 수업이 재미있었어요. — The class I had yesterday was interesting.
> 아침에 만든 음식이 맛있었어요. — The food I made this morning was delicious.

Note: V~(으)ㄴ N is not to be confused with the N~은/는 topic particle. The topic particle "은" is only attached to nouns. The "은" in "V~(으)ㄴ" is only attached to verbs.

V~(으)ㄹ N
Future tense noun-modifying form

살 집은 비싸지 않아요.
The house I'll buy isn't expensive.

You can add ~(으)ㄹ to an action verb stem to talk about a noun that you will interact with **in the future.** This means: "a noun that I will verb" or "a noun to verb (in the future)." For example: "the friend I'll meet," or, "a book to read."

ACTION VERBS

If the verb stem ends in a vowel sound, or ㄹ, attach ~ㄹ

사다	→	살 N	(a N to buy)
살다	→	살 N*	(a N to live in)
사랑하다	→	사랑할 N	(a N to love)
돕다	→	도울 N	(a N to help)

If the verb stem ends in a consonant sound, attach ~을

받다	→	받을 N	(a N to receive)
먹다	→	먹을 N	(a N to eat)
듣다	→	들을 N	(a N to listen to)

> 내일 아침에 **먹을** 빵이에요. — This is the bread I'll eat tomorrow morning.
> 사라가 **읽을** 책이에요. — This is the book Sara will read.
> **탈** 버스가 불편해요. — The bus I will ride is uncomfortable.
> **줄** 선물이 비쌌어요. — The present I will give was expensive.
> 우리는 **먹을** 음식을 발견했어요. — We found food to eat.
> 우리는 **볼** 영화를 골랐어요. — We picked a movie to watch.
> 마당에 **심을** 나무를 샀어요. — We bought a tree to plant in our yard.

Note: V~(으)ㄹ is not to be confused with the ~을/를 object particle. The object particle "을" is only attached to nouns. The "을" in "V~(으)ㄹ" is only attached to verbs.

---

* With this grammar form, the verbs "사다" (to buy) and "살다" (to live) conjugate the same way.

V~아/어 보다

For trying new things

인도에서 여행해 보고 싶어요.
I want to try traveling in India.

This grammar form is only used with action verbs. You can use this form to talk about things you try to do. This grammar includes the verb "보다" which means "to see." You can think about this grammar form literally meaning: to do something, and then **see how it goes**, or **see what happens**.

Grammar Form	Present Tense	Past Tense	Future Tense
~아/어 보다	~아/어 봐요	~아/어 봤어요	~아/어 볼 거예요

ACTION VERBS

This grammar form is only used with action verbs.

If the last vowel sound of the verb stem is ㅏ or ㅗ, attach **~아 보다**

    받다 → **받아 보다** (to try receiving)
    (!) 돕다 → **도와 보다** (to try helping)

If the last vowel sound of the verb is 하, attach **~해 보다**

    여행하다 → **여행해 보다** (to try traveling)
    사랑하다 → **사랑해 보다** (to try loving)

If the last vowel sound of the verb is something else, attach **~어 보다**

    읽다 → **읽어 보다** (to try reading)
    마시다 → **마셔 보다** (to try drinking)
    (!) 듣다 → **들어 보다** (to try listening)

> 김치를 먹**어 봐요**.   Try the kimchi.*
> 이 책을 읽**어 봐요**.   Try reading this book.
> 이 커피를 마셔 **봐요**.   Try this coffee.*
> 작년에 한국에 **가 봤어요**.   I went to Korea last year.*
> 한국에 **가 보고 싶어요**.   I want to go to Korea.*

Note: in English, the verb "to try" can include the meaning of "eating" and "drinking" without needing to include those words, whereas in Korean, you must say "먹어 보다" and "마셔 보다."

한국 사람이랑 같이 말**해 보**고 싶어요.	I want to try talking with a Korean person.
일본어를 공부**해 보**고 싶었어요.	I wanted to study Japanese.
강아지를 키**워 보**고 싶었어요.	I wanted to raise a dog.
여름 때 서핑**해 보**고 싶어요.	I want to try surfing in the summer.
먹**어 봤**지만 너무 매웠어요.	I tried eating it but it was too spicy.
배**워 봤**지만 너무 어려웠어요.	I tried learning it, but it was too difficult.
들**어 봤**지만 이해 못 했어요.	I tried to listen, but I couldn't understand.

It's not always natural to write "to try doing" in the English sentence. For example, "I want to try going to Korea" sounds a little bit unnatural in English, even though "한국에 가 보고 싶어요" sounds natural in Korean. Direct translations don't always work between languages.

WHAT'S THE DIFFERENCE?

Both ~아/어 보다 and ~아/어요 are used to talk about things you do. Both are grammatically correct and natural, it just depends on which (if any) additional feeling you want to add.

~아/어 보다	~아/어요
Something that you try doing with the intent to see what happens, or see how it goes.	*Just simple present tense with no additional meaning.*
한국에 **가 봐요**. I'm going to Korea. (I'm going to Korea and seeing how it goes) 작년에 한국어를 배**워 봤어요**. I tried learning Korean last year. (I learned Korean to see how it would go)	한국에 **가요**. I'm going to Korea. (Simple present/near future tense) 작년에 한국어를 배웠**어요**. I learned Korean last year. (Simple past tense)

PRACTICE EXERCISES

Given the English sentence, try writing an equivalent expression in Korean.

1. I want to try learning Japanese.

2. I wanted to try working at home last year.

3. Next year I will try going to a concert.

ANSWERS: 1. (저는) 일본어를 배워 보고 싶어요. 2. (저는) 작년에 집에서 일해 보고 싶었어요. 3. (저는) 내년에 콘서트에 가 볼 거예요.

USED IN WCK   542 times

V~(으)ㄴ 적이 있다/없다
For talking about your experiences

저는 중국에 가 본 적이 없어요.
I've never been to China.

This grammar form is used to talk about experiences you have or don't have. In Korean, the noun "적" means "experience," so you're literally saying that you have, (있다) or don't have (없다) the experience of doing some action (V) in the past.

Grammar Form	~아/어요 Conjugation
~(으)ㄴ 적이 있다	~(으)ㄴ 적이 있어요
~(으)ㄴ 적이 없다	~(으)ㄴ 적이 없어요

Note: ~(으)ㄴ 적이 있다/없다 is already talking about the past, you don't need to add the ~았/었 marker. This grammar form is not used in the future tense.

ACTION VERBS

If the verb stem ends in a consonant sound, attach **~은 적이 있다/없다**

| 받다 | → | **받은 적이 있다/없다** | (to have/not have ever received) |
| 읽다 | → | **읽은 적이 있다/없다** | (to have/not have ever read) |

If the verb ends in a vowel sound, or ㄹ, attach **~ㄴ 적이 있다/없다**

타다	→	**탄 적이 있다/없다**	(to have/not have ever ridden)
(!) 살다	→	**산 적이 있다/없다**	(to have/not have ever lived)
(!) 만들다	→	**만든 적이 있다/없다**	(to have/not have ever made)

EXPERIENCES YOU'VE HAD

To talk about something you **have** experienced, attach **~(으)ㄴ 적이 있다**

> 한국어를 공부**한 적이 있어요.**   I have studied Korean.
> 버스를 **탄 적이 있어요.**   I have ridden a bus.
> 책을 **쓴 적이 있어요.**   I have written a book.
> 한국에 **산 적이 있어요.**   I have lived in Korea.

EXPERIENCES YOU HAVEN'T EVER HAD
To talk about something you **haven't** experienced, attach ~(으)ㄴ 적이 없다

> 비행기를 **탄** 적이 없어요.	I haven't ever ridden on an airplane.
> 한국에 **산** 적이 없어요.	I haven't ever lived in Korea.
> 뼈가 부러**진** 적이 없어요.	I haven't ever broken a bone.
> 눈 사람을 만**든** 적이 없어요.	I haven't ever made a snowman.

OFTEN COMBINED WITH ~아/어 보다
This is used when talking about having the experience of trying something. Check the reference page below to learn more.

> 김치를 먹어 본 적이 있어요.	I've tried eating kimchi.
> 소주를 마셔 본 적이 있어요.	I've tried drinking soju.
> 오토바이를 타 본 적이 없어요.	I've never tried riding a motorbike.

COMMON USE: "HAVE YOU EVER...?"
This grammar form is used when asking people "have you ever?" questions.

> 한국에 가 본 적이 있어요?	Have you ever been to Korea?
> 비행기를 타 본 적이 있어요?	Have you ever ridden an airplane?
> 이사해 본 적이 있어요?	Have you ever moved house?
> 눈사람을 만들어 본 적이 있어요?	Have you ever made a snowman?

PRACTICE EXERCISES
Given the English sentences, write an equivalent expression in Korean.

1. I have tried making a snowman.

2. I haven't tried making music.

3. I've never bought expensive coffee.

4. I have tried eating expensive cheese.

ANSWERS: 1. (저는) 눈사람을 만들어 본 적이 있어요. 2. (저는) 음악을 만들어 본 적이 없어요. 3. (저는) 비싼 커피를 산 적이 없어요. 4. (저는) 비싼 치즈를 먹어 본 적이 있어요.

REFERENCE PAGES

V~아/어 보다 - page 147

USED IN WCK   36 times

N 때문에
To say "because of noun"

일 때문에 한국에 갔어요.
I went to Korea because of work.

You can place 때문에 after a noun to say; "because of that noun, some result occurs."

NOUNS
Place 때문에 after the noun with a space between the noun and 때문에.

눈	→	눈 **때문에** (because of the snow...)
시험	→	시험 **때문에** (because of the test...)
코로나	→	코로나 **때문에** (because of Coronavirus...)

> 눈 **때문에** 집에 못 가요.   I can't go home because of the snow.
> 일 **때문에** 미국에 갔어요.   I went to America because of work.
> 케이팝 **때문에** 한국어를 배우고 싶어요.   I want to learn Korean because of kpop.
> 코로나 **때문에** 한국에 못 갔어요.   I couldn't go to Korea because of Corona.
> 코로나 19 **때문에** 헬스장에 안 갔어요.   Because of Corona 19, I didn't go to the gym.
> 학업 **때문에** 일본에 살고 있어요.   I am living in Japan because of my studies.
> 코로나 **때문에** 마스크 해요.   Because of Corona, I wear a mask.
> 냄새 **때문에** 맛있지 않아요.   Because of the smell, it tastes gross.

ENDING A SENTENCE: "때문이에요"
You can also use 때문이에요 as a sentence ending. This is common when answering questions.

> Q. 왜 학교에 안 갔어요?   Why didn't you go to school?
> A. 눈 **때문이에요**.   Because of the snow.
> Q. 왜 한국에 왔어요?   Why did you come to Korea?
> A. 일 **때문이에요**.   Because of work.

SPECIAL CASE: N~이기 때문에

N~이기 때문에 means; "**because N1 is N2**, then..." For example:

> 오늘은 휴일**이기 때문에** 학교에 안 가요.   Today's a holiday so I'm not going to school.
> 오늘은 제 생일**이기 때문에** 파티를 열어요.   I'm having a party since today's my birthday.
> 제 친구의 생일**이기 때문에** 케이크를 먹었어요.   Since it's my friend's birthday, we ate cake.

WHAT'S THE DIFFERENCE?

There are times when you have to use N~이기 때문에 instead of N 때문에. Grammatically, you have to choose between one or the other. They are not interchangeable. Fortunately, it is relatively simple to know which one to use, because we follow the same rule in English.

N 때문에	N~이기 때문에
N 때문에 means: "because of"	N~이기 때문에 means: "because it is"
O 눈 때문에 집에 못 가요. I can't go home because of snow. X 일요일 때문에 직장에 안 가요. I'm not going to the office because of Sunday. O 약 때문에 졸려요. Because of the medicine, I feel sleepy.	X 눈이기 때문에 집에 못 가요. I can't go home because it is snow. O 일요일이기 때문에 직장에 안 가요. I'm not going to the office because it's Sunday. O 약이기 때문에 먹고 싶지 않아요. Because it's medicine, I don't want to take it.

PRACTICE EXERCISES

Given the English sentences, write an equivalent sentence in Korean.

1. I can't go to the park because of the rain.

2. I can't eat gluten because of an allergy.

3. I want to learn Korean because of my boyfriend.

4. I'm stressed because of exams.

5. I'm not going to school because it's Saturday.

ANSWERS: 1. (저는) 비 때문에 공원에 못 가요. 2. (저는) 알레르기 때문에 글루텐을 못 먹어요. 3. (저는) 남자친구 때문에 한국어를 배우고 싶어요. 4. (저는) 시험 때문에 스트레스를 받아요. 5. 토요일이기 때문에 학교에 안 가요/가지 않아요.

USED IN WCK **116 times**

A/V ~기 때문에

For joining clauses with "because"

그 음식이 너무 맵기 때문에 못 먹어요.
I can't eat that food because it's too spicy.

You can attach ~기 때문에 to action verbs and descriptive verbs to say "because of that verb, some result occurs." What follows must be a clause stating what occurred as a result of the first clause.

ACTION VERBS & DESCRIPTIVE VERBS

~기 때문에 can attach to action verbs and descriptive verbs. It doesn't matter what the last sound of the verb is, simply attach **~기 때문에**.

중요하다	→	중요하**기 때문에**	(because it's important...)
익숙하다	→	익숙하**기 때문에**	(because I'm used to it...)

> 이 시험은 중요하**기 때문에** 열심히 공부해요. — I study hard because this exam is important.
> 눈이 오**기 때문에** 학교에 못 가요. — I can't go to school because it's snowing.
> 스트레스를 받**기 때문에** 청소하고 있어요. — I'm cleaning because I'm stressed.
> 야근하**기 때문에** 스트레스를 받아요. — I'm stressed because I'm working overtime.
> 돈이 모자라**기 때문에** 집을 못 사요. — I can't buy a house because I don't have enough money.
> 시간이 없**기 때문에** 못 해요. — I can't do it 'cause I don't have enough time.

SENTENCE ENDING: ~기 때문이에요

You can also end a sentence using "**~기 때문이에요.**"

> 열심히 공부해요. 시험은 중요하**기 때문이에요**. — I'm studying hard. Because the test is important.
> 학교에 못 가요. 감기에 걸리**기 때문이에요**. — I can't go to school. Because I have a cold.
> 청소하고 있어요. 스트레스를 받**기 때문이에요**. — I'm cleaning. Because I'm stressed.

WHAT'S THE DIFFERENCE?

V~기 때문에	V~아/어서
~기 때문에 cannot be used to talk about a series of events.	~아/어서 can be used to talk about a series of events.
X 카페에 가기 때문에 커피를 샀어요. Because I went to a cafe, I bought a coffee. (This is awkward in Korean) X 일어나기 때문에 학교에 가요. Because I get up, I go to school. (This does not make sense)	O 카페에 가서 커피를 샀어요. I went to a cafe and then bought a coffee. O 일아나서 학교에 가요. I get up and then I go to school.
~기 때문에 is slightly more formal and is used more in written language.	~아/어서 is slightly more casual and used more in spoken language.
~기 때문에 implies a stronger correlation between the clauses. It is about direct cause and effect.	The connection between clauses in ~아/어서 can be slightly looser.
스트레스를 받기 때문에 청소하고 있어요. I'm cleaning because I'm stressed. Me cleaning at the moment is a direct result of being stressed.	스트레스를 받아서 청소하고 있어요. I'm stressed so I'm cleaning. Me cleaning at the moment is related to being stressed, but there might be other causes, or I might be cleaning for other additional reasons.

USAGE NOTE: 왜냐하면

"왜냐하면" means "because/since" and is used to **start** a sentence. Starting a sentence with "왜냐하면" and closing it with "~기 때문이에요" is considered a very neat and elegant way to structure "because" sentences in Korean.

> **왜냐하면** 내일 시험을 보**기 때문이에요**.	Because I have a test tomorrow.
> **왜냐하면** 거기는 완전 싸**기 때문이에요**.	Because it's totally cheap there.
> 내 친구는 당국을 안 믿어요. **왜냐하면** 개가 음모론자**이기 때문이에요**.	My friend doesn't trust the authorities. Because he's a conspiracy theorist.

Note: "때문에" is a slightly formal/written form. 왜냐하면 is also used more colloquially with grammar forms like ~(으)니까 and ~거든(요). Check the reference pages below to learn more.

REFERENCE PAGES

A/V~아/어서 N(이)라서 - page 115

A/V~(으)니까 - page 269
A/V~거든(요) - page 240

USED IN WCK **275 times**

V~(으)ㄹ 수 있다/없다
For things you can and can't do

원하면 제가 한국어로 말할 수 있어요.
I can speak in Korean if you want.

In Korean, "수" literally means "ability," or "way." Therefore, "수 있다" means to have an ability/way, and "수 없다" means to not have an ability/way. As you can likely guess, this grammar form is used to talk about things you have (or don't have) the ability to do.

Grammar Form	Present Tense	Past Tense	Future Tense
~(으)ㄹ 수 있다	~(으)ㄹ 수 있어요	~(으)ㄹ 수 있었어요	~(으)ㄹ 수 있을 거예요
~(으)ㄹ 수 없다	~(으)ㄹ 수 없어요	~(으)ㄹ 수 없었어요	~(으)ㄹ 수 없을 거예요

ACTION VERBS

~ㄹ/을 수 있다/없다 can only be attached to action verbs.
If the verb stem ends in a vowel sound, or ㄹ, attach **~ㄹ 수 있다/없다**

    하다 → **할 수 있다/없다**   (subj. can/cannot do)
    살다 → **살 수 있다/없다**   (subj. can/cannot live)
    (!) 돕다 → **도울 수 있다/없다**   (subj. can/cannot help)

If the verb stem ends in a consonant sound, attach **~을 수 있다/없다**

    받다 → **받을 수 있다/없다**   (subj. can/cannot receive)
    먹다 → **먹을 수 있다/없다**   (subj. can/cannot eat)
    (!) 듣다 → **들을 수 있다/없다**   (subj. can/cannot listen)

> 한국으로 이사할 **수 있어요**.   I can move to Korea.
> 일 때문에 파리에서 **살 수 있어요**.   I can live in Paris because of work.
> 너무 비싸기 때문에 보낼 **수 없어요**.   I can't send it because it's too expensive.
> 지금 너무 바빠서 주말에 만날 **수 없어요**.   I can't meet this weekend because I'm too busy at the moment.

PAST TENSE
Add ~(으)ㄹ 수 있었다 or ~(으)ㄹ 수 없었다 to talk about what you could/couldn't do in the past.

> 어렸을 때 농구를 **할 수 있었어요**. When I was young, I could play basketball.
> 취업 관련 조언을 많이 **받을 수 있었어요**. I could get a lot of job-hunting advice.
> 코로나 때문에 한국에 **갈 수 없었어요**. Because of Coronavirus, I couldn't go to Korea.
> 어제 눈이 와서 학교에 **갈 수 없었어요**. It snowed yesterday so I couldn't go to school.

USAGE NOTE: ~(으)ㄹ 수가 있다/없다
You may also see the ~이/가 subject particle used on the noun "수" (ability/way). The sentences are almost identical, but adding the particle gives the sentence more emphasis.

> 이길 **수가 있어요**. There is a way to win.
> 모기 때문에 잠을 **잘 수가 없어요**. Because of the mosquitoes I really can't sleep.

USAGE NOTE: ~(으)ㄹ 수도 있다/없다
Adding the ~도 particle indicates that something **might** or **might not** be possible.

> 이길 **수도 있어요**. We might be able to win.
> 학교에 **갈 수도 없고** 직업을 얻을 **수도 없어요**. They maybe can't go to school or get a job.

WHAT'S THE DIFFERENCE?

못	~(으)ㄹ 수 없다
못 **tends** to refer to things that you cannot do, but other people can. i.e. when you can't do something due to individual reasons.	~(으)ㄹ 수없다 **tends** to imply that there is some outside force that prevents everyone (or at least more than just yourself) from carrying out some action.
학교에 **못** 가요. I can't go to school. (For my own reasons, I can't go to school. I am sick, or busy, or tired, so I can't go to school.)	학교에 **갈 수 없어요**. I can't go to school. (There is no way to go to school. It's impossible. No one can go to school right now.)

Note: although 못 tends to be used with personal reasons and ~(으)ㄹ 수 없다 tends to be used with universal reasons, there is significant overlap and they are frequently interchangeable.

--- REFERENCE PAGES ---

못 V - page 65

USED IN WCK   24 times

A/V~았/었으면 좋겠다
For things you wish for

내년에 한국에 갈 수 있었으면 좋겠어요.
I wish I could go to Korea next year.

~았/었으면 좋겠다 can be added to the verb stem of action or descriptive verbs to say: "it would be nice if..." or "I wish I could do..." It combines a couple components, such as: ~았/었 (past tense), ~(으)면 (if/when) and ~겠다 (a future tense form). But you can treat it as one set grammar form.

ACTION VERBS & DESCRIPTIVE VERBS

If the last vowel sound of the verb stem is ㅏ or ㅗ, attach **~았으면 좋겠다**

싸다	→ 쌌으면 좋겠다	(to wish it was cheap)
살다	→ 살았으면 좋겠다	(to wish one could live)

If the verb stem ends in 하, it becomes **~했으면 좋겠다**

여행하다	→ 여행했으면 좋겠다	(to wish one could travel)
편하다	→ 편했으면 좋겠다	(to wish it was comfortable)

If the last vowel sound of the verb stem is something else, attach **~었으면 좋겠다**

주다	→ 줬으면 좋겠다	(to wish one could give)
마시다	→ 마셨으면 좋겠다	(to wish one could drink)
(!) 듣다	→ 들었으면 좋겠다	(to wish one could listen)

> 그 영화를 **봤으면** 좋겠어요.   I wish I could see that movie.
> 내년에 한국에 살 수 **있었으면** 좋겠어요.   I wish I could live in Korea next year.
> 그 사람을 도울 수 **있었으면** 좋겠어요.   I wish I could help that person.
> 그 때 소주를 **마셨으면** 좋겠어요.   I wish I could've drank soju back at that time.
> 날씨가 더 **더웠으면** 좋겠어요.   I wish the weather was hotter.
> 그 책이 더 **쌌으면** 좋겠어요.   I wish that book was cheaper.
> 비행기를 타는 게 더 **편했으면** 좋겠어요.   I wish riding planes was more comfortable.
> 이 해변이 깨끗**했으면** 좋겠어요.   I wish this beach was clean.

REFERENCE PAGES

A/V~았/었다 Past Tense - page 58   A/V~겠다 - page 218
A/V~(으)면 - page 125

Note: this grammar form can be used for present/future tense situations ("I wish I could") or past tense situations ("I wish I could have"). You can refer to past or future tense events by adding time-specifying words.

WHAT'S THE DIFFERENCE?	
~았/었으면 좋겠다	~(으)면 좋겠다
Emphasizes that you wish you could be doing something that is the opposite of your current situation. It implies that there is some obstacle preventing you from achieving your wish.	Simply wishes for something to happen that hasn't happened.
한국에 갈 수 있**었으면 좋겠어요**. I wish I could go to Korea. (But I cannot in my current situation)	한국에 갈 수 있**으면 좋겠어요**. I hope I can go to Korea. (Simple wish)
그 영화를 **봤으면 좋겠어요**. I wish I was watching that movie. (Instead of whatever I am currently doing)	그 영화를 **보면 좋겠어요**. I hope to see that movie. (Simple wish)
매일 한국어를 공부할 수 있**었으면 좋겠어요**. I wish I could study Korean every day. (Because right now I can't)	매일 한국어를 공부할 수 있**으면 좋겠어요**. I hope I can study Korean every day. (Simple wish)

PRACTICE EXERCISES

Given the Korean sentences, write an equivalent English expression.

1. 한국에서 여행할 수 있었으면 좋겠어요.

2. 그 사람을 만날 수 있었으면 좋겠어요.

3. 강아지를 키울 수 있었으면 좋겠어요.

4. 바다가 가까웠으면 좋겠어요.

5. 크리스마스에 눈이 왔으면 좋겠어요.

ANSWERS: 1. I wish I could travel in Korea. 2. I wish I could meet that person. 3. I wish I could raise a dog/puppy. 4. I wish the beach/ocean was nearby. 5. I wish it would snow on Christmas.

USED IN WCK   169 times*

N ~께/에게/한테
The "to" and "from" particles

한국 선생님에게 제가 한국어를 배웠어요.
I learned Korean from my Korean teacher.

~께, ~에게 and ~한테 are particles that can all mean either "to" or "from."

NOUNS

Attach either ~께, ~에게, or ~한테 to the noun. It does not matter if the noun ends on a vowel sound or a consonant sound.

부모님 →	부모님**께**	to/from one's parents
보스 →	보스**에게**	to/from one's boss
고양이 →	고양이**한테**	to/from one's cat

> 부모님**께** 선물을 보냈어요.   I sent a present to my parents. (honorific)
> 보스**에게** 이메일을 받았어요.   I received an email from my boss. (formal)
> 고양이**한테** 물을 줬어요.   I gave my cat some water. (casual)

WHAT'S THE DIFFERENCE?

Making the choice between ~께, ~에게 and ~한테 depends on how much respect you wish to show the **subject** you are attaching it to (i.e. the person giving or receiving some object or action).

~께	~에게	~한테
Honorific Particle, used for esteemed individuals. If the subject is someone you want to **honor**, for example your parents, grandparents, or your seniors at work, you should use the honorific form ~께.	Formal Particle, frequently used in written language. If you wish to be **formal**, but not necessarily honorific, you should use ~에게. This form is used most often in writing.	Casual particle, mostly used in spoken language. If you wish to refer **casually** to some subject, you can use ~한테. This form is commonly used in spoken Korean.

~께 - 15 times | ~에게 - 111 times | ~한테 - 26 times

~께	~에게	~한테
할머니**께** 선물을 주었어요. I gave my grandma a gift.	엄마**에게** 사과를 주었어요. I gave an apple to my mom.	강아지**한테** 먹이를 주었어요. I gave my dog some food.
저는 하느님**께** 빌었어요. I prayed to God.	친구**에게** 조언을 받았어요. I got some advice from a friend.	친구**한테** 선물했어요. I gave my friend a gift.
사장님**께** 이메일을 보냈어요. I sent an email to the CEO.	보스**에게** 이메일을 보냈어요. I sent an email to my boss.	남자친구**한테** 문자가 왔어요. I got a text from my boyfriend.

Note: If you use the wrong particle given the social context, your sentence might be awkward but the sentence is still grammatically correct and perfectly understandable.

DO THEY MEAN "TO" OR "FROM"?

~께, 에게, and 한테 are all dual-directional and can all mean **either** "to" or "from." The **verb** that is used in the sentence determines the direction of the action that is happening. For example:

1 저는 할머니께 선물을 **주었어요**.
I **gave** a present to my grandmother.

2 저는 할머니께 선물을 **받았어요**.
I **received** a present from my grandmother.

Notice how the sentences are identical except for the final verb. 1 uses the verb "주다" (to give), which by default is an action that you do **to** someone/something. But 2 uses the verb "받다" (to get/receive), which is innately an action that you get **from** someone/something. Just like in English, you would never say "I gave it from someone" or "I received it to someone."

The particle ~께 means either "to" or "from" and the meaning is inferred entirely from the verb. Here's another example, this time using ~에게:

3 엄마에게 사과를 **했어요**.
I **apologized** to my mom.

4 엄마에게 사과를 **받았어요**.
I **received** an apology from my mother.

Again, notice how these two sentences are the same except for the final verb. The particle can mean either "to" or "from," depending on the verb that is used.

Note: 사과 can mean either "apple" or "apology" depending on the context. They are homonyms.

PURE "FROM" PARTICLES: ~께서, ~에게서 & ~한테서

We just learned that ~께, ~에게 and ~한테 can **all** mean both "to" and "from" (see above). However there are particles that **only** mean "from," and they are: ~께서, ~에게서 and ~한테서.

Note: 께서, ~에게서 and ~한테서 are only used when you're receiving something from a person. If you're receiving something from something else (e.g. an animal or object), you should use ~(

으)로부터.

> 제 여자친구**한테서** 문자가 왔어요.   I got a text from my girlfriend.
> 우리 엄마**에게서** 전화가 왔어요.   I got a call from my mom.
> 한국 선생님**에게서** 한국어를 배워요.   I learn Korean from my Korean teacher.
> 저는 정부**로부터** 돈을 받았어요.   I got money from the government.

MULTIPLE FORMALITY LEVELS IN THE SAME SENTENCE
When you use the ~께/에게/한테 particles, you can very easily have different levels of formality happening in the same sentence. This is because the particle used depends on the **subject** that you're attaching it to, but the overall formality of the sentence (the ending) is determined by **who** you are directly addressing.

For example, imagine you are telling your friend about your day at work. You tell your friend that you sent an email to your boss. Because the subject you are attaching the ~께/에게/한테 particle to is your boss, you decide to use the honorific ~께 particle. But since you are talking to your friend, you are speaking casually (반말).
So you say: "오늘은 보스**께** 이메일을 **보냈어**." (Today I sent an email to my boss.)
Note: we haven't learned casual language (반말) yet, but you can learn about it by checking the reference page below.

Now imagine the inverse situation: you are telling your boss that you emailed your friend. Because the subject you're attaching the ~께/에게/한테 particle to is your friend, you decide to use the casual
~한테 particle. But because you're talking to your boss, you decide to conjugate the verb into it's honorific form.
So you say: "오늘은 친구**한테** 이메일을 **보냈습니다**." (Today I sent an email to my friend.)
Note: we haven't learned the honorific form (~(스)ㅂ니다) yet, but you can learn about it by checking the reference page below.

{ *The particle used depends on two things: 1 **your relationship with the subject**, and 2 whether you're speaking or writing. The formality of the final verb conjugation depends on **your relationship with who you are speaking to**.* }

―――――――――― **REFERENCE PAGES** ――――――――――
Banmal (반말) - page 169   A/V~(스)ㅂ니다 - page 172

USED IN WCK   **162 times**

V~(으)세요

For making requests

맛있게 드세요!
Please enjoy the meal!

You can make requests of others by adding ~(으)세요 to the verb stem of the action verb. This is a polite ending that you can use in most situations. It is roughly equivalent to adding "please" to English sentences.

ACTION VERBS

If the verb stem ends on a consonant sound, attach ~으세요

먹다	→	드세요*	(please eat)
앉다	→	앉으세요	(please sit)
(!) 듣다	→	들으세요	(please listen)

If the verb stem ends on a vowel sound, or ㄹ, attach ~세요

사다	→	사세요	(please buy)
주다	→	주세요	(please give)
(!) 만들다	→	만드세요	(please make)
(!) 돕다	→	도우세요	(please help)

> 샌드위치를 드세요.*   Please eat a sandwich.
> 여기에 앉으세요.   Please sit here.
> 확인할 수 있으세요?   Can you please check it?
> 이 책을 읽으세요.   Please read this book.
> 한국어로 말하세요.   Please speak in Korean.
> 할 수 있으면 영어로 말씀하세요.*   Please speak English if you can.
> 가능하면 이것을 만드세요.   Please make this if possible.

* Some verbs (and nouns) have two forms: a regular form and an honorific form. Because ~(으)세요 is a formal/honorific form, it activiates the verb's honorific version. E.g. 먹다 → 드시다.

REFERENCE PAGES

Honorific Vocabulary - page 290

A/V~지 마세요

For telling someone not to do something

외국어를 배우는 건 어렵지만 포기하지 마세요~
Learning a foreign language is hard, but don't give up~

If you want to request that someone **not** do something, you can use the ~지 마세요 form. Note that "~지 마세요" is the polite version - if you want to speak informally, you can just add "~지마." But be careful, because this can come off as rude in some situations.

ACTION VERBS

Attach ~지 마세요 regardless of whether the verb ends on a vowel sound or a consonant sound.

먹다	→	드시**지 마세요*** (please don't eat)
듣다	→	듣**지 마세요** (please don't listen)
돕다	→	돕**지 마세요** (please don't help)

> 그 매운 새우를 드시**지 마세요**.   Please don't eat that spicy shrimp.
> 그 사람의 조언을 듣**지 마세요**.   Please don't listen to that person's advice.
> 그 넥타이 사**지 마세요**. 천에 흠이 있어요.   Don't buy the tie. There's a defect in the material.
> 도운 걸 싫어하면 돕**지 마세요**.   If you don't want to help, then don't help.
> 벌들을 무서워하**지 마세요**.   Please don't be scared of bees.

DESCRIPTIVE VERBS

This grammar form can also be attached to descriptive verbs. This is most commonly used with feeling words. Recommended: check the "Passive & Active Verbs" reference page below.

If the descriptive verb ends in ㅏ or ㅗ, attach ~아하지 마세요

     (!) 나쁘다   →   나**빠하지 마세요**.   (please don't feel bad)

If the descriptive verb ends in 하 it becomes ~해하지 마세요

     우울하다   →   우울**해하지 마세요**   (please don't be down)

If the descriptive verb ends in something else, attach ~어하지 마세요.

REFERENCE PAGES

V~(으)세요 - page 162   Passive & Active Verbs - page 282

(!) 슬프다	→	슬퍼하지 마세요	(please don't be sad)
(!) 무섭다	→	무서워하지 마세요	(please don't be afraid)
(!) 노엽다	→	노여워하지 마세요	(please don't be offended)

> 큰 일이 아니라서 우울해하지 마세요. — It's not a big deal so don't be down.
> 제 이야기에 노여워하지 마세요. — Please don't be offended at what I said.
> 거기서 일어난 일에 기분 나빠하지 마세요. — Don't feel bad for what happened over there.
> 방학은 끝났지만 슬퍼하지 마세요. — Vacation is over but don't be sad.

USAGE NOTE: INFORMAL LANGUAGE

If you want to speak informally, add "~지 마" instead. Careful - this can sound rude in some situations.

> 그 매운 새우를 먹지 마. — Don't eat that spicy shrimp.
> 여기에 앉지 마. — Don't sit here.
> 그 사람의 조언을 듣지 마. — Don't listen to that person's advice.
> 방학은 끝났지만 슬퍼하지 마. — Winter vacation is over but don't be sad.

WHAT'S THE DIFFERENCE?

A/V~지 마세요	A/V~지 않다
Used to make suggestions/commands.	Used to make statements.
그 우유를 사지 마세요.	그 우유를 사지 않아요.
Please don't buy that milk.	I don't buy that milk.
사라씨, 슬퍼하지 마세요.	사라는 슬퍼하지 않아요.
Sara, please don't be sad.	Sara is not sad.

PRACTICE EXERCISES

Given the English sentences, write an equivalent Korean expression using ~지 마세요.

1. Please don't get up too early.

2. Please don't give me a birthday present.

3. Please don't be afraid of the dog.

ANSWERS: 1. 너무 일찍 일어나지 마세요. 2. 제게/저에게 생일 선물을 주지 마세요. 3. 강아지/개를 무서워하지 마세요.

REFERENCE PAGES

Banmal (반말) - page 169

A/V~지 않다 - page 63

으 Irregular - page 294

V~아/어 주다

For asking for favors

저에게 한국어를 좀 가르쳐 주세요!
Please teach me some Korean!

"주다" is the Korean verb meaning "to give." You can ask people to do things for you by attaching ~아/어 주다 to the verb stem of action verbs. When you use this form, you are implying that you want someone to do something **for your benefit**.

Grammar Form	Present Tense	Past Tense	Future Tense
~아/어 주다	~아/어 줘요	~아/어 줬어요	~아/어 줄 거예요

ACTION VERBS

If the last vowel sound of the verb stem is ㅏ or ㅗ, attach ~아 주다

- 사다 → **사 주다** (to buy for subj.)
- 보다 → **봐 주다** (to watch something for subj.)
- 찾다 → **찾아 주다** (to look for something for subj.)

If the verb stem ends in 하, it becomes 해 주다.

- 말하다 → **말해 주다** (to say something for/to subj.)
- 청소하다 → **청소해 주다** (to clean for subj.)

If the last sound of the verb stem is something else, attach ~어 주다

- 열다 → **열어 주다** (to open something for subj.)
- 만들다 → **만들어 주다** (to make something for subj.)
- 가르치다 → **가르쳐 주다** (to teach something for/to subj.)

> 이 영화를 봐 줘요.   Watch this movie for me.
> 이 노래를 들어 줘요.   Listen to this song for me.
> 저에게 이 책을 읽어 줘요.   Read this book to me.
> 우유를 사 줘요.   Buy me some milk.

DECREASING POLITENESS WITH ~줘 ENDING

If you're talking to a close friend, someone much younger than you, out loud to yourself, or to an animal, you can use the ~줘 ending. This is an informal ending (반말), and should be used with caution.

>	말해 줘.	Tell me.
>	기다려 줘.	Wait for me.
>	피자를 사 줘.	Buy me pizza.

INCREASING POLITENESS WITH ~세요 ENDING

"주다" is often written with the ~세요 ending (주세요) to make the sentence feel a little bit more polite. It is common to add the word "좀" in your sentence to soften your request. It is similar to adding "a little" or "some," or even like saying "pretty please."

>	좀 말해 주세요.	Please tell me.
>	좀 기다려 주세요.	Please wait a bit for me.
>	피자를 좀 사 주세요.	Please buy me some pizza.

INCREASING POLITENESS FURTHER WITH ~시겠어요 ENDING

To make the sentence even more polite, you can use "~시겠어요" as an ending. Use this form when you are in a formal setting (e.g. an office meeting, a presentation, interview, etc.)

>	좀 말씀해* 주시겠어요.	(Sir/madam), could you please tell me.
>	좀 기다려 주시겠어요.	(Sir/madam), could you please wait a bit for me.
>	피자를 좀 사 주시겠어요.	(Sir/madam), could you please buy me some pizza.

Note: the English translations are rough approximations of the meaning.
* Some words have "honorific forms." Check the reference page below to learn more.

PRACTICE EXERCISES

Given the Korean sentences, write an equivalent English expression.

1. 물 좀 주세요.

2. 이메일을 확인해 주세요.

3. 치킨하고 맥주 한 병 주세요.

ANSWERS: 1. Please give me some water. 2. Please check your emails. 3. Please give me some (fried) chicken and a bottle of beer.

--- REFERENCE PAGES ---

Banmal (반말) - page 169
V~(으)세요 - page 162

A/V~겠다 - page 218
Honorific Vocabulary - page 290

Level Four

Developing Your Sentences

DIFFICULTY LEVEL: MEDIUM!
The example sentences are adapted from conversational sentences made by real Korean people. You can expect the difficulty to increase slightly compared to Level Three.

Level Four Grammar

What we will learn

한국어 문법을 공부하자!
Let's study Korean grammar!

Banmal (반말)	169
A/V~(스)ㅂ니다	172
A/V~ㄴ다/는다/다	175
V~(으)려고 [하다]	177
V~다가, V~았/었다가	180
V~기 전에	183
V~(으)ㄴ 후에/다음에	184
V ~(으)ㄹ 줄 알다/모르다	186
V~아/어야 하다/되다	189
N~처럼	191
N~마다	192
A/V~아/어도, N(이)라도	193
A~아/어지다	195
V~게 되다	197
V~은/는/을 것 같다	199
A/V~(ㄴ/는)다고 생각하다	204
N 중에(서)	207
A~게/이/히	209
V~기	211
N~에 대해(서)	213
V~는 대신(에), N 대신(에)	215

Banmal (반말)
Casual Language

조금만 더 기다려!
Just wait a little longer!

In Korea, casual language is used between people who have a close relationship - generally with people who are the same age (or younger) than you. You might be tempted to speak banmal (반말) to Korean people to indicate that you are being friendly. However, the cultural significance of language formality goes far deeper than mere friendliness in Korean. Using casual language inappropriately will make people feel awkward and uncomfortable, and can easily be construed as rude.

We advise you to use the ~아/어요 form with people **unless you both agree** to speak in 반말.

Grammar Form	Present Tense	Past Tense	Future Tense
Descr. & Action V	~아/어	~았/었어	~(으)ㄹ 거야
Nouns	~(이)야	~이었어/였어	~일 거야

ACTION VERBS & DESCRIPTIVE VERBS

Casual language (반말) can be applied to any sentence by adjusting the final verb ending.
If the final vowel sound of the verb is ㅏ or ㅗ, attach **~아**

타다	→	**타**	(subj. rides)
오다	→	**와**	(subj. comes)
알다	→	**알아**	(subj. knows)
(!) 아프다	→	**아파**	(subj. hurts)
(!) 모르다	→	**몰라**	(subj. does not know)

If the final character of the verb is 하, it becomes **해**

공부하다	→	공부**해**	(subj. studies)
시작하다	→	시작**해**	(subj. starts)

If the final vowel sound of the verb is something else, attach **~어**

있다	→	있**어**	(subj. has)

기다리다	→	기다**려**	(subj. waits)
(!) 예쁘다	→	예**뻐**	(subj. is pretty)
(!) 걷다	→	걸**어**	(subj. walks)
(!) 아름답다	→	아름다**워**	(subj. is beautiful)

> 저는 한국어를 공부하고 있**어**. — I'm studying Korean.
> 아침을 먹고 학교에 **갔어**. — I had breakfast and then went to school.
> 한국에 가면 김치를 먹어 **봐**. — If you go to Korea, try kimchi.
> 버스를 타는 게 좀 불편**해**. — Riding the bus is a bit uncomfortable.
> 그냥 반말 **해**. — Just speak casually.
> 이 단어를 **몰라**. — I don't know this word.

NOUNS

If applying banmal to a noun, attach ~(이)야

If the noun ends on a consonant sound, attach **~이야**

빵	→	빵**이야**	(it's bread)
사람	→	사람**이야**	(it's a person)
톰	→	톰**이야**	(it's Tom/I am Tom)

If the noun ends on a vowel sound, attach **~야**

사라	→	사라**야**	(it's Sara/I am Sara)
김치	→	김치**야**	(it's kimchi)
한국어	→	한국어**야**	(it's Korean)

WHAT'S THE DIFFERENCE?

반말	~아/어요
Casual language. It is used when talking to people younger than you, talking to yourself, to animals, or close friends.	Polite language. It is used when you want to be polite, yet still friendly.

"I," "ME," AND "YOU" IN CASUAL LANGUAGE

When speaking banmal with someone, there are different words used for "I," "me" and "you." These casual forms are also used when writing in plain form (referenced below).

REFERENCE PAGES

Honorifics in Korean - page 21

	I/me	My	You
Polite language (존댓말)	저는/제가	제/저의	당신(은/이)
Casual language (반말)	나는/내가	내/나의	너는/네가

Note: while "당신" means "you" in polite language, people tend to avoid using it because it has a variety of nuanced meanings. People prefer to use titles or names instead of "당신." To learn more about these, see referenced page below.

> 나는 아이디어가 떠오를 때마다 메모해. — Every time I think of an idea, I jot it down.
> 나는 내 갈 길을 가. — I walk my own path.
> 나는 기본 카메라로 찍는 셀카를 좋아하지 않아. — I don't like selfies taken with the default camera.
> 내가 저런 상황에 처하게 된다면 어떻게 될까? — What would I do in a situation like that?
> 내가 어렸을 때 절대 먹지 않는 음식은 굴이었어. — A food I never ate when I was young was oysters.
> 내가 고양이를 싫어하는 건 아니야. — It's not that I dislike cats.
> 내 눈 앞에 해야할 일이 더 걱정돼. — I'm more worried about the things facing me.
> 내 삶에 가장 영향을 준 사람은 우리 가족이야. — My family has had the most impact on my life.

INFORMAL "YOU": "너"

When speaking banmal, there is a word you can use for "you." This word is "너" but when combined with particles, it becomes either 너는 (topic particle) or 네가 (subject particle).

Note: "네가" is pronounced [니가] when spoken.

Remember that this word is **not** to be used outside of banmal, as it can be considered rude. When speaking in polite language (~아/어요 or ~(스)ㅂ니다) you should use a different method (see the reference pages below).

PRACTICE EXERCISES

Given the English sentences, write an equivalent Korean expression using 반말.

1. I am studying Korean.

2. I don't like going to parties.

3. My favorite food is pizza.

ANSWERS: 1. (나는) 한국어를 공부하고 있어. 2. (나는) 파티에 가는 것을 안 좋아해/좋아하지 않아. 3. 내가 가장 좋아하는 음식은 피자야.

REFERENCE PAGES

A/V~ㄴ다/는다/다 - page 175
Words for People - page 288

제가/저는/제 - page 35
"You" in Korean - page 37

A/V ~(스)ㅂ니다

Honorific Language

다 괜찮습니다. 문제가 없습니다.
Everything is fine. There's no problems.

~(스)ㅂ니다 is another formality ending like ~아/어요 or banmal. Any of the sentences we've learned so far using ~아/어요 can have ~(스)ㅂ니다 substituted in to raise the formality of the sentence. Most grammar books introduce ~(스)ㅂ니다 very early on. In fact, many teach ~(스)ㅂ니다 before they teach ~아/어요. We waited this long to teach ~(스)ㅂ니다 because it is a very formal, honorific form, and we wished to prioritize conversational language.

WHAT IS HONORIFIC LANGUAGE?

In Korea, honorific language is used with people you wish to show respect to; such as your boss at work, your partner's parents, and the elderly. It's also used in official occasions like weddings, job interviews, news broadcasts, and so on.

Grammar Form	Present Tense	Past Tense	Future Tense
Desc. & Action V	~(스)ㅂ니다	~았/었습니다	~(으)ㄹ 겁니다
Nouns	~입니다	~이었/였습니다	~일 겁니다

ACTION VERBS & DESCRIPTIVE VERBS

Honorific language can be applied to any sentence by adjusting the final verb ending.
If the verb ends in a vowel sound, or ㄹ, attach **~ㅂ니다**

하다	→	**합니다**	(subj. does it)
바쁘다	→	**바쁩니다**	(subj. is busy)
(!) 힘들다	→	**힘듭니다**	(it's difficult)

If the verb ends in a consonant sound, attach **~습니다**

먹다	→	**먹습니다**	(subj. eats)
괜찮다	→	**괜찮습니다**	(it's fine)
좋다	→	**좋습니다**	(it's good)

REFERENCE PAGES

Honorifics in Korean - page 21

› 저는 한국어를 공부**합니다.**	I study Korean.
› 전문적으로 배워 본 적은 **없습니다.**	I've never learned professionally.
› 화장실에 가는 것으로 하루를 시작**합니다.**	I start my day by going into the bathroom.
› 심신의 밸런스를 맞춰가는 것이 **좋습니다.**	It's good to balance your mind and body.
› 장거리 연애를 해 본 적은 **없습니다.**	I've never tried long-distance dating.

NOUNS

When using a noun, attach **~입니다** to the noun. It doesn't matter if it ends on a vowel or a consonant sound.

빨래	→	빨래**입니다**	(it is laundry)
일본어	→	일본어**입니다**	(it is Japanese)

› 가장 싫어하는 집안일은 빨래**입니다.**	The chore I hate most is laundry.
› 제가 유창하게 할 수 있는 언어는 한국어와 일본어**입니다.**	The languages I can speak fluently are Korean and Japanese.
› 한복은 정말 아름다운 한국의 전통 의복**입니다.**	Hanbok is Korea's really beautiful traditional clothing.

ASKING QUESTIONS: ~(스)ㅂ니까?

When you want to ask a question using honorific language, attach "~(스)ㅂ니까?" to the verb stem, or "입니까?" to the noun.

› 요즘 바**쁩니까?**	Are you busy these days?
› 점심을 먹었**습니까?**	Have you eaten lunch?
› 당신의 베프는 동성**입니까?**	Is your best friend the same gender as you?
› 기적을 본 적이 있**습니까?**	Have you ever seen a miracle?

PRACTICE EXERCISES

Given the English sentences, write an equivalent Korean expression using ~(스)ㅂ니다 form.

1. I am teaching English at a school.

2. I like rainy days.

3. My favorite season is fall.

ANSWERS: 1. (저는) 학교에서 영어를 가르치고 있습니다. 2. (저는) 비가 오는 날을 좋아합니다. 3. 제가 가장/제일 좋아하는 계절은 가을입니다.

WHAT'S THE DIFFERENCE?

~(스)ㅂ니다	~아/어요
Honorific language.	Polite, yet casual language.
그 사람은 선생님**입니까?** Is that person the teacher? (When asking a question in honorific ~(스)ㅂ니다 form, you use the question form: ~(스)ㅂ니까?)	그 사람은 선생님이**에요?** Is that person the teacher? (When asking a question in ~아/어요 form, just raise the inflection at the end of the sentence)
Used more in formal writing/speaking.	Used more in casual polite conversation.

WHAT'S THE DIFFERENCE?

~(스)ㅂ니다	~아/어
Honorific language.	Informal language.
저는 사라**입니다.** (When introducing yourself formally, for example in interviews, presentations, news broadcasts, etc.)	나는* 사라야. (When introducing yourself casually, for example to children, animals, etc.)
Used more in formal writing/speaking.	Used in casual, informal situations between close friends or people younger than you.

* Notice how 저는 has changes to 나는 in this sentence. This is because "저" is the way you refer to yourself in formal language, and "나" is how you refer to yourself in casual language.

WHAT FORMALITY LEVEL SHOULD I USE?

Unfortunately, there is no single right answer to this question. It depends on the social context of the situation. In addition, different people have different personal preferences when it comes to formality. You may find that younger people are more lax about formality, but this is not always the case. Overall, we recommend using ~(스)ㅂ니다 ending in writing & ~아/어요 when speaking, unless someone suggests you do otherwise.

A/V~ㄴ다/는다/다

Plain form/diary form

오늘 아침에 한국어를 공부했다.
I studied Korean this morning.

Plain form is a type of ending that does not strongly connotate any level of formality, however it is closer to informal than formal. This form is commonly used making general exclamations and observations out loud (e.g. "wow, the weather is great!" or "oh, that dog is so cute!"). It is a form of self-talk. It is also used in situations where there is no relationship between the writer and the reader, like books and magazines, news articles, tests and exams, and social media comments.

Grammar Form	Present Tense	Past Tense	Future Tense
Descriptive Verbs	~다	~았/었다	~(으)ㄹ 것이다
Action Verbs	~ㄴ/는다	~았/었다	~(으)ㄹ 것이다
Nouns	~(이)다	~이었다/였다	~일 것이다

ACTION VERBS

If the action verb ends in a vowel sound, attach ~ㄴ다

하다	→	**한다**	(subj. does)
보내다	→	**보낸다**	(subj. sends)
타다	→	**탄다**	(subj. rides)

If the action verb ends in a consonant sound, attach ~는다

먹다	→	**먹는다**	(subj. eats)
받다	→	**받는다**	(subj. receives)

> 춤을 추거나, 복싱, 요가 등을 좋아**한다**.   I like dancing or boxing, yoga, etc.
> 저는 생 미역을 못 먹**는다**.   I can't eat raw seaweed.
> 직장에서 나는 부당한 대우를 받**는다**.   I'm being treated unfairly at work.
> 여성 목소리가 더 익숙해서 여성보컬을 선호**한다**.   I'm more used to female voices, so I prefer female vocals.

REFERENCE PAGES

Honorifics in Korean - page 21

DESCRIPTIVE VERBS

If you are attaching it to a **descriptive verb**, simply attach ~다 (identical to dictionary form)

예쁘다 →	예쁘**다**	(subj. is pretty)
춥다 →	춥**다**	(subj. is cold)
귀엽다 →	귀엽**다**	(subj. is cute)

> 나는 늙는 것이 두렵**다**. — I'm scared of getting old.
> 요즘 가장 행복하**다**. — These days are my happiest.
> 내 커리어가 떨어진다는 것이 가장 두렵**다**. — I'm most afraid of failing in my career.
> 나의 삶에 만족하며 살고 있고 즐기고 있**다**. — I'm satisfied with my life and enjoying living.
> 돈이 샘솟는 마법의 주머니가 있었으면 좋겠**다**. — I wish I had a magic pocket of endless money.

NOUNS

Attach ~(이)다 when you are talking about a noun using plain form.
If the noun ends in a consonant sound, attach ~이다

선택 →	선택**이다**	(it's a choice)
사람 →	사람**이다**	(it's a person)

If the noun ends in a vowel sound, attach ~다

필수 →	필수**다**	(it's a must)
나라 →	나라**다**	(it's a country)

Note: to say something is not something in plain form, attach ~이/가 아니다.

> 와, 바다**다**! — Wow, it's the ocean!
> 행복은 선택이 아니**다**. — Happiness is not a choice.
> 껌을 씹는 것도 필수**다**. — Chewing gum is also a must.
> 한국은 정말 아름다운 나라**다**. — Korea is a very beautiful country.

WHAT'S THE DIFFERENCE?

~ㄴ다/는다/다	~아/어
Plain language, common in writing.	Informal language, common in speaking.
나는 사라**다**.	나는 사라**야**.
I am Sara.	I am Sara.
(For example when introducing yourself in a diary)	(When introducing yourself to someone much younger than you, or to an animal)

USED IN WCK   60 times

V~(으)려고 [하다]

1. "In order to" / 2. For things you plan on doing

이번 주말에 친구를 만나려고 해요.
I plan on meeting a friend this weekend.

~(으)려고 [하다] has two main usages.
    1 To mean "in order to" do something
    2 To talk about things you plan on doing in the future: "I'm intending/planning on..."

Grammar Form	Present Tense	Past Tense	Future Tense
~(으)려고 [하다]	~(으)려고 [해요]	~(으)려고 [했어요]	~(으)려고 [할 거예요]

1 "IN ORDER TO"

You can use the form A~(으)려고 B to mean: "in order to achieve A, I do B." In this form, it only attaches to action verbs.

If the action verb ends in a consonant sound, attach **~으려고**

    받다   →   받**으려고**   (in order to get/receive)
    읽다   →   읽**으려고**   (in order to read)

If the action verb ends in a vowel sound, or ㄹ, attach **~려고**

    보내다   →   보내**려고**   (in order to send)
    만들다   →   만들**려고**   (in order to make)

> 그 책들을 보내**려고** 쌌어요.   I packaged up the books to send.
> 주목을 받**으려고** 이상한 옷을 입어요.   She wears weird clothes to get attention.
> 피자를 만들**려고** 치즈를 샀어요.   In order to make pizza, I bought some cheese.

2 PLANS/INTENTIONS

~(으)려고 하다 can be attached to action verbs to talk about your future plans and intentions.
If the action verb ends in a final consonant, attach **~으려고 하다**

    먹다   →   먹**으려고 하다**   (to intend on eating)
    (!) 듣다   →   들**으려고 하다**   (to intend on listening)

If the action verb ends in a vowel sound, or ㄹ, attach ~려고 하다

| 연습하다 | → | 연습하려고 하다 | (to intend on practicing) |
| (!) 돕다 | → | 도우려고 하다 | (to intend on helping) |

> 한국어를 배우려고 해요. I'm planning on learning Korean.
> 오늘은 저녁을 요리하려고 했어요. I planned on cooking dinner today.
> 주말에 이메일을 확인하려고 하지 않아요. I don't intend on checking my emails on the weekend.

Note: ~(으)려고 하다 has more intent than ~고 싶다 (which is used to talk about things you want to do, but may not have any plan on doing), and less intent than ~(으)ㄹ 것이다 (which is used to talk about things you will highly likely do).

DESCRIPTIVE VERBS

If you want to use ~(으)려고 [하다] with a descriptive verb, you have to add in the ~아/어지다 form (referenced below) first. This creates the conjugation: ~아/어 지려고 하다.

| 건강하다 | → | 건강해지려고 [하다] | (in order to get healthy/I plan to be healthy) |
| 행복하다 | → | 행복해지려고 [하다] | (in order to get happy/I plan to be happy) |

> 건강해지려고 매일 물을 마셔요. In order to be healthy, I drink water every day.
> 행복해지려고 새로운 걸 배우고 있어요. In order to be happy, I'm learning new things.
> 내년에 건강해지려고 해요. I plan on being healthy next year.

FOLLOWING WITH NON-하다 VERBS

The grammar form introduced was "~(으)려고 하다" but you can use other verbs at the end instead of 하다. The English equivalents of these sentences may vary, but it usually involves the feeling of doing something for the purpose of, or in order to achieve, something else. For example:

1 ~(으)려고 준비하다   To prepare to to something.
하고싶은 일을 하려고 준비해요. I'm getting ready to do what I want to do.
여행하려고 준비해요. I'm preparing to go traveling.

2 ~(으)려고 노력하다   To make an effort to do something.
한국어를 배우려고 노력해요. I'm making an effort to learn Korean.
매일 운동하려고 노력해요. I'm making an effort to exercise every day.

— REFERENCE PAGES —

A~아/어지다 - page 195

WHAT'S THE DIFFERENCE?

~고 싶다	~(으)려고	~(으)ㄹ 것이다
Used to talk about things you want to do (weak will).	Used to talk about things you intend on doing (medium will).	Used to talk about things you will do (strong will).
한국에 가고 **싶어요**. I want to go to Korea. (You want to do something, but you may not have a plan on doing so.)	한국에 **가려고 해요**. I plan on going to Korea. (You are intending to do something, but it still may or may not actually happen.)	한국에 **갈 거예요**. I will go to Korea. (Unless things unexpectedly change, you are going to go to Korea.)

USAGE NOTE: CANNOT BE USED IN IMPERATIVE SENTENCES

An imperative sentence is one where you are demanding or requesting some action.
In sentences like these, you cannot use ~(으)려고 하다. For example:

✗ 한국 여행을 가려고 한국어를 배우세요.　　✗ 한국어를 배우려고 이 책을 사세요.
This sentence is not correct.　　　　　　　　This sentence is not correct.

You can use other grammar forms in imperative sentences, for example the 위해(서) grammar form.
To learn about the 위해(서) grammar form, check the reference page below.

○ 한국 여행을 가기 위해 한국어를 배우세요.　　○ 한국어를 배우기 위해 이 책을 사세요.
Please learn Korean for your travels in Korea.　Please buy this book for learning Korean.

ENDING A SENTENCE WITH ~(으)려고(요)

You can end a sentence with ~(으)려고(요). This is just a casual contraction of "~(으)려고 해요."
This contraction is often used as a response to a question.
In this situation, attach the appropriate politeness level given the situation. With ~아/어요, this becomes ~(으)려고요. With 반말, it becomes ~(으)려고. When used as a sentence ending like this, is a conversational form and not used with honorific language (~(스)ㅂ니다).
Note: the honorific version of the full grammar form is: ~(으)려고 합니다.

> Q: 왜 도서관에 갔어요?　　　　Why did you go to the library?
> A: 책을 읽**으려고요**.　　　　　To read some books.
> Q: 왜 한국어를 배워?　　　　　Why'd you learn Korean?
> A: 한국에서 일하**려고**.　　　　To work in Korea.

REFERENCE PAGES

V~고 싶다 - page 93　　　　　　V~기 위해(서) N 위해(서) - page 222
A/V~(으)ㄹ 것이다 Future Tense - page 60　　V~(으)세요 - page 162

USED IN WCK   49 times

V~다가, V~았/었다가
For actions that abruptly changed

잠을 자다가 좋은 꿈을 꿨어요.
I was dreaming and then had a nice dream.

PRESENT TENSE: ~다가

~다가 is used when one action abruptly ends, and another action immediately starts. The first action was interrupted and **not completed**. It is often translated to "then" or "but then" in English. ~다가 is only attached to action verbs. It is also sometimes translated to "while" or "when."
Note: when using ~다가, both clauses must have the same subject.

ACTION VERBS - PRESENT TENSE

Attach ~다가 to all verb stems regardless of final vowel sound or consonant sounds.

공부하다 →	공부하**다가**	(subj. was studying and then...)
잠을 자다 →	잠을 자**다가**	(subj. was sleeping and then...)
울다 →	울**다가**	(subj. was crying and then...)

> 공부를 하**다가** 졸려서 잤어요.	I was studying and then dozed off and slept.
> 집에 가**다가** 친구를 만났어요.	While going home, I met a friend.
> 길을 걷**다가** 휘청거렸어요.	While walking on the street, I staggered.
> 비가 오**다가** 갤 때도 있어요.	Sometimes it clears up after rain.
> 서울에 살**다가** 지금은 대구에 살아요.	I lived in Seoul but now I live in Daegu.
> 몇년간 편지로만 연락을 하**다가** 헤어졌어요.	After a few years of only contact by letter, we broke up.
> 잠을 자**다가** 무서운 꿈을 꿨어요.	I was sleeping when I had a scary dream.

PAST TENSE: ~았/었다가

When used in the past tense, ~았/었다가 shows that one action is **completed** and then another action begins. Like with ~다가, the subjects in both clauses must be the same.

ACTION VERBS - PAST TENSE

If the action verb ends in ㅏ or ㅗ, attach ~았다가

| 가다 | → | **갔다가** | (subj. went somewhere and then...) |
| 오다 | → | **왔다가** | (subj. came somewhere and then...) |

If the action verb ends in 하, it becomes 했다가

| 예약하다 | → | 예약**했다가** | (subj. reserved sth and then...) |
| 준비하다 | → | 준비**했다가** | (subj. prepared sth and then...) |

If the action verb ends in something else, attach ~었다가

열다	→	열**었다가**	(subj. opened sth and then...)
끄다	→	**껐다가**	(subj. turned sth off and then...)
켜다	→	**켰다가**	(subj. turned sth on and then...)

> 창문을 열**다가** 다시 닫았어요. I opened the window and then closed it again.
> 컴퓨터를 껐**다가** 다시 켰어요. I turned the computer off and on again.
> 주말에 부산에 갔**다가** 왔어요. On the weekend I went to Busan and back.
> 바지를 샀**다가** 너무 커서 환불했어요. I bought some pants but they were too big so I returned them.

WHAT'S THE DIFFERENCE?

V~다가	V~았/었다가
The second action happens **before** the first is complete.	The second action happens **after** the first is complete.
The first action was not completed in the eyes of the speaker. They were still in the middle of the first action, but it was interrupted by the second action.	The first action was completed in the eyes of the speaker. Then the second action began.
집에 가**다가** 친구를 만났어요. When I was going home I met a friend. The first action is NOT complete, therefore you're saying you met the friend on the way home. The action of meeting a friend happens BEFORE you reach home.	집에 갔**다가** 친구를 만났어요. I went home and then met a friend. The first action IS complete, therefore you are saying you went home and then (after getting home) you met a friend. The action of meeting a friend happens AFTER you reach home.

USAGE NOTE: "WHILE"

In English, "while" can be used in a wide variety of sentences, and though one of the possible translations for ~다가 is "while," it's important to remember that ~다가 is only used as "while" when the second action **interrupts** the first action. You can think of it as "while in the middle of doing X, Y happened." If you want to talk about doing two actions at the same time, you should use a grammar form like ~(으)면서 (referenced below).

WHAT'S THE DIFFERENCE?	
V~다가	V~(으)면서
The second action **interrupts** the first action.	Both actions occur **concurrently.**
밥을 먹다가 전화가 왔어요. I was eating and then got a phone call. (I stopped eating to take the phone call) O 공부를 하다가 졸려서 잤어요. I was studying and then dozed off and slept. (The action of sleeping interrupted the action of studying)	밥을 먹으면서 전화가 왔어요. I ate my food while taking a phone call. (I ate and talked on the phone concurrently) X 공부를 하면서 졸려서 잤어요. (This sentence is awkward because it implies that you were sleeping and studying at the same time)

PRACTICE EXERCISES

Given the following Korean sentences, write an equivalent English expression.

1. 내가 다림질을 하다가 드레스를 눌게 태웠다.

2. 그는 좀도둑질을 하다가 잡혔다.

3. 마이크는 면도를 하다가 베였다.

4. 나는 축구를 하다가 다리가 부러졌다.

5. 너무 심하게 운동을 하다가 허리를 다쳤다.

6. 어젯밤에 공부를 하다가 코피를 흘렸다.

ANSWERS: 1. I burned my dress while ironing it. 2. He got caught stealing. 3. Mike cut himself shaving. 4. I broke my leg playing football/soccer. 5. I overdid my workout and hurt my back. 6. I was studying last night and got a nosebleed.

— REFERENCE PAGES —

V~(으)면서, N(이)면서 - page 135

USED IN WCK — 33 times

V~기 전에
Before doing some action

저는 운동하기 전에 스트레칭을 해요.
Before I work out, I do some stretches.

You can join two clauses together with ~기 전에. Use the following format:
"Clause 1~기 전에 Clause 2" which means: "before I do Clause 1, I do clause 2."

ACTION VERBS
You can attach ~기 전에 to any action verb, regardless of final consonant or vowel sound.

운동하다	→ 운동하**기 전에**	(before exercising)
마시다	→ 마시**기 전에**	(before drinking)
만나다	→ 만나**기 전에**	(before meeting)

> 잠을 자**기 전에** 읽어요.   Before going to sleep, I read.
> 학교에 가**기 전에** 아침을 먹어요.   Before going to school, I eat breakfast.
> 출근하**기 전에** 커피를 마셔요.   Before going to work, I drink coffee.

ORDER OF THE CLAUSES MATTERS
The verb that you attach ~기 전에 to is always the verb that you are saying "before this verb."

1 잠을 자**기 전에** 읽어요.   2 읽**기 전에** 잠을 자요.
Before going to sleep, I read.   Before reading, I sleep.

NOUNS
You can also add 전에 after a noun to mean before that noun. Some common nouns you will encounter 전에 being used with are: "그 **전에**" (before that) and "얼마 **전에**" (not long ago).

> 그 **전에** 헬스장에 갔어요.   Before that, I went to the gym.
> 얼마 **전에** 커피를 마셨어요.   I drank coffee not long ago.
> 얼마 **전에** 다큐멘터리를 봤어요.   I watched a documentary just recently.

USED IN WCK 42 times*

V~(으)ㄴ 후에/다음에
After doing some action

저는 일어난 후에 아침식사를 먹어요.
After I get up, I eat breakfast.

You can join two clauses together with ~(으)ㄴ 후에 or ~(으)ㄴ 다음에. Use the following format: "Clause 1 ~(으)ㄴ 후에/다음에 Clause 2" which means: "after doing clause 1, I do clause 2."

ACTION VERBS

If the verb stem ends in a vowel sound, or ㄹ, attach ~ㄴ 후에 or ~ㄴ 다음에

| 일어나다 | → | 일어난 후에 | or | 일어난 다음에 | (after getting up) |
| (!) 만들다 | → | 만든 후에 | or | 만든 다음에 | (after making) |

If the verb stem ends in a consonant sound, attach ~은 후에 or ~은 다음에

| 받다 | → | 받은 후에 | or | 받은 다음에 | (after receiving) |
| 읽다 | → | 읽은 후에 | or | 읽은 다음에 | (after reading) |

> 저는 일어난 후에 물을 마셔요.   After I get up, I drink some water.
> 한국으로* 이사한 후에 한국어를 배웠어요.   After I moved to Korea, I learned Korean.
> 한국에서 여행한 다음에 일본에 가요.   After I travel in Korea, I'm going to Japan.
> 이 책을 읽은 다음에 그 책을 읽을 거예요.   After I read this book, I will read that book.

NOUNS

You can also use 후에 or 다음에 after nouns to say "after this noun."

> 그 후에 헬스장에 갔어요.   After that, I went to the gym.
> 그 다음에 숙제를 했어요.   After that, I did my homework.
> 식사 후에 설거지를 해요.   After a meal, I do the dishes.

Note: the ~(으)로 particle can be used to talk about a direction of movement (like the ~에 particle). You can use it with the verb "이사하다," to mean "to move to a place." I.e. "한국으로 이사해요" means "I move to Korea."

* 후에 - 34 times | 다음에 - 8 times

WHAT'S THE DIFFERENCE?

후에	다음에
Slightly more formal, used more in writing.	*Slightly more casual, used more in speaking.*
일어**난 후에** 물을 마셔요. After I get up, I drink some water.	일어**난 다음에** 물을 마셔요. After I get up, I drink some water.
Wider usage available. "후에" can be used after all action verbs and after many nouns, particularly time nouns.	Narrower usage available. "다음에" can be used with all action verbs, but **not many nouns**.
O 점심 후에 책을 읽어요. After I eat lunch, I read a book.	X 점심 다음에 책을 읽어요. This sentence is understandable but awkward because 다음에 is not commonly used with many nouns including 점심.

Note: although 후에 is more common in writing, and 다음에 is more common in speaking, it is not a hard rule and both are commonly seen in both writing and speaking.

NOTE: "뒤에"

You might also see "뒤에" used in the same way as 후에 and 다음에. "뒤에" means "after." It can be used with verbs (V~(으)ㄴ 뒤에) and with nouns (N 뒤에). There seems to be no particular instances where it's better to use 뒤에, it's just another possible option for you to use.

PRACTICE EXERCISES

Given the English sentences, write an equivalent Korean expression using 후에.

1. After I get up, I go to the bathroom.

2. I will do my homework after dinner.

3. After graduation I traveled in Europe.

4. Two years later, I became a doctor.

5. I like jogging after work.

ANSWERS: 1. (저는) 일어난 후에 화장실에 가요. 2. (저는) 저녁을 먹은 후에 숙제를 할 거예요. 3. (저는) 졸업 후에 유럽에서 여행했어요. 4. (저는) 2년 후에 의사가 됐어요/되었어요. 5. (저는) 퇴근 후에 조깅하는 것을 좋아해요.

4

USED IN WCK — 29 times

V ~(으)ㄹ 줄 알다/모르다
For things you've learned

저는 한국어를 할 줄 알아요.
I've learned how to speak Korean.

You can attach ~(으)ㄹ 줄 알다/모르다 to action verbs to talk about things you've learned (or not learned) how to do. 알다 is the verb "to know," and "모르다" is the verb "to not know." 모르다 is a 르 irregular verb - check the reference page below to learn more.

Grammar Form	Present Tense	Past Tense	Future Tense
~(으)ㄹ 줄 알다	~(으)ㄹ 줄 알아요	~(으)ㄹ 줄 알았어요	~(으)ㄹ 줄 알 거예요
~(으)ㄹ 줄 모르다	~(으)ㄹ 줄 몰라요	~(으)ㄹ 줄 몰랐어요	~(으)ㄹ 줄 모를 거예요

ACTION VERBS

Attach **~(으)ㄹ 줄 알다** to talk about things you've **learned**. (The verb "알다" means "to know"). Attach **~(으)ㄹ 줄 모르다** for things you **haven't learned**. (The verb "모르다" means "to not know")

If the verb stem ends in a vowel sound, **or ㄹ**, attach **~ㄹ 줄 알다/모르다**

하다	→	할 줄 알다/모르다	(to know/not know how to do)
만들다	→	만들 줄 알다/모르다	(to know/not know how to make)
사용하다	→	사용할 줄 알다/모르다	(to know/not know how to use)

If the verb stem ends in a consonant sound, attach **~을 줄 알다/모르다**

| 닫다 | → | 닫을 줄 알다/모르다 | (to know/not know how to close) |
| 입다 | → | 입을 줄 알다/모르다 | (to know/not know how to wear) |

> 저는 수영할 줄 알아요.   I've learned how to swim.
> 저는 수영할 줄 몰라요.   I haven't learned how to swim.
> 저는 피자를 만들 줄 알아요.   I know how to make pizza.
> 저는 피자를 만들 줄 몰라요.   I don't know how to make pizza.

--- REFERENCE PAGES ---

르 Irregular - page 295

NOUNS

When using this grammar form with nouns, attach ~인 줄 알다/모르다. Attach ~인 줄 알다/모르다 whether the noun ends on a vowel sound or a consonant sound. When using with nouns, ~인 줄 모르다 is usually conjugated in the past tense.

제 코트	→	제 코트**인 줄 알다/모르다**	(to know/not know it's my coat)
여자	→	여자**인 줄 알다/모르다**	(to know/not know subj. is a woman)
랩	→	랩**인 줄 알다/모르다**	(to know/not know it's rap)

> 죄송해요. 제 코트**인 줄 알아요**. — My apologies. That's my coat. (I know this)
> 인정머리 없는 여자**인 줄 알아요**. — You're a woman without a heart. (I know)
> 지금 나오는 음악이 **랩인 줄 몰랐어요**. — I didn't know this music was rap.

WHAT'S THE DIFFERENCE?

V ~(으)ㄹ 줄 알다/모르다	~(으)ㄹ 수 있다/없다
Used to talk about things you've learned, or not learned, how to do.	Used to talk about things you are able or unable to do.
한국어를 **할 줄 알아요**. I've learned how to speak Korean. 한글을 **읽을 줄 알아요**. I've learned how to read Hangeul.	한국어를 **할 수 있어요**. I can speak Korean. 한글을 **읽을 수 있어요**. I can read Hangeul.
Is unnatural to use for abilities that everyone knows how to do (sleeping, breathing, etc.)	Can be used for abilities that everyone knows how do to.
X 친구 집에서 잠을 줄 알아요. I know how to fall asleep at my friend's house. (This sentence is unnatural because everyone knows how to fall asleep. It's not something you have to learn)	O 친구 집에서 잠을 잘 수 있어요. I can sleep at my friend's house. (You are able to fall asleep. There is nothing preventing you from doing this.)
Is unnatural to use for possibilities.	Can be used for possibilities.
X 내일 생일 파티에 갈 줄 알아요. I know how to go to your birthday party tomorrow. X 이번 주말에 여행 할 줄 알아요. I've learned how to travel this weekend.	O 내일 생일 파티에 갈 수 있어요. I can go to your birthday party tomorrow. O 이번 주말에 여행 할 수 있어요. I can travel this weekend.

REFERENCE PAGES

V~(으)ㄹ 수 있다/없다 - page 155

V ~(으)ㄹ 줄 알다/모르다	~(으)ㄹ 수 있다/없다
Can be used with nouns.	Cannot be used with nouns.
O 제 모자인 줄 알아요. I know that's my hat. (When you know/don't know about some noun)	X 제 모자일 수 있어요. I am able my hat. (This does not make sense)

	~(으)ㄹ 줄 알다/모르다	~(으)ㄹ 수 있다/없다
Things you learn	O	O
Things everyone can do	X	O
Possibilities	X	O
Nouns	O	X

PAST TENSE: ~(으)ㄹ 줄 알았다/몰랐다

When conjugated in the past tense, this grammar form is commonly used to say "I knew that..." "I didn't know that..." or even "I thought that..."

> 죄송해요. 제 코트인 **줄 알았어요.** My apologies. I thought that was my coat.
> 그거면 될 **줄 알았어요.** I knew that would work.
> 인정머리 없는 여자**인 줄 알았어요.** I thought you were a woman without a heart.
> 생일 파티에 올 **줄 알았어요?** Did you know I would come to your party?
> 주택이 그렇게 비**싼 줄 몰랐어요.** I didn't know houses were so expensive.
> 진동으로 해 두어서 전화 온 **줄 몰랐어요.** It was on vibrate so I didn't know you called.

FUTURE TENSE: ~(으)ㄹ 줄 알 것이다/모를 것이다

When conjugated in the future tense, this grammar form is commonly used to say "people will think that..." or "people won't know that..."

> 정말 사진 찍기 좋아하는 사람들인 **줄 알 거예요.** People will think we really love taking photos.
> 그 남자가 제가 떠난 줄 절대 **모를 거예요.** That man will never know that I've left.
> 한국 거리를 탐험하면서 시간 가는 **줄 모를 거예요.** You'll loose track of time while exploring the streets of Korea.

REFERENCE PAGES

A/V~았/었다 Past Tense - page 58   A/V~(으)ㄹ 것이다 Future Tense - page 60

USED IN WCK   109 times

V~아/어야 하다/되다

Things you should do

월요일이라서 출근해야 해요.
It's Monday so I have to go to work.

You can attach **~아/어야 하다** or **~아/어야 되다** to action verbs to talk about something you should do, have to do, or must do.

Grammar Form	Present Tense	Past Tense	Future Tense
~아/어야 하다	~아/어야 해요	~아/어야 했어요	~아/어야 할 거예요
~아/어야 되다	~아/어야 돼요	~아/어야 됐어요 or ~아/어야 되었어요	~아/어야 될 거예요

ACTION VERBS

~아/어야 하다 can only be attached to action verbs.

If the last vowel sound in the verb is ㅏ or ㅗ, attach **~아야 하다** or **~아야 되다**

    만나다 → 만나**야 하다** or 만나**야 되다**   (to have to meet)
    (!) 돕다 → 도와**야 하다** or 도와**야 되다**   (to have to help)

If the last vowel sound in the verb is 하 it becomes **~해야 하다**

    연습하다 → 연습**해야 하다** or 연습**해야 되다**   (to have to practice)
    시작하다 → 시작**해야 하다** or 시작**해야 되다**   (to have to start)

If the last vowel sound in the verb is anything else, attach ~어야 하다

    쉬다 → 쉬**어야 하다** or 쉬**어야 되다**   (to have to rest)
    기다리다 → 기다려**야 하다** or 기다려**야 되다**   (to have to wait)
    (!) 듣다 → 들**어야 하다** or 들**어야 되다**   (to have to listen)

> 늦어서 지금 가**야 돼요**.   I'm late so I have to go now.
> 3시에 친구를 만나**야 해요**.   I have to meet my friend at 3 o'clock.
> 다른 사람을 도와**야 돼요**.   You should help other people.
> 너무 힘들어서 쉬**어야 해요**.   It's too difficult so I have to rest.

USAGE NOTE: NEGATIVE FORMS

If you want to talk about something you **shouldn't** do, there are two options:

    1 V~지 않아도 되다 - to suggest some action is not necessary, not required
    2 V~(으)면 안 되다 - to suggest some action is prohibited, not allowed

>	1 걱정하**지 않아도 돼요**.	There's no need to worry.
>	1 아직 정하**지 않아도 돼요**.	You don't have to decide yet.
>	1 불안해하**지 않아도 돼요**.	You don't need to be nervous.
>	1 일일이 다 알려주**지 않아도 돼요**.	You don't need to spoon-feed them.
>	2 약속시간에 우리 늦**으면 안 돼요**.	You must not be late for your appointment.
>	2 차를 여기 주차하**면 안 돼요**.	You can't park your car here.

PAST TENSE: ~아/어야 했다/~아/어야 됐다

To talk about things you had to do in the past, you can use the past tense form: ~아/어야 했어요 or ~아/어야 됐어요 (sometimes it is spelled ~아/어야 되었어요 - no difference in meaning).

>	3시에 친구를 만**나야 됐어요**.	I had to meet my friend at 3 o'clock.
>	월요일에 직장에 **가야 했어요**.	I had to go to the office on Monday.
>	급하게 먹고 이동**해야 했어요**.	I had to quickly eat and run.
>	아쉽게도 자리를 내려놓**아야 했어요**.	Unfortunately I had to resign.
>	저는 어렸을 때 집안일을 **해야 했어요**.	When I was young I had to do chores.

WHAT'S THE DIFFERENCE?

~아/어야 했다 and ~아/어야 됐다 are very similar and are interchangeable in most all situations.

~아/어야 했다	~아/어야 됐다
Slightly more formal, more common in written language.	Slightly more casual, more common in spoken language.
3시에 친구를 만**나야 해요**. I have to meet my friend at 3 o'clock. (More common while writing)	3시에 친구를 만**나야 돼요**. I have to meet my friend at 3 o'clock. (More common while speaking)

REFERENCE PAGES

A/V~지 않다 - page 63
안 A/V - page 61

A/V~(으)면 - page 125

USED IN WCK   38 times

N~처럼
Like, as if

일주일 동안 개처럼 일했어요.
I worked like a dog this week.

You can attach ~처럼 to nouns to create similes and metaphors: i.e. to say some noun is "like" or "as ___ as" some other noun.

NOUNS
Simply attach ~처럼 to the noun whether that noun ends on a vowel or consonant.

한국 사람	→ 한국 사람**처럼**	(like a Korean person)
어제	→ 어제**처럼**	(like yesterday)

> 한국어는 모국어**처럼** 말할 수 없어요. I can't speak Korean like my native language.
> 오늘은 어제**처럼** 쉬고 싶어요. Today I want to rest like I did yesterday.
> 치즈**처럼** 느끼한 식감을 좋아하지 않아요. I don't greasy textures like cheese.
> 돼지**처럼** 코를 골아요! You snore like a pig!
> 산**처럼** 커요! You're as tall as a mountain!

ACTION VERBS
If you want to attach ~처럼 to an action verb, use **~는 것처럼** to put the verb in it's noun form.

피해주다	→ 피해주**는 것처럼**	(like harming)
넘어지다	→ 넘어지**는 것처럼**	(like falling)

> 피해주는 것**처럼** 느껴요. I feel like someone is harming me.
> 넘어지는 것**처럼** 보였어요. You looked like you were falling.
> 우는 것**처럼** 보였어요. You looked like you were crying.

REFERENCE PAGES

V~는 것 - page 69

USED IN WCK — 28 times

N~마다

Each or every

요즘에는 사람마다 핸드폰이 있어요.
Nowadays everyone has a cellphone.

You can add ~마다 to nouns to say "each noun" or "every noun." When added to a time noun, ~마다 expresses the repetition of an event over a set period of time, e.g. "every week" or "every year." ~마다 can be added to other nouns to indicate that every one of them is included with no exceptions.

NOUNS

Simply attach ~마다 to the noun whether that noun ends on a vowel or consonant.

날	→	날마다	(every day)
사람	→	사람마다	(every person)
15분	→	15분마다	(every 15 mins)

> 15분마다 버스가 와요.   The bus comes every 15 minutes.
> 일요일마다 청소해요.   I clean every Sunday.
> 할 때마다 결국이 달라요.   Every time I do it, the result is different.
> 사람마다 핸드폰이 있어요.   Every person has a cellphone.

Some specific time nouns can also use "매~N." For these time nouns, you can use either expression.

	Every day	Every week	Every month	Every year
N~마다	날마다	일주일마다	달마다	해마다
매~N	매일	매주	매월 or 매달	매년

Note: N~마다 comes from pure Korean and 매~N derives from 한자 (Chinese characters)

> 매일 한국어를 공부해요. / 날마다 한국어를 공부해요.   I study Korean every day.
> 매주 영화관에 가요. / 일주일마다 영화관에 가요.   I go to the movies every week.

A/V~아/어도, N(이)라도

Even so, even if

아무리 바빠도 아침을 꼭 먹어요.
No matter how busy I am, I always eat breakfast.

You can add ~아/어도 when talking about a situation that occurs regardless of the previous action or state. In English, this is often translated to "even if" or "regardless of." This grammar form is used to join two clauses together.

	Present Tense	Past Tense	Future Tense
Descriptive & Action V	~아/어도	~았/었어도	~(으)ㄹ 거라도
Nouns	~(이)라도	~이었어도/였어도	~일 거라도

ACTION VERBS & DESCRIPTIVE VERBS

~아/어도 can be added to action verbs and descriptive verbs.
If the last vowel sound of the verb is ㅏ or ㅗ, attach **~아도**

알다	→	알**아도**	(even if subj. knows)
O 바쁘다	→	바빠**도**	(even if subj. is busy)
(!) 다르다	→	달라**도**	(even if it's different)

If the last vowel sound of the verb is 하 it becomes **~해도**

| 이해하다 | → | 이해**해도** | (even if subj. understands) |
| 연습하다 | → | 연습**해도** | (even if subj. practices) |

If the last vowel sound of the verb is something else, attach **~어도**

| 힘들다 | → | 힘들**어도** | (even if it's difficult) |
| 가르치다 | → | 가르**쳐도** | (even if subj. teaches) |

> 돈을 쓰지 않**아도** 운동할 수 있어요.   You can exercise even if you don't spend money.
> 보고만 있**어도** 힐링 되는 기분이 들어요.   Even if I just look at it, it makes me feel refreshed.
> 무슨 일이 있**어도** 너 자신을 잃지 마세요.   Whatever happens, don't lose yourself.

> 잘 다루지는 못 **해도** 금방 배워요.   Even if I can't manage it well, I learn quickly.

NOUNS

Attach ~(이)라도 to nouns.
If the noun ends on a consonant sound, attach **~이라도**

| 학생 | → | 학생**이라도** | (even if subj. is a student) |
| 선생님 | → | 선생님**이라도** | (even if subj. is a teacher) |

If the noun ends on a vowel sound, attach **~라도**

| 부자 | → | 부자**라도** | (even if subj. is a rich man) |
| 아이 | → | 아이**라도** | (even if subj. is a child) |

> **부자라도** 법규를 지켜야 해요.   Even if you're rich, you have to follow the law.
> **학생이라도** 할인을 받지 못해요.   Even if you're a student, you can't get a discount.
> 재미가 없는 영화**라도** 끝까지 봐요.   Even if it's a boring movie, I watch until the end.

ADDING "아무리"

You can add the word "아무리" into the sentence to add emphasis. This is equivalent to saying something like "no matter how," or "no matter how much" in English.

> 아무리 바빠**도** 아침을 꼭 먹어요.   No matter how busy I am, I always eat breakfast.
> 아무리 반대**해도** 꼭 결혼할 거예요.   No matter the opposition, we will get married.
> 아무리 피곤**해도** 매일 운동해요.   I exercise every day, no matter how tired I am.

STARTING A SENTENCE WITH "EVEN SO": 그래도

Until now we've been talking about the sentence connecting form "~아/어도." However there is also the word "그래도" that can be used to start a sentence. "그래도" means something like: "but," "even so," "nevertheless," or "regardless of."

> **그래도** 나는 단거리가 좋아요.   Even so, I like short-distance (relationships).
> **그래도** 언니는 저의 가장 소중한 친구예요!   Even so, my older sister is my dearest friend!
> **그래도** 친구와 재미있는 추억이 생겼어요.   Even so, I made fun memories with my friend.

Note: "그래도" is a combination of the verb "그렇다" (to be some way) with the grammar form ~아/어도.

A~아/어지다

To become

날씨가 추워졌어요.
The weather has gotten colder.

You can add ~아/어지다 to descriptive verbs to say that someone (or something) is becoming that descriptive verb. It is commonly combined with "더" and "덜" to mean "more" and "less."

	Present Tense	Past Tense	Future Tense
Descriptive Verbs	~아/어져요	~아/어졌어요	~아/어질 거예요

DESCRIPTIVE VERBS

~아/어지다 can only be attached to descriptive verbs.

If the last vowel sound of the descriptive verb is ㅏ or ㅗ, attach **~아지다**

- 비싸다 → 비싸**지다** (to become expensive)
- 많다 → 많**아지다** (to become many)

If the last vowel sound of the descriptive verb is 하, it becomes **~해지다**)

- 편하다 → 편**해지다** (to become comfortable)
- 건강하다 → 건강**해지다** (to become healthy)

If the last vowel sound of the descriptive verb is something else, attach **~어지다**

- 없다 → 없**어지다** (to become gone)
- (!) 나쁘다 → 나빠**지다** (to become bad)
- (!) 춥다 → 추워**지다** (to become cold)
- (!) 다르다 → 달라**지다** (to become different)

> 과일은 비싸**져요**. — Fruit's gotten expensive.
> 사람이 더 많**아졌어요**. — There's more people than before.
> 돈이 없**어져서** 못 먹어요. — The money's run out so I can't eat.
> 운동을 자주 해서 더 강**해져요**. — I exercise often, so I'm getting stronger.

REFERENCE PAGES

더 & 덜 - page 119

ATTACHING ~고 싶다 TO DESCRIPTIVE VERBS: "~아/어지고 싶다"

The ~아/어지다 grammar form acts as a connecting piece to allow you to attach ~고 싶다 to descriptive verbs. This is similar to how in English we can't say, "I want to pretty" or "I want to smart." We have to say, "I want to **become** prettier" or "I want to **get** smarter." This addition of "become/get" is the role that ~아/어지다 plays in the sentence.

Therefore, if you wish to attach ~고 싶다 to descriptive verbs, you have to attach ~아/어지다 to the verb stem of the descriptive verb first. So V + ~아/어지다 + ~고 싶다 = **V~아/어지고 싶다.**

똑똑하다	→	X 똑똑하고 싶어요.	I want to smart.
		O 똑똑해지고 싶어요.	I want to get smarter.
예쁘다	→	X 예쁘고 싶어요.	I want to pretty.
		O 예뻐지고 싶어요.	I want to become prettier.
키가 크다	→	X 키가 크고 싶어요.	I want to tall.
		O 키가 커지고 싶어요.	I want to get taller.

> 더 **똑똑해지고 싶**어서 열심히 공부해요.   I want to get smarter so I study hard.
> 더 키가 **커지고 싶**어서 야채를 많이 먹어요.   I want to get taller so I eat a lot of veggies.
> 더 **강해지고 싶**어서 헬스장에 가고 있어요.   I want to get stronger so I'm going to the gym.

Note: adding "더" or "덜" is optional in your sentences, but it can be natural to do so.
Note: while sentences like "똑똑하고 싶어요" are technically not correct, you might see them used in the real world. This is because native speakers break the "official" rules all the time. We recommend you stick to "똑똑해지고 싶어요." in your own sentences.

PRACTICE EXERCISES

Given the Korean sentences, write an equivalent English expression.

1. 행복했던 날의 기억이 들어서 기분이 좋아져요. _____

2. 저는 실수를 할 때 우울해져요. _____

3. 지구온난화가 심각해져서 걱정돼요. _____

4. 그 뒤로 친해져서 베프가 됐어요. _____

ANSWERS: 1. I feel better when I think about those happy days. 2. I get depressed when I make mistakes. 3. I'm worried that global warming has gotten severe. 4. After that, we got close and became best friends.

REFERENCE PAGES

V~고 싶다 - page 93

USED IN WCK   54 times

V~게 되다
To end up doing something

친구들이랑 점심을 먹게 되었어요.
I ended up eating lunch with my friends.

You can attach ~게 되다 to the verb stems of action verbs to talk about something you ended up doing. Using this form indicates that the events that occurred happened out of one's control, without the subject having much influence on the outcome.

Grammar Form	Present Tense	Past Tense	Future Tense
Action Verbs	~게 돼요	~게 됐어요 or ~게 되었어요	~게 될 거예요

Note: "됐" is a contraction of "되었" and is more common in spoken language.

ACTION VERBS

~게 되다 can only be attached to action verbs.
Attach ~게 되다 to the verb stem of the action verb regardless of whether it ends in a vowel sound or a consonant sound.

취직하다	→ 취직하게 되다	(to end up being hired)
받다	→ 받게 되다	(to end up receiving)
돕다	→ 돕게 되다	(to end up helping)

> 예상한 시간보다 더 자게 돼요.
> I end up sleeping more than expected.
>
> 걱정을 하고 있는지 잊게 돼요.
> I end up forgetting what I was worrying about.
>
> 사소한 불편감 쯤은 금방 잊게 돼요.
> I end up forgetting about the minor issues.
>
> 운동하기 싫어질 때도 친구의 잔소리 덕분에 꾸준히 하게 돼요.
> Even when I hate working out, I end up doing it regularly thanks to my friend bugging me.
>
> 같이 방송부에 붙게 돼서 그때 처음 만났어요!
> We met for the first time because I ended up in the broadcasting club!

4

PAST TENSE

To conjugate into the past tense, attach ~게 됐어요 or ~게 되었어요.

› 한국에서 살**게 되었어요**.	I ended up living in Korea.
› 고등학생 시절 이 책을 읽**게 됐어요**.	I ended up reading this book in high school.
› 가지를 최근에 좋아하**게 되었어요**.	I recently found myself liking eggplant.
› 점점 커가면서 오이를 잘 먹**게 됐어요**.	As I got older, I got better with eating cucumber.
› 실천했을 때 오는 성취감으로 하루하루 살아가**게 됐어요**.	When I practiced, I ended up living with a sense of satisfaction every day.

FUTURE TENSE

To conjugate into the future tense, attach ~게 될 거예요.

› 한국에서 살**게 될 거예요**.	I will end up living in Korea.
› 뜨거운 햇살을 그리워하**게 될 거예요**.	I will end up missing the warm sunshine.
› 못하**게 될** 것 같아서 망설이고 있어요.	I'm hesitating since I think I'll end up failing.
› 결국 부모님을 원망하**게 될 거예요**.	In the end, you'll end up blaming your parents.
› 미래의 후손들이 힘든 상황이 처하**게 될** 거 같아서 걱정돼요.	I worry that I think we'll end up leaving future generations facing a difficult situation.

PRACTICE EXERCISESS

Given the English sentences, write an equivalent Korean expression using ~게 됐어요.

1. We ended up living together. _____

2. I ended up getting hired after graduation. _____

3. I ended up meeting good friends in Korea. _____

4. I will end up missing Korean food. _____

5. I'm scared because I think I might fail. _____

ANSWERS: 1. (저는) 우리는 같이 살게 됐어요. 2. (저는) 졸업 후에 고용되게 됐어요. 3. (저는) 한국에서 좋은 친구들을 만나게 됐어요. 4. (저는) 한국 음식을 그리워하게 될 거예요. 5. (저는) 못하게 될 것 같아서 무서워요.

REFERENCE PAGES

A/V~았/었다 Past Tense - page 58   A/V~(으)ㄹ 것이다 Future Tense - page 60

USED IN WCK   250 times

V~은/는/을 것 같다
To talk about your thoughts

엄마가 잠을 자는 것 같아요.
I think mom is sleeping.

~은/는/을 것 같다 is a very useful form to use when you're talking about your thoughts and opinions. You can use it to make sentences with the feeling of: "I think...," "I guess...," or "it seems like..."

	Present Tense	Past Tense	Future Tense
Action Verbs	~는 것 같아요	~(으)ㄴ 것 같아요	~(으)ㄹ 것 같아요
Descriptive Verbs	~(으)ㄴ 것 같아요	N/A	~(으)ㄹ 것 같아요
Nouns	~인 것 같아요	N/A	~일 것 같아요

ACTION VERBS: PRESENT TENSE

~는 것 같다 is used to talk about a situation in the present tense. ("I think subj. is...)
It is also used for 있다 and 없다 verbs (even though they are descriptive verbs).

오다	→	오는 것 같다	(to think subj. is coming)
있다	→	있는 것 같다	(to think there is something)
없다	→	없는 것 같다	(to think there is not something)
(!) 울다	→	우는 것 같다	(to think subj. is crying)

> 사라가 오는 것 같아요.   I think Sara is coming.
> 돈이 없는 것 같아요.   I think I have no money.
> 그 사람이 우는 것 같아요.   I think that person is crying.
> 엄마가 잠을 자는 것 같아요.   I think mom is sleeping.
> 지금 우는 것 같지만 얼마전에 웃었어요.   I think they're crying now but just before they were laughing.

ACTION VERBS: PAST TENSE

~(으)ㄴ 것 같다 is used for action verbs in the past tense. ("I think subj. was...")
If the verb ends in a consonant sound, attach ~은 것 같다

먹다	→	먹**은 것 같다**	(to think subj. ate)
읽다	→	읽**은 것 같다**	(to think subj. read)

If the verb ends in a vowel sound, attach ~ㄴ 것 같다

오다	→	오**ㄴ 것 같다**	(to think subj. came)
(!) 울다	→	우**ㄴ 것 같다**	(to think subj. cried)

> 사라가 **온 것 같**아요.   I think Sara came.
> 그 사람이 **운 것 같**아요.   I think that person cried.
> 그 사람이 넘어**진 것 같**아요.   I think that person fell over.

ACTION VERBS & DESCRIPTIVE VERBS: FUTURE TENSE

~(으)ㄹ 것 같다 is used to talk about a situation in the future tense. This form is used for both action verbs and descriptive verbs. ("I think I will" or "I think it will be...")
If the verb ends in a consonant sound, attach ~을 것 같다

있다	→	있**을 것 같다**	(to think there will be something)
받다	→	받**을 것 같다**	(to think subj. will receive something)

If the verb ends in a vowel sound, attach ~ㄹ 것 같다

오다	→	올 **것 같다**	(to think subj. will come)
울다	→	울 **것 같다**	(to think subj. will cry)

> 사라가 **올 것 같**아요.   I think Sara will come.
> 비행기에서 **먹을 것 같**아요.   I'm guessing I'll eat on the plane.
> 그 영화를 보면 **울 것 같**아요.   I think I'll cry if I watch that movie.
> 화성에서 살 수 있**을 것 같**아요.   I think I could live on Mars.

PRACTICE EXERCISES

Given the English sentences, write an equivalent Korean expression.

1. I think Tom is studying.   ....

2. If I watch that movie, I think I'll cry.   ....

3. I think I ate some food that was off.   ....

ANSWERS: 1. 톰이 공부하는 것 같아요. 2. (저는) 그 영화를 보면 울 것 같아요. 3. (저는) 상한 음식을 먹은 것 같아요.

~은/는/을 것 같다	Present Tense	Past Tense	Future Tense
Descriptive Verbs	~(으)ㄴ 것 같아요	N/A	~(으)ㄹ 것 같아요

DESCRIPTIVE VERBS: PRESENT TENSE

When you're conjugating a descriptive verb in the present tense, add ~ (으)ㄴ 것 같다. Descriptive verbs in present tense have the same conjugation as action verbs in past tense.

If the descriptive verb ends in a consonant sound, attach **~은 것 같다**

| 많다 | → | **많은 것 같다** | (to think there is many) |
| (!) 덥다 | → | **더운 것 같다** | (to think it is hot) |

If the verb ends in a vowel sound, or ㄹ, attach **~ㄴ 것 같다**

나쁘다	→	**나쁜 것 같다**	(to think it is bad)
(!) 멀다	→	**먼 것 같다**	(to think it is far)
불편하다	→	**불편한 것 같다**	(to think it is uncomfortable)

> 여기에는 식당이 많**은 것 같아요**. I think there are lots of restaurants here.
> 오늘은 정말 더**운 것 같아요**. I think it's really hot today.
> 그 사람은 나**쁜 것 같아요**. I think that person is bad.
> 비행기를 타는 것이 불편**한 것 같아요**. I think riding planes is uncomfortable.

DESCRIPTIVE VERBS: PAST TENSE

When talking about descriptive verbs in the past tense, just conjugate the **final verb** into the past tense using the form "~(으)ㄴ 것 같**았어요**." See the example sentences below.

> 여기에는 식당이 많**은 것 같았어요**. I thought there were lots of restaurants here.
> 오늘은 정말 더**운 것 같았어요**. I thought it was really hot today.
> 그 사람은 나쁜 것 같**았어요**. I thought that person was bad.
> 비행기를 타는 것이 불편**한 것 같았어요**. I thought riding planes was uncomfortable.

~은/는/을 것 같다	Present Tense	Past Tense	Future Tense
Nouns	~인 것 같아요	N/A	~일 것 같아요

NOUNS: PRESENT TENSE

You can attach this grammar form to nouns if you use the form: N~인 것 같다.

| 학생 | → | **학생인 것 같다** | (to think subj. is a student) |

강아지	→	강아지인 것 같다	(to think subj. is a puppy)
복숭아	→	복숭아인 것 같다	(to think it is a peach)

> 그 사람은 학생인 것 같아요.   I think that person is a student.
> 그 동물은 강아지인 것 같아요.   I think that animal is a puppy.
> 이 과일은 복숭아인 것 같아요.   I think this fruit is a peach.
> 아이를 키우는 것이 부담인 것 같아요.   I think raising kids is a burden.

NOUNS: FUTURE TENSE

You can attach this grammar form to nouns if you use the form: N~일 것 같다

무리	→	무리일 것 같다	(to think there will be a crowd)
부담	→	부담일 것 같다	(to think it will be a burden/problem)
축복	→	축복일 것 같다	(to think it will be a blessing)

> 그 사람은 학생일 것 같아요.   I think that person will be a student.
> 그 곳에 가면 큰 무리일 것 같아요.   If you go there I think there'll be a big crowd.
> 강아지를 키우는 것이 부담일 것 같아요.   I think raising puppies will be a burden.
> 아이를 키우는 것이 축복일 것 같아요.   I think raising kids will be a blessing.

NOUNS: PAST TENSE

When using this grammar form with nouns in the past tense, just conjugate the **final verb** into the past tense using the form: "~인 것 같았어요." See the example sentences below.

> 그 사람은 학생인 것 같았어요.   I thought that person was a student.
> 그 동물은 강아지인 것 같았어요.   I thought that animal was a puppy.
> 이 과일은 복숭아인 것 같았어요.   I thought this fruit was a peach.
> 아이를 키우는 것이 부담인 것 같았어요.   I thought raising kids was a burden.

PRACTICE EXERCISES

Given the English sentences, write an equivalent Korean expression.

1. I think kimchi is delicious.

2. I thought coffee was cheap.

3. I thought Tom was a student.

ANSWERS: 1. 김치가 맛있는 것 같아요. 2. 커피가 싼 것 같았어요. 3. 톰이 학생인 것 같았어요.

WHAT'S THE DIFFERENCE?

~은/는/을 것 같다	~은/는/을 것 같았다
Used when talking about things you **think** (about situations in the past, present, or future).	Used when talking about things you **thought** (about situations in the past, present, or future).
그 사람이 **우는 것 같아요**. I think that person is crying. 오늘 정말 **추운 것 같아요**. I think it's really hot today. 오늘 사라가 우리 집에 **올 것 같아요**. I think Sara will come to our house today.	그 사람이 **우는 것 같았어요**. I thought that person was crying. 어제 절말 **추운 것 같았어요**. I thought it was really hot yesterday. 오늘 사라가 우리 집에 **올 것 같았어요**. I thought Sara would come to our house today.

WHAT'S THE DIFFERENCE?

~은/는/을 것 같다	~았/었던 것 같다
For things you think, but **don't have personal experience with**.	For things you think, but **do have personal experience with**.
오늘 정말 **추운 것 같아요**. I think it was cold today. I think today was cold, but I haven't been outside at all so I'm just guessing. 서울은 **붐빈 것 같아요**. I think Seoul is crowded. I haven't been to Seoul (at least recently) but I think it is crowded.	어제 정말 **추웠던 것 같아요**. I think it was cold today. I went outside today and thought it was pretty cold. So I think it was cold today. 서울은 **붐볐던 것 같아요**. I think Seoul is crowded. I've been to Seoul and I thought it was pretty crowded. So I think Seoul is crowded.

PRACTICE EXERCISES

Given the English sentences, write an equivalent Korean expression using ~은/는/을 것 같다.

1. I think that person is laughing.

2. I thought that person was sick.

3. I think it'll rain tomorrow.

ANSWERS: 1. 그 사람은 웃는 것 같아요. 2. 그 사람은 아픈 것 같았어요. 3. 내일은 비가 올 것 같아요.

REFERENCE PAGES

A/V~았/었던 N - page 261

USED IN WCK **176 times**

A/V~(ㄴ/는)다고 생각하다
To tell someone what you think

20대 후반에 결혼하는 것이 좋다고 생각합니다.
I think it's good to get married in your late twenties.

~다고 생각하다 is a type of quoted form that involves the verb "생각하다," which means "to think." You can use this grammar form to say things like "I think that..." It's direct and asserts your personal opinion on matters.

Grammar Form	Present Tense	Past Tense	Future Tense
Descriptive Verbs	~다고 생각해요	~다고 생각했어요	~(으)ㄹ 거라고 생각하다
Action Verbs	~ㄴ/는다고 생각해요	~ㄴ/는다고 생각했어요	~(으)ㄹ 거라고 생각하다
Nouns	~(이)라고 생각해요	~(이)라고 생각했어요	~(일)거라고 생각하다

DESCRIPTIVE VERBS
For descriptive verbs, attach **~다고 생각하다** to the verb stem.

부담스럽다	→	부담스럽**다고 생각하다**	(to think subj. is burdensome)
빠르다	→	빠르**다고 생각하다**	(to think subj. is fast)
없다	→	없**다고 생각하다**	(to think there is none)

> 담배는 몸에 안 좋**다고 생각해요**. I think smoking is bad for you.
> 우정에서 나이가 중요하**다고 생각해요**. I think age is important to a friendship.
> 우정에 나이가 큰 영향은 없**다고 생각해요**. I think age has no big effect on friendships.
> 친구의 용기가 저는 늘 대단하**다고 생각해요**. I think my friend's bravery is so amazing.
> 눈이 제일 중요하**다고 생각해요**. I think one's eyes are most important.

ACTION VERBS
If the action verb ends in a vowel sound, or ㄹ, you attach **~ㄴ다고 생각하다**

잘하다	→	잘한**다고 생각하다**	(to think subj. does something well)
나오다	→	나온**다고 생각하다**	(to think subj. comes out)

(!) 만들다	→	만든다고 생각하다	(to think subj. makes)

If the action verb ends in a consonant sound, attach ~는다고 생각하다

먹다	→	먹는다고 생각하다	(to think subj. eats)
읽다	→	읽는다고 생각하다	(to think subj. reads)
듣다	→	듣는다고 생각하다	(to think subj. listens)

> 감정은 솔직하게 말해줘야 **한다고 생각해요**. I think one should speak their emotions honestly.
> 강아지는 좀 더 맹목적인 사랑을 **준다고 생각해요**. I think dogs give more unconditional love.
> 내가 쓰레기를 줄여야 **된다고 생각해요**. I think my trash should be reduced.
> 제가 낯선 기계를 빨리 배**운다고 생각해요**. I think I learn unfamiliar machines quickly.

PAST TENSE

There are multiple ways past tense can be used, depending on what you wish to say. If you use ~았/었다고, you're indicating that the **action** you're thinking about happened in the past. If you use 생각했어요, it means that your **thinking** happened in the past (i.e. "subj. thought").

> 민수가 한국에 간다고 생각해요. I think Minsu is going to Korea. (present tense)
> 민수가 한국에 **갔**다고 생각**해**요. I think Minsu **went** to Korea.
> 민수가 한국에 간다고 생각**했**어요. I **thought** Minsu **was going** to Korea.
> 민수가 한국에 **갔**다고 생각**했**어요. I **thought** Minsu **went** to Korea.

FUTURE TENSE

The same is true for future tense conjugations. If you use ~(으)ㄹ 거라고, you're saying that the **action** will happen in the future, but if you use 생각할 것이다, you're saying the **thinking** will happen in the future (i.e. subj. will think). You can have all sorts of tense combinations depending on context - see the example sentences below.

> 민수가 한국에 **갈 거라고 생각해요**. I think Minsu **will** go to Korea.
> 하람이 숙제를 **할 거라고 생각해요**. I think Haram **will** do his homework.
> 다른 사람들은 우리가 미친다고 생각**할 거예요**. Other people **will** think we **are** crazy.
> 다른 사람들은 우리가 미쳤다고 생각**할 거예요**. Other people **will** think we **were** crazy.

REFERENCE PAGES

V~은/는/을 것 같다 - page 199

4

WHAT'S THE DIFFERENCE?	
A/V~다고 생각하다	~ㄴ/는/을 것 같다
Slightly more formal, often used in written language.	*Slightly more casual, often used in spoken language.*
친구의 용기가 저는 늘 대단하**다고 생각해요**. I think my friend's bravery is so amazing. 우정에 나이가 큰 영향은 없**다고 생각해요**. I think age has no big effect on friendships	친구의 용기가 저는 늘 대단**한 것 같아요**. I think my friend's bravery is so amazing. 우정에 나이가 큰 영향은 없**는 것 같아요**. I think age has no big effect on friendships.
More direct - when using this grammar form, you are being assertive in saying that these are your thoughts on the matter. You can use this form when you feel strongly about something.	*Less direct - when using this grammar form, you are indicating that you think/guess/suppose something, but you don't feel too strongly about it either way.*
친구의 용기가 저는 늘 대단하**다고 생각해요**. I think my friend's bravery is so amazing. (The speaker is stating their opinion directly/assertively) 우정에 나이가 큰 영향은 없**다고 생각해요**. I think age has no big effect on friendships. (The speaker is stating their opinion directly/assertively)	친구의 용기가 저는 늘 대단**한 것 같아요**. I think my friend's bravery is so amazing. (The speaker is stating their opinion indirectly/softly) 우정에 나이가 큰 영향은 없**는 것 같아요**. I think age has no big effect on friendships. (The speaker is stating their opinion indirectly/softly)

PRACTICE EXERCISES

Given the English sentences, write an equivalent Korean expression using ~(ㄴ/는)다고 생각하다.

1. I think drinking alcohol is bad for you. ....

2. I think language learning is important. ....

3. I think we need to talk. ....

4. I believe I had a reservation. ....

ANSWERS: 1. (저는) 술을 마시는 것이 몸에 안 좋다고 생각해요. 2. (저는) 언어/외국어를 배우는 것이 중요하다고 생각해요. 3. (저는) 우리가 얘기해야 한다고 생각해요. 4. (저는) 예약을 했다고 생각해요.

USED IN WCK — 75 times

N 중에(서)
Out of, among

가 본 곳 중에서 가장 아름다운 도시는 로마였어요.
Of all the places I've been, Rome was the most beautiful.

중 is derived from a Chinese character meaning "middle" or "center." 중에서 means "among," "between," or "out of all." 중에서 is placed after the noun. Often 중에서 is shortened to just 중에.

NOUNS

한국 음식	→	한국 음식 **중에(서)**	(out of all Korean foods)
고기	→	고기 **중에(서)**	(out of all meats)
운동	→	운동 **중에(서)**	(out of all exercises)

› 한국 음식 **중에서** 무엇이 제일 맛있어요?	Among Korean foods, what tastes best?
› 소고기하고 생선 **중에** 저는 소고기를 더 좋아해요.	Between beef and fish, I prefer beef.
› 이 세 개 **중에서** 저는 이것을 사고 싶어요.	Among these 3 things, I want to buy this one.
› 운동 **중에** 걷기와 요가를 제일 좋아합니다.	Of all the exercises, walking and yoga are my favorite.
› 가 본 곳 **중에** 가장 아름다운 도시는 로마였어요.	Of all the places I've been, Rome was the most beautiful.

USAGE NOTE: "OR"

This grammar form can also be translated to "or" in some sentences. When asking people to choose between two (or more) options, we use "or" in English. For example, "do you prefer coffee or tea?" or, "do you like cats or dogs?" Although we use "or" in English, it is most natural to use "중에" or "중에서" in sentences like this in Korean. You can follow this format: **N1하고 N2 중에 어떤 것을 V?**

› 커피와 차 **중에서** 어떤 것을 선호하세요?	Do you prefer coffee or tea?
› 강아지랑 고양이 **중에** 어떤 것을 좋아하세요?	Do you like cats or dogs?

REFERENCE PAGES

N~와/과, N~(이)랑, N~하고 - page 96

> 책을 읽는 것하고 텔레비전을 보는 것 **중에** 어떤 것을 더 선호하세요?
Do you prefer reading books or watching television?

> 저는 커피와 차 **중에서** 커피가 더 좋아요.
Out of coffee and tea, coffee is better.

> 강아지랑 고양이 **중에서** 강아지를 더 좋아해요.
Out of cats and dogs, I like dogs more.

WHAT'S THE DIFFERENCE?

In Level 3, we learned that ~나/거나 can be used to say "or" in Korean. So what's the difference?

N 중에(서)	~나/거나
When you're asking someone to make a choice between several options (i.e. out of this thing or that), it is more natural to use 중에서.	It is more natural to use ~나/거나 when listing things that you do (e.g. I do this thing or that thing...) etc.
X 차하고 커피 중에 마시고 싶어요. I want to drink between tea or coffee. O 차과 커피 중에서 어떤 것을 더 좋아해요? Do you prefer coffee or tea? O 강아지랑 고양이 중에 어떤 것을 더 선호해요? Do you prefer cats or dogs?	O 차나 커피를 마시고 싶어요. I want to drink coffee or tea. X 차나 커피를 더 좋아해요? This sentence is unnatural. X 강아지나 고양이를 더 선호하세요? This sentence is unnatural.

PRACTICE SENTENCES

Given the following English sentences, write an equivalent sentence in Korean using 중에(서).

1. Out of all Korean food, I like bibimbap the best.

2. Out of all exercise, I like yoga the most.

3. Out of tea and coffee, I like tea more.

4. Out of beer and wine, I drink wine more.

5. Mary is the prettiest of all my friends.

6. Tom is the smartest of all people I know.

ANSWERS: 1. 한국 음식 중에(서) 비빔밥이 가장/제일 좋아해요. 2. 운동 중에(서) 요가를 가장/제일 좋아해요. 3. 차하고 커피 중에(서) 차를 더 좋아해요. 4. 맥주하고 와인 중에(서) 와인을 더 마셔요. 5. (내) 친구 중에(서) 마리가 가장/제일 예뻐요. 6. 아는 사람 중에(서) 이 톰이 가장/제일 똑똑해요.

V~거나, N(이)나 - page 141

USED IN WCK   538 times

A~게/이/히
Making adverbs

어제는 남자친구랑 시간을 재미있게 보냈어요.
I had a great time with my boyfriend yesterday.

When you add ~게 to the verb stem of a descriptive verb, it turns that descriptive verb into an adverb. Such as, "quickly," "softly," "easily," etc. It can only be used with descriptive verbs.

DESCRIPTIVE VERBS

Simply attach ~게 to the verb stem of the descriptive verb. It does not matter if the verb ends in a vowel sound or a consonant sound.

편하다	→	편하게	(comfortably)
자연스럽다	→	자연스럽게	(naturally)
쉽다	→	쉽게	(easily)

> 책을 읽으면서 크게 웃은 적이 있나요?   Have you ever laughed out loud while reading a book?
> 맛있게 먹는 음식은 뭐예요?   What is a food you love to eat?
> 그 영화를 가장 재미있게 봤어요.   I enjoyed watching that movie the most.
> 유일하게 해외여행으로 가 본 나라가 터키예요.   The only country I've been to overseas is Turkey.

Note: You can add ~게 to descriptive verbs that might sound strange when directly translated into English. However, these sentences are completely natural in Korean. For example:

맛있게 먹다   =   to eat deliciously (to enjoy eating)
재미있게 보다   =   to watch funly/interestingly (to enjoy watching)

MAKING ADVERBS WITH ~이 OR ~히

Many descriptive verbs can be changed into adverbs by adding ~이 or ~히 to the verb stem. Here are some common adverbs ending in ~이 or ~히.

Descriptive Verb	~이 or ~히 Adverb	Meaning	Example Sentence
빠르다	빨리	Quickly	빨리 오세요. Please come quickly.
많다	많이	Many	저는 많이 있어요. I have many.
없다	없이	Without	저 없이 가지 마세요. Don't go without me.
N/A*	천천히	Slowly	천천히 말하세요. Please talk slowly.
조용하다	조용히	Quietly	조용히 말하세요. Please talk quietly.
편하다	편히	Comfortably	편히 있어요. I am comfortable.

* "천천히" exists only as an adverb. The verb "천천하다" does not exist.

WHICH ONE DO I USE?

Sometimes the ~이 or ~히 form of the verb sounds more natural than the ~게 adverb form. For example, "빠르다" can become "빠르게" (quickly), and "많다" can become "많게" (many). However, "빨리" and "많이" are more commonly used. Other verbs **only** use the ~게 form and do not have an ~이 or ~히 form. For example, "쉽다" always becomes "쉽게" (easily) and "자연스럽다" always becomes "자연스럽게" (naturally). Still other verbs only have an ~이 or ~히 form and do not have a ~게 form (like 천천히). Unfortunately, **you will have to memorize** adverbs like these as there is no set rule to follow. If you use ~게 on a descriptive verb that usually uses ~이 or ~히, or vice versa, it may sound unnatural, but everyone will still understand what you mean.

PRACTICE EXERCISES

Given the following Korean sentences, write an equivalent English expression.

1. 여행을 편하게 즐기기 위해 차편을 마련했어요.

2. 불안할 때에는 자연스럽게 보이기가 어렵다.

ANSWERS: 1. We arranged transportation in order to enjoy our vacation comfortably. 2. It's difficult to look natural when you're feeling nervous.

| USED IN WCK | 301 times |

V~기

Nominalization (another method)

야채를 먹기가 좋아요.
I like eating vegetables.

We already learned one way to perform nominalization in Korean, which is to add ~는 것 (referenced below). Adding ~기 is another commonly used method of changing a verb into it's noun form.

ACTION VERBS
~기 can only be attached to action verbs. Attach ~기 regardless of whether the verb ends on a vowel sound or a consonant sound.

먹다	→ 먹기	(eating)
청소하다	→ 청소하기	(cleaning)
혼자 있다	→ 혼자 있기	(being alone)

> 야채를 먹기를 싫어해요. — I hate eating vegetables.
> 청소하기가 괜찮아요. — Cleaning is okay.
> 혼자 있기가 힘들어요. — It's difficult being alone.
> 다른 사람들과 쉽게 친해지기 어려워요. — It's difficult to get close to others quickly.
> 내 감정은 꺼내놓기 어려워요. — It's difficult to let out my feelings.
> 운동하기 싫어질 때도 있어요. — There's also times when I hate exercising.

SOME FUN IDIOMS USING ~기

"식은 죽 먹기!" "It's a piece of cake!" (lit. "eating cold porridge")
"하늘의 별 따기!" "It's impossible!" (lit: "catching a star in the sky")
"서울에서 김서방 찾기." "Like finding a needle in a haystack." (lit: "looking for Mr. Kim in Seoul")

REFERENCE PAGES

V~는 것 - page 69

WHAT'S THE DIFFERENCE?	
V~기	~는 것
Slightly more casual and used more in spoken language.	Slightly more formal and used more in written language.
혼자 있**기**가 힘들어요. Being alone is hard. (Slightly more casual)	혼자 있**는 것이** 힘들어요. It's hard to be alone. (Slightly more formal)
There are some fixed grammar forms that can only use ~기.	There are some fixed grammar forms that cannot use ~는 것.
O 한국어를 공부하기 시작했어요. I started learning Korean. O 내 생일이기 때문이야. Because it's my birthday. O 중요한 일을 하기 전에 잘 자려고 노력해요. I make an effort to sleep well before doing something important.	X 한국어를 공부하는 것을 시작했어요. This sentence is awkward. X 내 생일이는 것 때문이야. This sentence is awkward. X 중요한 일을 하는것 전에 잘 자려고 노력해요. This sentence is awkward.
Generally used to talk about specific circumstances.	Used to talk about universal truths about yourself.
손 잡**기**가 싫어요. I don't want to hold your hand. (As for this specific moment, I don't want to hold your hand) 야채를 먹**기**를 좋아해요. I like eating vegetables. (I may not always like vegetables, but at this time, I do)	손 잡**는 것이** 싫어요. I don't like holding hands. (In general, I don't like holding hands) 야채를 먹**는 것을** 좋아해요. I like eating vegetables. (In general, eating vegetables is good. I like it)

{ Although there are subtle differences, **don't stress** about the details. ~기 and ~는 것 are interchangeable in most situations. }

USED IN WCK · 90 times

N ~에 대해(서)
About something

회의에서 자료에 대해 질문했습니다.
In the meeting I asked about the data.

You can add ~에 대해(서) to indicate that you are talking **about that noun.** For example, "learning about Korean" or "reading about sports." The 서 is purely optional, and is often dropped.

NOUNS
~에 대해(서) is attached to nouns. Attach ~에 대해(서) regardless of whether the noun ends on a vowel sound or a consonant sound.

삶	→	삶에 대해(서)	(about life)
저	→	저에 대해(서)	(about myself)
주제	→	주제에 대해(서)	(about the subject)

> 부모님은 제 삶에 대해 조언해 주셨어요. — My parents gave me advice about my life.
> 그 친구가 저에 대해서 뒷담화했어요. — That friend talked about me behind my back.
> 어떤 주제에 대해 항상 의견을 말해요? — About what subject must you always speak your opinion?

USAGE NOTE: ~에 대해(서) IS NOT NECESSARILY REQUIRED

~에 대해(서) is **not required in every situation** that we use "about" in English. For example, we frequently use "about" when talking about emotions (e.g. I'm worried about, happy about, wondering about), but in Korean, you don't necessarily need ~에 대해(서) in these sentences, you only need the verb and the particle.

> 시험이 걱정돼요. — I'm worried about the test.
> 어제 한 일을 생각하고 있어요. — I'm thinking about what I did yesterday.
> 저는 그 결과에 만족해요. — I'm happy about the result.

4

"A NOUN ABOUT SOMETHING": N~에 대한 N

You might see this grammar in it's noun-modifying form:~에 대한. This is useful when you want to describe a noun as being about something else. For example:

> 시험**에 대한** 질문이 있어요.   I have a question about the test.
> 사라**에 대한** 소문을 들었어요.   I heard a rumor about Sara.
> 레스토랑**에 대한** 리뷰를 읽었어요.   I read a review about a restaurant.

"RELATED TO/ABOUT": N~에 관해 OR N관련

~에 관해 and N관련 are less common than ~에 대해, but have a very similar meaning.

> 처음으로 차를 운전했을 때**에 관해** 써보세요.   Try writing about the first time you drove a car.
> 인생**에 관한** 내용을 좋아합니다.   I like the contents related to life.
> 어릴 때부터 꿈**에 관한** 질문들을 받아요.   Since a young age, we get questioned about our dreams.
> 프로젝트**관련** 책을 읽었어요.   I read a book related to the project.
> 취업**관련** 조언도 많이 받을 수 있었어요.   I could also recieve lots of job related advice.
> 예술**관련** 학위가 돈 낭비 아니라고 생각해요.   I don't think arts degrees are a waste of money.

PRACTICE EXERCISES

Given the following English sentences, write an equivalent Korean expression.

1. I wrote a book on the subject.

2. I want to learn about Korean culture.

3. We talked about marriage.

4. We talked about buying a house next year.

5. Do you have a question about me?

6. How do you feel about rainy days?

ANSWERS: 1. (저는) 주제에 대한(서)/관련 책을 썼어요./주제에 대한 책을 썼어요. 2. 한국 문화에 대해 배우고 싶어요. 3. (우리는) 결혼에 대해 이야기했어요. 4. (우리는) 내년에 집을 사는 것에 대해/관련 이야기했어요. 5. 저에 대한 질문이 있어요? 6. 비가 오는 날에 대해(서) 어떻게 생각해요?

USED IN WCK — 11 times

V~는 대신(에), N 대신(에)
Instead of

물 대신 소주 어때?
Instead of water, how about some soju?

You can use this grammar form in the format: **V1~는 대신에 V2** to mean "V2 instead of V1." And you can place "대신(에)" after a noun using the format: **N1 대신 N2** to mean: "N2 instead of N1."

ACTION VERBS

Attach ~는 대신(에) to the verb stem of action verbs. Simply attach ~는 대신(에) regardless of whether the verb ends on a consonant sound of a vowel sound. The "에" at the end is optional.

쓰다	→	쓰는 대신(에)	(instead of writing/using)
요리하다	→	요리하는 대신(에)	(instead of cooking)
읽다	→	읽는 대신(에)	(instead of reading)

> 안경을 쓰**는 대신에** 렌즈를 끼고 있어요. I'm wearing lenses instead of glasses.
> 요리하**는 대신** 밖에 나가서 외식을 했어요. Instead of cooking, I went out for a meal.
> 취직하**는 대신에** 진학할 거예요. I'm going to pursure higher education instead of finding a job.

NOUNS

For use with a noun (i.e. "this noun instead of that noun") just leave a space after the first noun then write "대신." Again, the ~에 is optional here.

밥	→	밥 **대신(에)**	(instead of rice)
저	→	저 **대신(에)**	(instead of myself)

> 음료 **대신** 차를 마시고 싶어요. I want to drink tea instead of soda.
> 고양이 **대신** 강아지를 키워요. I raise a dog instead of a cat.
> 젓가락 **대신에** 포크를 써요. I use a fork instead of chopsticks.

Level Five

Developing Your Sentences

DIFFICULTY LEVEL: HIGH
Most of the example sentences in this Level are taken directly from real conversational sentences made by real Korean people. You can expect the difficulty to increase compared to Level Four.

Level Five Grammar

What we will learn

한국어 문법을 공부하자!
Let's study Korean grammar!

A/V~겠다	218
V~기 위해(서) N 위해(서)	222
A/V~(으)ㄹ까(요)	225
A/V~잖다 N(이)잖다	228
A/V~죠/지(요), N(이)죠/지요	231
A/V~네(요), N(이)네요	234
A/V~더라고(요)	236
A/V~(으)ㄴ/는 편이다	238
A/V~거든(요)	240
A/V ~(으)ㄴ/는/~(으)ㄹ지	243
A/V~ㄴ/는다면, N(이)라면	246
A/V~(으)ㄹ 정도(로)	249
V~(으)러 가다/오다	251
A/V~기도 하다, N이기도 하다	253
A/V~(으)ㄴ/는데	255
V~던 N	259
A/V~았/었던 N	261
A~구나, V~는구나, N~(이)구나	263
A~(으)ㄴ가요? V~나요?	266
A/V~(으)니까	269
"N"~(이)라는 N	273

A/V ~겠다

Strong will & suppositions

수업을 시작하겠습니다.
I will start the lesson.

The ~겠다 grammar form can be used in a number of ways. In this chapter we are going to discuss seven of these uses, with a stronger focus on the following: 1 to make declarations of strong will, and 2 to make suppositions, guesses, or observations.

Grammar Form	Present Tense	Past Tense	Future Tense
Descr. & Action V	~겠어요	~았/었겠어요	~겠어요

Note: ~겠다 can mean the present tense or the future tense depending on the context. The form for present tense and future tense is the same.

1 STRONG WILL & INTENTIONS

In first-person statements, the ending ~겠 expresses **intention or will**.

시작하다	→	시작하겠다	(I will start)
공부하다	→	공부하겠다	(I will study)
기다리다	→	기다리겠다	(I will wait)

> 내가 즉시 그걸 하겠어요. — I'll do it right away.
> 나는 프루트 샐러드로 하겠어요. — I'll have the fruit salad.
> 다음번에는 우리가 그걸 제대로 하겠어요. — We'll get it right next time.
> 당신 상급자들에게 항의를 하겠어요. — I'm going to complain to your superiors.
> 매일 한국어를 공부하겠습니다. — I'm going to study Korean every day.
> 지금부터 더 열심히 공부하겠습니다. — I'm going to study harder from now on.
> 제가 제안서를 작성하고 서류를 제출하겠습니다. — I'll draw up the proposal and submit the paperwork.

WHAT'S THE DIFFERENCE?

~겠다	~을 것이다
Use when you have strong will and determination to do something no matter what, even if the situation changes.	Used when you have strong will to do something, but your plans could change if the situation changes.
매일 한국어를 공부하기 시작하**겠**습니다. I will start studying Korean every day. (My intention is to do this, and I am determined to do so even if my circumstances change) 한국에 가**겠**습니다. I will go to Korea. (I'm determined to go to Korea no matter what)	매일 한국어를 공부하기 시작**할 거예요**. I will start studying Korean every day. (I will do this, unless something was to happen that changed my current circumstances) 한국에 **갈 거예요**. I will go to Korea. (I am going to Korea in the future, unless something happens to disrupt my plans)

"INTENTION" GRAMMAR FORMS

There are many ways to talk about intent in Korean. Here is an ordering of some common grammar forms used to talk about intention. This ordering is not necessarily to scale.

~고 싶다   ~(으)려고 하다   ~(으)ㄹ 것이다   ~겠다

Least Intention ●────────────────────────────────▶ Most Intention

Note: to learn more about the grammar forms above, check the reference pages below.

2 SUPPOSITIONS & GUESSES

~겠다 can also convey a **supposition, a guess, a thought or observation**.

살다	→	살**겠**다	(would you live?)
가다	→	가**겠**다	(would you go?)
할 수 있다	→	할 수 있**겠**다	(could you do it?)

> 나무 위 집에서 살**겠**어요?   Would you ever live in a tree house?
> 돈이 필요하면 배달기사를 하**겠**어요?   Would you be a delivery driver if you needed money?
> 이혼했던 사람과 사귀**겠**어요?   Would you date someone who is divorced?
> 중요한 것은 그 사람의   I suppose the important thing is that person's
>   가치관이**겠**지요.   values.
> 첫눈에 반 할 수도 있**겠**어요!   I suppose love at first sight could happen!

REFERENCE PAGES

V~고 싶다 - page 93   A/V~(으)ㄹ 것이다 Future Tense - page 60

V~(으)려고 [하다] - page 177

3 "I GUESS I SHOULD...": ~아/어야 겠다

This grammar form is commonly combined with the ~아/어야 (하다) form to say things like, "well, I guess I'd better..." or "okay, I guess I should..."

> 지금 전화를 끊어야 **겠**어요.	Well, I guess I should hang up now.
> 집에서 한번 해봐야 **겠**습니다.	Okay, I guess I should try it at home.
> 이만 가봐야 **겠**어요.	Well, looks like I've got to go now.
> 습관을 고쳐서 아침마다 해를 봐야**겠**다.	I guess I should fix my habits and see the sun every morning.

4 HOPES & WISHES: ~았/었으면 좋겠다

When combined with ~았/었으면 and 좋다, it can be used to express a hope or wish for your current situation to change.

> 한국에 갈 수 있**었으면 좋겠**어요!	I wish I could go to Korea!
> 한국어를 배울 수 있**었으면 좋겠**어요.	I wish I could learn Korean.

5 FORMAL REQUESTS: N~주시겠다? V~아/어 주시겠다?

When combined with the honorific marker 시 and the verb 주다, it is a polite way to request or ask for something or some action to be done.

> 물을 좀 **주시겠**어요?	Could you please bring me some water?
> 그 일을 해 **주시겠**어요?	Could you please do that work item?
> 그 회의에 참석**해주시겠**어요?	Could you please attend that meeting?

6 POLITELY SAYING "I KNOW" OR "I DON'T KNOW": 알겠어요/모르겠어요

~겠다 can also be added to 알다 (to know) and 모르다 (to not know) to raise the politeness. 알겠어요/모르겠어요 sound softer and more polite than 알아요/몰라요, though they have the same meaning.

> 왜인지 정확히 모르**겠**어요.	I don't exactly know why.
> 제 친구중엔 잘 모르**겠**네요.	Out of my friends, I'm not sure.
> 저만 그런 건지 모르**겠**는데...	I'm not sure if it's just me, but...

REFERENCE PAGES

V~아/어야 하다/되다 - page 189   V~아/어 주다 - page 165

A/V~았/었으면 좋겠다 - page 157

7 "I BET IT WAS...": ~았/었겠다

When used in the past tense, you can say things like, "it must have been...," or, "I bet it was..."
Note: it's usually used when talking about the actions of someone else - for example, when reacting to a story someone tells you.

> 와, 좋**았겠**네요. — Oh wow, that must have been nice.
> 그 영화는 무서**웠겠**다. — That movie must have been scary.
> 여행은 대단**했겠네요**. — Your vacation must have been amazing.
> 근데 가족이랑 좋은시간 보**냈겠죠**? — But you must've had a good time with your family, right?

PRACTICE EXERCISES
Given the following Korean sentences, write an equivalent English expression.

1. 두통이 있어서 누워야 겠다.

2. 복어로 만든 음식은 무서워서 못 먹겠습니다.

3. 전기 없이 일주일 살 수 있겠어요?

4. 그 영화는 꽤 재미있었겠어요.

5. 일본의 그런류 영화를 정말 못 보겠어요.

6. 양배추 샐러드는 좋아하지만 삶은 양배추 못 먹겠어요.

7. 나비효과가 되었으면 좋겠어요.

8. 나를 아껴줄 수 있는 사람이었으면 좋겠어요.

9. 첫 데이트는 따뜻한 분위기였으면 좋겠어요.

10. 좀비와의 전쟁은 제가 빨리 죽는다는 건 알겠어요.

ANSWERS: 1. I have a headache so I guess I should lie down. 2. I'm scared of foods made with pufferfish, so I won't eat them. 3. Could you live for a week without electricity? 4. That movie must have been pretty funny. 5. I really can't watch Japanese movies like that. 6. I like cabbage salad, but I can't eat boiled cabbage. 7. I hope it has a butterfly effect. 8. I want someone who can take care of me. 9. I'd like the first date to have a warm atmosphere. 9. I know I'm going to die quickly in a zombie apocalypse.

V~기 위해(서) N 위해(서)
For the sake of, in order to

꿈을 이루기 위해 제 미래에 투자 할 거예요.
I will invest in my future to achieve my dream.

You can attach ~기 위해(서) to a verb to say "in order to do" that verb, or place it after a noun to say "for the sake of" that noun. The -서 is optional, and is often dropped, particularly in conversation.

ACTION VERBS

When using an action verb, attach ~기 위해(서) to the verb stem of the action verb. Attach ~기 위해(서) regardless of whether the verb ends on a vowel sound or a consonant sound.

만나다	→	만나**기 위해(서)**	(in order to meet)
시작하다	→	시작하**기 위해(서)**	(in order to start)
돕다	→	돕**기 위해(서)**	(in order to help)

> 의사가 되**기 위해서** 열심히 공부한다. — I study hard in order to become a doctor.
> 추울 때 몸을 따뜻하게 하**기 위해** 뭘 해요? — When it's cold, what do you do to warm up?
> 변하는 세상에 적응하**기 위해** 컴퓨터를 배우려 해요. — I intend to learn computers to adapt to this changing world.

DESCRIPTIVE VERBS

When using a descriptive verb, attach **~아/어지기 위해(서)** to the verb stem of the descriptive verb. This is a combination of the ~아/어지다 grammar form and the ~기 위해서 grammar form.

건강하다 →	건강해지기 위해(서)	(in order to get healthy)
따뜻하다 →	따뜻해지기 위해(서)	(in order to get warm)

> 하루하루 더 나아**지기 위해** 노력하고 있어요. — I am making an effort to get better every day.
> 더 건강해지**기 위해** 할 수 있는 일은 뭐예요? — What can you do in order to become healthier?
> 주말은 쉬**기 위해** 존재하는 거예요. — Weekends exist in order to relax.

── REFERENCE PAGES ──

A~아/어지다 - page 195

NOUNS

For nouns, attach ~을/를 위해서 to the noun. This combines the ~을/를 object particle and 위해서.

친구	→	친구를 위해(서)	(for subj.'s friend)
사랑	→	사랑을 위해(서)	(for love)

> 엄마를 **위해** 선물을 샀어요. I bought a present for my mom.
> 가족이나 친구를 **위해** 요리를 하는 것을 즐겨요. I enjoy cooking for my friends and family.
> 은퇴 후를 **위해** 돈을 모으고 있나요? Are you saving money for retirement?

FOLLOWING WITH A NOUN: "위한"

You can also follow 위해(서) with a noun to signify that the noun is for some purpose or goal. When 위해(서) is followed by a noun, it becomes **위한**. This turns the base verb, "위하다" (to care for, honor) into it's noun-modifying form. This noun-modifying form can then be used to describe nouns. For example:

나를 **위한** 시간   Time for myself
건강을 **위한** 음식   Food for my health

> 나를 **위한** 시간으로 만들 수 있었어요. I could make time for myself.
> 어른들을 **위한** 색칠공부를 해 본 적이 있어요. I've tried a coloring book for adults.
> 100명을 **위한** 식사를 준비해야 한다면 무엇을 만드시겠어요? If you had to make a meal for 100 people, would you make?

WHAT'S THE DIFFERENCE?

N 위해	N 위한
Emphasizes the action that comes after 위해	*Emphasizes the noun that comes after 위한*
엄마를 **위해** 선물을 샀어요. I **bought** a present for my mom. (Emphasizes **buying the present** was something you did for your mom. This emphasizes the verb.)	엄마를 **위한** 선물을 샀어요. I bought a **present** for my mom. (Emphasizes that the **present** you bought was for your mom. This emphasizes the noun.)
Can be followed by an action or a noun, but must include some action.	*Can only be followed by a noun.*

REFERENCE PAGES

V~(으)ㄴ N - page 145

N 위해	N 위한
O 가족을 위해 샀어요. I bought it for my family. X 가족을 위해 선물이에요. This sentence is awkward because 선물이에요 (it is a gift/present) is not an action.	X 가족을 위한 샀어요. This sentence is awkward because 사다 (to buy) is not a noun. O 가족을 위한 선물이에요. This is a present for my family.

WHAT'S THE DIFFERENCE?

위해(서)	~(으)려고
Slightly more common in written language.	Slightly more common in spoken language.
Used for grand goals or large schemes.	More commonly used for everyday things.
O 세계의 기아를 줄이기 위해 일한다. We work to alleviate world hunger.	O 건강해지려고 운동해요. I work out to be healthy.
Can be used in imperative sentences.	Cannot be used in imperative sentences.
O 선물을 사기 위해서 돈을 모으세요. Please save money in order to buy that present.	X 선물을 사려고 돈을 모으세요. (This sentence is awkward because you cannot ask people to do things using ~(으)려고)
Can be used with nouns.	Used only with verbs.
O 친구를 위한 케이크를 만들었어요. I made a cake for my friend.	X 친구려고 케이크를 만들었어요. This sentence is awkward because 친구 is not a verb.

PRACTICE EXERCISES

Given the following Korean sentences, write an equivalent English expression.

1. 사람들과 친해지기 위해서 시간이 좀 걸리는 편입니다. _____

2. 더 건강해지기 위해 비타민을 챙겨 먹고 있어요. _____

3. 정신건강을 위해서는 일기를 쓰는 게 도움이 돼요. _____

ANSWERS: 1. It tends to take a long time to get close to people. 2. I'm taking vitamins in order to get healthier. 3. Keeping a diary is good for your mental health.

REFERENCE PAGES

V~(으)려고 [하다] - page 177

V~(으)세요 - page 162

A/V~(으)ㄹ까(요)

Making suggestions & suppositions

점심을 먹을까?
Shall we eat lunch?

This grammar form is commonly used to make suggestions to the listener ("shall we do this...?") and also to ask yourself questions or wonder out loud to yourself ("will I...? will it...?").

1 SUGGESTIONS

When making a suggestion, ~(으)ㄹ까(요) is usually attached to action verbs.
If the verb ends in a consonant sound, attach ~을까(요)

먹다	→	먹을까(요)	(shall we eat?)
(!) 듣다	→	들을까(요)	(shall we listen?)

If the action verb ends in a vowel sound, or ㄹ, attach ~ㄹ까(요)

시작하다	→	시작할까(요)	(shall we start?)
연습하다	→	연습할까(요)	(shall we practice?)
만들다	→	만들까(요)	(shall we make?)

> 점심을 먹을까요? — Shall we eat lunch?
> 오늘 점심에 뭐 먹을까요? — What should we eat for lunch today?
> 일요일에 만날까요? — Shall we meet on Sunday?
> 일 끝난 후에 한잔 할까? — Shall we have a drink after work?
> 케이크를 만들까? — Shall we make a cake?

2 QUESTIONS, THOUGHTS & GUESSES

Whether ~(으)ㄹ까 means a suggestion or a question depends on context. The verb conjugation is the same.

살 수 있다	→	살 수 있을까(요)	(will subj. live?)
예쁘다	→	예쁠까(요)	(will subj. be pretty?)
비가 오다	→	비가 올까(요)	(will it rain?)

› 한국에서 살 수 있**을까요**?	Would I be able to live in Korea?
› 여자가 예**쁠까요**?	Will the girl be pretty?
› 내일 비가 **올까**?	Will it rain tomorrow?
› 이 셔츠가 비**쌀까**?	Will this shirt be expensive?

PAST TENSE: ~았/었을 까(요)?

When combined with the past tense marker (~았/었) you make guesses or suppositions about things that happened in the past. This is also generally used when talking to yourself out loud, like: "I wonder if something happened?" or, "would something have been...?"

› 톰은 이 책을 읽**었을까요**?	I wonder if Tom read this book?
› 사라는 이 영화를 보면서 울**었을까**?	I wonder if Sara cried while watching this movie?
› 한국에 친구가 없었다면 한국에서 10년 동안 살 수 있**었을까**?	If I didn't have friends in Korea, would I have been able to live there for 10 years?
› 여름에 호주에 갔으면 좋**았을까**?	Would it have been nice if I'd gone to Australia in the summer?

COMMON USAGE: ~지 않을 까(요)

The ~(으)ㄹ까 grammar form is often combined with the ~지 않다 grammar form (referenced below) to create ~ 지 않을 까(요)? which means something like; "wouldn't it be?," or "don't you think?" This is commonly used to make hypothetical questions.

› 좋지 않**았을까요**?	Wouldn't it be good?
› 가능하지 않**을까요**?	Wouldn't it be possible?
› 둘 다이지 않**을까요**?	Wouldn't it be both?
› 더 많은 진실을 알고 있지 않**을까요**?	Wouldn't we know more facts?
› 일하는 것은 좀 편하지 **않을까**?	Wouldn't working be a bit easier?

WHAT'S THE DIFFERENCE?

~(으)ㄹ까?	~(으)ㄹ 것 같다?
Used more often when asking hypothetical questions (suppositions).	Used more often when asking a question about a specific situation.

--- REFERENCE PAGES ---

A/V~았/었다 Past Tense - page 58   A/V~지 않다 - page 63

~(으)ㄹ까?	~(으)ㄹ 것 같다?
한국에 살 수있**을까요**? Would I be able to live in Korea? (Hypothetical question)	한국에 살 수있**을 것 같아요**? Do you think you could live in Korea? (A question about someone's thoughts)
Used more often when talking out loud to yourself.	*Used more often when asking someone a question.*
흠... 비가 **올까**? Hmm... will it rain? (Talking to yourself out loud)	비가 **올 것 같아요**? Do you think it will rain? (Asking someone else a question)
Commonly used to make suggestions. When you use ~(으)ㄹ까, you're often involving yourself in some future action. ("shall we?/ shall I?")	*When using ~(으)ㄹ 것 같다, you're just asking about some situation, not necessarily involving yourself in the future action. ("will it?")*
일 끝난 후에 한잔 **할까요**? Shall we grab a drink after work? (Making a suggestion about doing something together after work)	일 끝난 후에 한잔 **할 것 같아요**? Do you think you'll have a drink after work? (Asking someone about their after work plans)

Note: these are not hard rules, just some general tendencies of how these two grammar forms are used.

PRACTICE EXERCISES

Given the following Korean sentences, write an equivalent English expression.

1. 학교에서는 거의 동갑의 친구만 사귈 수 있죠. _____

2. 제가 첫 눈에 반한 적이 없기 때문이죠. _____

3. 하지만 그 조언을 무시해서도 안되겠죠. _____

ANSWERS: 1. Because you can only really meet friends your own age at school, you know? 2. Because I've fallen in love at first sight, you see. 3. But we shouldn't ignore that advice, right?

REFERENCE PAGES

V~은/는/을 것 같다 - page 199   Banmal (반말) - page 169

USED IN WCK — 48 times

A/V ~잖다   N(이)잖다
Of course, obviously

저는 매일 운동하잖아요.
I work out every day, of course.

You can add ~잖다 to the end of a sentence to remind the listener of something they should be aware of, or that they've possibly forgotten. In English it is similar to how we sometimes end a sentence with; "obviously" or, "of course." It can even be similar to "duh" or "you know that, right?"

Note: ~잖아(요) is a conversational grammar form that should be avoided in formal situations.

Grammar Form	Present Tense	Past Tense	Future Tense
Desc. & Action V	~잖아(요)	~았/었잖아(요)	~(으)ㄹ 거잖아(요)
Nouns	~(이)잖아(요)	~이었잖아(요)/였잖아(요)	~일 거잖아(요)

DESCRIPTIVE VERBS & ACTION VERBS

~잖다 can be attached to action verbs and descriptive verbs. Add ~잖아(요) to the verb stem regardless of whether it has a final consonant sound or vowel sound.

맛있다	→	맛있**잖아(요)**	(it's delicious, you know)
공부했다	→	공부했**잖아(요)**	(subj. studied it, of course)
할 줄 알다	→	할 줄 알**잖아(요)**	(subj. knows how to do it, obviously)

> 그 가수가 멋있**잖아요**. That singer is obviously so handsome.
> 그 여자가 한국에서 공부하**잖아요**. That girl studies in Korea, of course.
> 한국어를 할 줄 알**잖아요**. I do know Korean, you know.
> 변화를 바로바로 느낄 수 있**잖아요**. You can feel the change immediately, of course.
> 고양이는 보통 산책 잘 안 하**잖아요**. You obviously don't really take cats for walks.

Caution!
Using ~잖아(요) can come off as condescending in some situations.

NOUNS

~잖다 can be attached to nouns in the form of ~(이)잖아(요).

If the noun ends on a consonant sound, attach **~이잖아(요)**

학생	→	학생**이잖아(요)** (subj. is a student, you know)
외국인	→	외국인**이잖아(요)** (subj. is a foreigner, you know)

If the noun ends on a vowel sound, attach **~잖아(요)**

친구	→	친구**잖아(요)** (subj. is a friend, you know)
고양이	→	고양이**잖아(요)** (subj. is a cat, you know)

> 우리 그냥 친구**잖아요**. — We're just friends, you know.
> 그냥 고양이**잖아요**. — It's just a cat, of course.
> 그 사람이 외국인**이잖아요**. — That person is a foreigner, obviously.

CASUAL LANGUAGE

If you want to use ~잖아요 in casual language (반말), just remove -요.

> 우리가 친구**잖아**. — We're friends, you know.
> 그냥 고양이**잖아**. — It's just a cat, of course.
> 내가 너를 사랑하**잖아**! — I love you, you know that right!?

PAST TENSE

To talk about situations in the past tense, attach ~았/었잖아(요).

> 날 차로 칠 뻔 **했잖아**! — You could have run me over!
> 한 시간 전에 여기 왔어야 **했잖아**. — You were supposed to be here an hour ago.
> 너 왜 그래? 오전 내내 한 마디도 안 **했잖아**. — What's up with you? You haven't said a word all day.
> 네가 항상 그러고 싶어**했잖아**. — You know you've always wanted to.
> 글쎄, 너 공부 정말 열심히 **했잖아**. — Well, you know you studied really hard for it.

FUTURE TENSE

To talk about situations in the future tense, attach ~(으)ㄹ 거잖아(요).

> 난 정말 안 걸을 **거잖아**. — I'm obviously not going to do any walking.
> 넌 날 잊지 않을 **거잖아**, 맞지? — You're not going to forget me, right?

REFERENCE PAGES

Banmal (반말) - page 169

> 그냥 며칠 동안 떠나있을 거잖아.	I'm just leaving for a few days, of course.
> 네가 날 어차피 죽일 거잖아.	You're obviously just going to kill me anyway.

USAGE NOTE: GIVING REASONS

You can use the ~잖아요 grammar form to give reasons for doing something. This is particularly common when responding to "why" questions. Using this grammar form is similar to adding "of course" or "obviously" to the end of a sentence in English. Along with some "eye-rolling" attitude.

> 왜 그 책을 샀어? 진짜 쌌**잖아**.	Why did you buy that book? 'Cause it was so cheap, of course.
> 왜 점심을 안 먹었어? 너무 아프**잖아**.	Why didn't you eat lunch? 'Cause I'm too sick, obviously.
> 오늘 왜 청소하지 않았어? 일 때문에 너무 피곤하**잖아**.	Why didn't you clean today? Since I'm obviously too tired from work.

"YOU TOLD ME THAT....!" ~(ㄴ/는)다고 했잖아(요)

A very common way that ~잖다 is used in conversational Korean is to exclaim about what someone has (or hasn't) said. This involves the use of what's known as "quoted forms" in Korean. While we don't dive into quoted forms in this book, essentially it involves attaching ~(ㄴ/는)다고 하다 to the verb stem. You might recognize it from when we learned the grammar form "A/V~(ㄴ/는)다고 생각하다" in Level Four (see reference page below).

Note: there are many other quoted forms in Korean, check online if you wish to learn more.

> 이곳에 10시에 **온다고 했잖아요**!	You said you'd be here at 10 o'clock!
> 나도 한 몫 떼어 **준다고 했잖아**!	You promised me a cut of the deal!
> 너 배에 왕자 있**다고 했잖아**.	You told me you had washboard abs.
> 확실하게 끊을 수 있**다고 했잖아**.	I told you I could quit cold turkey.

Note: because subjects can be dropped in Korean, knowing who told who (e.g. "I told you..." or "You told me...") will often come from context. Therefore, a sentence like "이곳에 10시에 온다고 했잖아요!" can mean either "I told you I'd be here at 10 o'clock!" OR "you told me you'd be here at 10 o'clock!"

REFERENCE PAGES

A/V~(ㄴ/는)다고 생각하다 - page 204

A/V~죠/지(요), N(이)죠/지요

You know? Right? Isn't it?

126 times

> 날씨가 좋지.
> The weather's nice, right?

You can add ~죠 or ~지요 to the end of a sentence to suggest an answer, or to reconfirm something with the other person. It is similar to how we sometimes add "right?," "you know?," or, "isn't it?" to the end of a sentence in English. When you use ~죠 or ~지요, the speaker is seeking some agreement or affirmation from the listener.

Note: in English, although we usually end "right?" with a question mark, in Korean it's more common to use a full stop after ~죠/지요.

Grammar Form	Present Tense	Past Tense	Future Tense
Desc. & Action V	~죠/지(요)	~았/었죠/지(요)	~(으)ㄹ 죠/지(요)
Nouns	~(이)죠/지(요)	~이었죠/였죠 or ~이었지요/였지요	~일 거죠 or ~일 거지요

DESCRIPTIVE VERBS & ACTION VERBS

~죠/지(요) can be added to descriptive verbs and action verbs. Simply attach ~죠/지(요) to the verb stem. It does not matter if the verb stem ends on a vowel sound or a consonant sound.

재미있다	→	재미있**죠** / 재미있**지(요)**	(it's fun, right?)
좋다	→	좋**죠** / 좋**지(요)**	(it's good, right?)
했다	→	했**죠** / 했**지(요)**	(subj. did it, right?)

> 단 한 번의 전화도 소중하**죠**. — Even one phone call is invaluable, you know?
> 중학교 다닐 때 우리는 처음 만**났죠**. — We first met while at middle school, right?
> 나중에 비가 **올죠**. — It's going to rain later, right?
> 첫 데이트엔 마주보고만 있어도 좋**죠**. — It's nice just to see each other face-to-face on a first date, you know?
> 어렵기 때문에 대부분은 지키지 못하**죠**. — It's difficult so not all can stick to it, eh?

NOUNS

~죠/지(요) can be added to nouns in the form ~(이)죠/(이)지(요).
If the noun ends in a consonant sound, attach ~이죠/이지요

좋은 점	→	좋은 점**이죠** / 좋은 점**이지(요)**	(it's a good thing, right?)
주말	→	주말**이죠** / 주말**이지(요)**	(it's the weekend, right?)

If the noun ends in a vowel sound, attach ~죠/지(요)

도시	→	도시**죠** / 도시**지(요)**	(it's a city, right?)
커피	→	커피**죠** / 커피**지(요)**	(it's coffee, right?)

> 친척들을 오랜만에 본다는 게 제일 좋은 점**이죠**.
> The best thing is seeing my family members again after a long time, you know?

> 요코하마는 한국의 인천과도 닮은 곳이 많은 도시**죠**.
> Yokohama is a city that has a lot of places that look like Incheon in Korea, right?

> 애인이랑 데이트 하는 것이 가장 행복한 주말이**죠**.
> My happiest weekend is going for a date with my significant other, you know?

CASUAL LANGUAGE

If you want to use ~죠/지요 in casual language, just take off the -요. This means you attach ~지 if you're attaching to a verb, and ~(이)지 if you're attaching to a noun.

> 봄과 가을은 꽃가루 때문에 괴롭**지**.
> Because of the pollen, spring and fall are the worst, aren't they?

> 떨어지면 어떡하**지***..' 라는 생각에 두려웠어요.
> "What if I fail...?" that's what I was afraid of.

> 자유시간을 혼자 즐기는 거**지**.
> I'm enjoying my free time alone, you know?

* '어떡하지' is a set expression meaning, "what do I do if...?" or, "now what do I do...?"

WHAT'S THE DIFFERENCE?

~죠	~지요
Just a contraction of "~지요." It is most common in spoken language.	More common in written language.
지금 비가 오고 있**죠**. It's raining right now, right?	지금 비가 오고 있**지요**. It's raining right now, right?

REFERENCE PAGES

Banmal (반말) - page 169

WHAT'S THE DIFFERENCE?

~잖아(요)	~죠/지요
Used when you're positive the other person knows what you're talking about. ("Come on, you know this.")	More tentative, and more of a question. ("This is how it is, right?")
Imagine you're at home and you see that your older sister ate all your favorite cookies. So you ask her: 언니, 왜 쿠키 다 먹었어? Sis, why'd you eat all the cookies? She says to you: 맛있**잖아**! They're delicious, duh! (What kind of question is that? They're so dang good. You know how good they are)	Now imagine you bought your favorite cookies and you're sharing them with your friend. Your friend tries a cookie and says: 와, 이 쿠키 왜 이렇게 맛있어? Wow, why are these cookies so dang good? You reply: 맛있**지**! They're so good, right?? (I'm pretty sure you like them, but I'm still looking for affirmation)
Let's look at another example: imagine you're leaving the house and your sibling asks you: 왜 우산을 가지고 있어? Why do you have an umbrella? 비가 **올 거잖아**! 'Cause it's gonna rain later, duh! (I know you know it's going to rain - you can see those clouds outside)	Versus: 왜 우산을 가지고 있어? Why do you have an umbrella? 비가 **올 거지**. 'Cause it's gonna rain later, right? (I think it's going to rain later, don't you?)

{ ~죠/지요 may come across as more polite than ~잖아요.
It depends on context and tone of voice. }

───────────── REFERENCE PAGES ─────────────

A/V~잖다 N(이)잖다 - page 228

A/V~네(요), N(이)네요

For expressing an emotional reaction to something new

와, 경치가 너무 좋네요!
Wow, the view is so nice!

This grammar form is used to add a special sort of emphasis to your sentence. It's used when you experience something (often for the first time) and you wish to convey that you had an **emotional reaction** (i.e. surprise, joy, fear, shock, etc.) to that experience.

For example, one of the most common ways you will hear this used is: when you speak Korean to a Korean person and they say; "한국어 잘하시네요!" Which means something like; "wow, your Korean is so good!" The Korean person is experiencing you speaking Korean for the first time, and they are having an emotional reaction (surprise, admiration, happiness, etc.) to this experience.

Using ~네요 is kind of like adding "wow" to a sentence in English.

Note: ~네요 can be used to express positive or negative emotional reactions. You will be expected to infer their emotional reaction through context, tone of voice, and/or facial expressions.

Grammar Form	Present Tense	Past Tense	Future Tense
Desc. & Action V	~네(요)	~았/었네(요)	~겠네(요)
Nouns	~(이)네(요)	~이었네요/였네(요)	~이겠네(요)

DESCRIPTIVE VERBS & ACTION VERBS

Simply attach ~네(요) to the verb, whether the verb is an action verb or a descriptive verb, and whether the verb stem ends on a vowel sound or a consonant sound.

잘하다 →	잘하네(요)	(wow, you're good)
좋다 →	좋네(요)	(wow, it's nice)
예쁘다 →	예쁘네(요)	(wow, it's pretty)

> 오늘은 날씨가 정말 좋네요.   The weather is so nice today. (wow)
> 영어를 정말 잘하네요.   Your English is so good. (wow)

> 그 여자가 예쁘**네요**.   That girl is pretty. (wow)
> 그 남자가 멋있**네요**.   That guy is handsome. (wow)
> 강아지가 정말 귀엽**네요**!   Your dog is so cute! (wow)

WHAT'S THE DIFFERENCE?

~네(요)	~죠/지(요)
Implies that you are having an emotional reaction to a first-time experience.	Implies that you're seeking affirmation or agreement on something.
오늘은 날씨가 좋**네요**. The weather is nice today. (wow) (I'm experiencing this great weather and it's making me feel some sort of way)	오늘은 날씨가 좋**죠**. The weather is nice today, isn't it? (I think the weather is nice, do you think the weather is nice?)

WHAT'S THE DIFFERENCE?

~네(요)	~잖아(요)
Implies that you are having an emotional reaction to a first-time experience.	Used when you're reminding someone of something they know, and have possibly forgotten.
오늘은 날씨가 좋**네요**. The weather is nice today. (wow) (I'm experiencing this great weather for the first time and it's making me feel something)	2 오늘은 날씨가 좋**잖아요**. You know the weather is good. (come on) (Of course the weather is good, you should know this already)
Cannot be used to give reasons for something.	Can be used to give reasons for something.
Q. 오늘 왜 공원에 갔어요? Why did you go to the park today? X 오늘은 날씨가 좋네요. The weather is nice today. (wow) This sentence is grammatically correct, but it's an awkward response to the question.	Q. 오늘 왜 공원에 갔어요? Why did you go to the park today? O 오늘은 날씨가 좋잖아요. (Because) the weather is good today, of course. (You're reminding them the weather is good, so of course that's why you went to the park)

REFERENCE PAGES

A/V~죠/지(요), N(이)죠/지요 - page 231   A/V~잖다 N(이)잖다 - page 228

A/V~더라고(요)

For telling someone about what you experienced

한국어 공부하기가 어렵더라고요.
Studying Korean is difficult (in my experience).

더라고(요) is used when you're telling someone about something you **directly experienced** at some point in the past. For example, something you personally saw, heard, or did. It's commonly used when you want to tell someone something and emphasize that you're speaking from personal experience. It's also accompanied by that feeling of discovery from having experienced something first-hand.

ACTION VERBS & DESCRIPTIVE VERBS

You can attach ~더라고(요) to all verb stems regardless of whether they end on a vowel sound or a consonant soun, and regardless of whether they're an action verb or descriptive verb.

보다	→	보더라고(요)	(I directly saw...)
듣다	→	듣더라고(요)	(I directly heard...)
하다	→	하더라고(요)	(I personally did...)
많다	→	많더라고(요)	(there are many, in my experience)
없다	→	없더라고(요)	(there are none, in my experience)

> 옛날엔 많았는데 최근에는 별로 없**더라고요**. — In the old days there was a lot, but nowadays there aren't really (in my experience).

> 설거지는 청소기 돌리는 것보다 더 싫**더라고요**. — Doing dishes is worse than vacuuming (in my experience).

> 영어보단 수학을 잘 하는게 돈 벌이에 도움이 되**더라고요**. — More than English, I've found that being good at math is better for earning money.

> 빨간색 속옷을 입으면 조금 마음이 편해지는 것 같**더라고요**. — I think wearing red undies makes me feel a little bit more at ease (in my experience).

> 달팽이 요리를 입에 넣을 용기가 나지 않**더라고요**. — I found that I wasn't brave enough to put the escargo in my mouth.

USAGE NOTE: PAST TENSE ~았/었더라고(요)

The regular grammar form ~더라고(요) is **already** talking about an event that happened in the past, so in most cases you do not need to add the ~았/었 past tense marker. If you do use the past tense form ~았/었더라고(요) in your sentence, you indicate that you directly experienced a **completed action**, i.e. an action that started and finished **before** you directly experienced it yourself.

> 한국에 도착했을 때 눈이 **왔더라고요**.	When I arrived in Korea, I saw it had been snowing.
> 정말 잘 **했더라고요**.	I saw that they had done a really good job.
> 약간 좀 연구를 **했더라고요**.	I noticed that you'd done a bit of practice.
> 저한테 보낸 편지에 보니까 타이핑 미스를 **했더라고요**.	I saw there was a typing mistake in the email you sent to me.

USAGE NOTE: DECREASING FORMALITY

You can make your sentence less formal by dropping the -요 and just saying ~더라고. You may even hear people just saying ~더라.

USAGE NOTE: ~더라구(요)

An alternative spelling you might encounter is ~더라구(요). The meaning is the same, it just sounds cuter and more friendly. While it's technically not the "proper" spelling, it is very commonly used, particularly with younger people. In *Writing Conversational Korean*, they were used almost an equal amount, with "~더라고(요)" used 14 times and ~더라구(요) used 15 times.

> 생각보다 어렵**더라구요**.	I found it was harder than I thought.
> 엉덩이를 박아서 아파하**더라구요**.	I (directly) saw him hit his butt and get hurt.
> 지는 팀은 벌칙이 있기 때문에 꼭 이기고 싶**더라구요**.	There's a penalty for the losing team, so you really want to win (in my experience).
> 제사상에 올라가는 밥이 더 맛있**더라구요**.	The rice on the ceremonial table is more delicious (in my experience).
> 기차에서 그를 봤는데 그는 슬퍼하**더라구요**.	I saw him on the train and he looked so sad.
> 저는 처음에 이 영화가 로맨틱 코미디라고 생각했는데 액션무비 **더라구요**.	I thought the movie was supposed to be a romantic comedy at first, but it turned out to be an action movie.

USED IN WCK   244 times

A/V ~(으)ㄴ/는 편이다

For talking about tendencies

저는 돈을 모으는 편이에요.
I tend to save my money.

This is a grammar form used to talk about the way things tend to be. It's often used to soften expressions when talking about one's own characteristics. We do this in English as well: for example, instead of saying; "I am smart," it's more humble to say; "I **tend** to be smart," "I'm **kind of** smart," or, "I'm **pretty** smart." You use the ~(으)ㄴ/는 편이다 grammar form to do this in Korean.
Note: "편" is a noun meaning "side" in Korean, so this grammar form literally means "to be on the side" of something. i.e. "I'm on the smart side" or "I'm on the tall side."

Grammar Form	Present Tense	Past Tense	Future Tense
Descriptive Verbs	~(으)ㄴ 편이에요	~(으)ㄴ 편이었어요	N/A*
Action Verbs	~는 편이에요	~는 편이었어요	N/A*

DESCRIPTIVE VERBS

This grammar form can be attached to descriptive verbs using the form: ~(으)ㄴ 편이다.
If the descriptive verb ends on a consonant sound, attach **~은 편이다**.

| 맑다 | → | 맑**은 편이다** | (to tend to be sunny) |
| 머리가 좋다 | → | 머리가 좋**은 편이다** | (to tend to be smart) |

If the descriptive verb ends on a vowel sound, or ㄹ, attach **~ㄴ 편이다**.

키가 크다	→	키가 크**ㄴ 편이다**	(to tend to be tall)
(!) 힘들다	→	힘든 **편이다**	(to tend to be difficult)
(!) 덥다	→	더운 **편이다**	(to tend to be hot)

If the descriptive verb ends in 있 or 없 attach **~는 편이다**.

| 재미있다 | → | 재미있**는 편이다** | (to tend to be fun/interesting) |
| 맛없다 | → | 맛없**는 편이다** | (to tend to taste gross/disgusting) |

> 저는 머리가 좋**은 편이에요**.   I'm kind of smart.
> 약속은 꼭 지키**는편이에요**.   I definitely tend to keep my promises.

---

*~(으)ㄴ/는 편이다 is only used to talk about the past or present, not the future.

> 100%는 아니지만, 솔직한 편이에요.   Not 100%, but I tend to be honest.
> 완전히 믿는 것은 아니지만 그래도   I don't completely believe in it, but I tend to be
> 조심하는 편이에요.   careful nonetheless.

ACTION VERBS

This grammar form can be attached to action verbs using the form: ~는 편이다. It does not matter if the action verb ends on a vowel sound or a consonant sound.

Note: descriptive verbs ending in ~있/없 (재미있다, 맛없다, etc.) also use this form.

먹다 →	먹는 편이다	(to tend to eat)
이해하다 →	이해하는 편이다	(to tend to understand)
돕다 →	돕는 편이다	(to tend to help)
(!) 울다 →	우는 편이다	(to tend to cry)

> 저는 김치를 잘 먹는 편이에요.   I tend to be fine with eating kimchi.
> 한국어를 이해하는 편이에요.   I tend to understand Korean.
> 저는 엄마를 돕는 편이에요.   I tend to help my mom.
> 그 영화를 봤을 때 우는 편이었어요.   I tended to cry when I watched that movie.

USAGE NOTE: NOT USED FOR DEFINITE THINGS

~(으)ㄴ/는 편이다 cannot be used for things that are definite. Like heights, lengths, weights, etc.

O 키가 작은 편이에요.   I tend to be on the short side.
X 키가 150cm 편이에요.   My height tends to be 150cm.

USAGE NOTE: NOT USED IN FUTURE TENSE

~(으)ㄴ/는 편이다 is not used in the future tense. For example:

X 주말에 바쁜 편일 거예요.   This sentence is awkward in Korean.

If you want to say; "I will tend to be busy on the weekend," you can use an option like:

O 주말에 바쁠 거예요.   I will be busy on the weekend.
O 주말에 좀 바쁠 거예요.   I'll be kind of busy on the weekend.
O 주말에 바쁠 것 같아요.   I think I'll be busy on the weekend.
O 주말에는 좀 바쁜 편이에요.   I tend to be busy on weekends. (in general)

A/V~거든(요)

For giving reasons

피자를 많이 샀어요. 정말 좋아하거든요.
I bought a lot of pizza. Since I love pizza.

This grammar form is used in two main ways.
  1 "If/when" - similar to ~(으)면
  2 "Because/since" - similar to ending with ~아/어서요, ~기 때문이에요, or ~잖아요.
  Note: in *Writing Conversational Korean*, 2 was used much more than 1

Grammar Form	Present Tense	Past Tense	Future Tense
Action & Desc. V	~거든(요)	~았/었거든(요)	~(으)ㄹ 거든(요)
Nouns	~(이)거든(요)	~이었거든(요)/ ~였거든(요)	N/A

1 "IF / WHEN"

In this first usage, ~거든 is used to connect two clauses together with the idea of "if something is true" or "if something turns out to be true." To conjugate, simply attach ~거든 to the verb stem of the first verb. It does not matter if it ends on a vowel sound or a consonant sound.

아프다	→	아프거든	(if they turn out to be sick...)
싸다	→	싸거든	(if they turn out to be cheap...)
도착하다	→	도착하거든	(if/when you arrive)

> 아프거든 병원에 가세요.   If you're sick, please go to the hospital.
> 사과가 싸거든 많이 사세요.   If the apples are cheap, please buy a lot.
> 공항에 도착하거든 연락하세요.   Please contact me when you arrive at the airport.

Note: when used this way, ~거든 is frequently used with imperative forms like "~(으)세요." To learn more about ~(으)세요, check the reference page below.

REFERENCE PAGES

A/V~(으)면 - page 125
A/V~아/어서 N(이)라서 - page 115

A/V~기 때문에 - page 153
V~(으)세요 - page 162

WHAT'S THE DIFFERENCE?	
~거든(요)	~(으)면
Cannot be used to state general facts and truths.	Can be used to state general facts and truths.
X 봄이 가거든 여름이 와요. This sentence is awkward in Korean. X 물은 100도가 되거든 끓는다. This sentence is awkward in Korean.	O 봄이 가면 여름이 와요. When spring goes, summer comes. O 물은 100도가 되면 끓는다. When water reaches 100°C it boils.
Cannot be used in suppositions.	Can be used in suppositions.
X 취직하거든 얼마나 좋을까? This sentence is awkward in Korean.	O 취직하면 얼마나 좋을까? How good would it be if I get hired?
Can be used to end a sentence.	Cannot be used to end a sentence.
O 병원에 갔어요. 아프거든요. I went to the hospital. 'Cause I'm sick. (In the above sentence, ~거든요 is being used for it's second usage - see below).	X 병원에 갔어요. 아프면요. I went to the hospital. If sick. (~으면 cannot be used to give reasons)

2 "BECAUSE/SINCE"

In this second usage, ~거든 is used to indicate that the statement is obviously true by citing the preceding statement as an example. It's often used to give a reason for something that you do/have done. When used this way, it's usually a sentence ending instead of a connecting clause. It's often used in the past tense (~았/었거든) to give a reason for something you **did** in the past.

아팠다	→	아팠거든(요)	(because I was sick)
쌌다	→	쌌거든(요)	(because they were cheap)
좋아하다	→	좋아하거든(요)	(because I like them)

> 병원에 갔어요. 아**팠거든요**.   I went to the hospital. Because I was sick.
> 사과를 많이 샀어요. 정말 **쌌거든요**. I bought a lot of apples. Since they were so cheap.
> 피자를 많이 샀어요. 정말 좋아**하거든요**.I bought a lot of pizza. Since I love pizza.

CASUAL LANGUAGE

If you want to use ~거든 in casual language, just drop the -요. For example:

>	피자를 많이 샀어. 정말 좋아하**거든**.	I bought a lot of pizza. 'Cause I like it a lot.
>	고양이를 좋아해. 정말 귀엽**거든**.	I like cats. 'Cause they're so cute.
>	병원에 갔어. 아**팠거든**.	I went to the hospital. 'Cause I was sick.

NOUNS

To use this grammar form with nouns, attach ~(이)거든(요).

If the noun ends on a vowel sound, attach **~거든(요)**

    보너스 →   보너스**거든(요)**   (because it's a bonus)

If the noun ends on a consonant sound, attach **~이거든(요)**

    꿈 →   꿈**이거든(요)**   (because it's a dream)
    같은 반 →   같은 반**이거든(요)**   (because of the same class)

>	그것이 제겐 매출 보너스**거든요**.	Because that's a sales bonus for me.
>	초등학교 때 같은 반**이었거든요**.	Because we were in the same class in elementary.
>	프랑스로 유학을 가고 싶어. 현재 제 꿈**이거든**.	I want to study abroad in France. 'Cause it's my dream.
>	왠만하면 서로 대화로 푸는 편**이거든요**.*	Because we both tend to fix (problems) by talking to each other.

*편 comes from the grammar form "~(으)ㄴ/는 편이다" but " 편 is a noun that means "side." Therefore when saying "because I tend to be some way," you can use: ~(으)ㄴ/는 편이거든(요). Check the reference page below to learn more about ~(으)ㄴ/는 편이다.

WHAT'S THE DIFFERENCE?

~거든(요)	~잖아(요)
Gives a reason the listener doesn't know.	Gives a reason the listener should know.
병원에 갔어. 아팠**거든**. I went to the hospital. 'Cause I was sick. The other person didn't know you were sick, and you're telling them that's the reason.	병원에 갔어. 아팠**잖아**. I went to the hopsital. 'Cause I was sick. (duh) The other person knew you were sick, you you're reminding them of that fact.

REFERENCE PAGES

A/V~(으)ㄴ/는 편이다 - page 238

USED IN WCK   56 times

A/V ~(으)ㄴ/는/~(으)ㄹ지

For adding uncertainty

어디에 가는지 몰라.
I don't know where it is that I'm going.

This grammar form is used to indicate an ambiguous reason or judgment about the following statement. It's commonly used when you want to tell the listener that you don't know, or you're not sure, about something. It can often be translated to "whether," e.g. "I do A whether B," or "I'm not sure whether A or B." It can be a sentence connector or a sentence ending.

Grammar Form	Present Tense	Past Tense	Future Tense
Descriptive Verbs	~(으)ㄴ지	~았/었는지	~(으)ㄹ지
Action Verbs	~는지	~았/었는지	~(으)ㄹ지
Nouns	~인지	~이었는지/였는지	

DESCRIPTIVE VERBS (PRESENT TENSE)

If the verb stem of the descriptive verb ends in a consonant sound, attach **~은지**

많다	→	많**은지**	(whether/if there's a lot)
괜찮다	→	괜찮**은지**	(whether/if it's okay)
좋다	→	좋**은지**	(whether/if it's good)

If the verb stem of the descriptive verb ends in a vowel sound, or ㄹ, attach **~ㄴ지**

비싸다	→	비싼**지**	(whether/if it's expensive)
편리하다	→	편리한**지**	(whether/if it's convenient)
(!) 멀다	→	먼**지**	(whether/if it's far)
(!) 춥다	→	추운**지**	(whether/if it's cold)

If the verb stem of the descriptive verb ends in 있 or 없, attach **~는지**

| 있다 | → | 있**는지** | (whether/if there is) |
| 재미없다 | → | 재미없**는지** | (whether/if it's boring) |

> 음식이 좋**은지** 모르겠어요.   I don't know whether the food is good.
> 이 치즈가 비**싼지** 확인했어요.   I checked to see if the cheese is expensive.

> 아이가 괜찮**은지** 물어봤어요.　　I asked whether the child is okay.
> 이것을 할수 있**는지** 몰라.　　I don't know if I can do this.
> 지금 돈이 있**는지** 없**는지** 몰라.　　Right now I'm not sure whether I have money or not.

ACTION VERBS (PRESENT TENSE)

Attach **~는지** to action verbs regardless of whether they end on a vowel sound or a consonant sound.

가다	→	가**는지**	(whether/if subj. goes)
만나다	→	만나**는지**	(whether/if subj. meets)
(!) 알다	→	아**는지**	(whether/if subj. knows)
이해하다	→	이해하**는지**	(whether/if subj. understands)

> 우리가 어디에 가**는지** 모르겠어요.　　I don't know where we are going.
> 어디에서 만나**는지** 모르겠어요.　　I don't know where we are meeting.
> 이 단어를 아**는지** 물어봤어요.　　I asked whether they knew this word.
> 이 문법을 이해할 수있**는지** 확인했어요.　　I checked if they could understand this grammar form.

NOUNS (PRESENT TENSE)

To add uncertainty to a noun, attach **~인지**. It does not matter if the noun ends on a vowel sound or a consonant sound.

Note: ~인지 is a combination of the descriptive verb "이다" (to be), with ~ㄴ지.

학생	→	학생**인지**	(whether subj. is a student)
한국 사람	→	한국 사람**인지**	(whether subj. is Korean)
여자	→	여자**인지**	(whether subj. is a girl/woman)

> 그 사람은 학생**인지** 모르겠어요.　　I don't know whether that person is a student.
> 한국 사람**인지** 물어봤어요.　　I asked whether they were Korean.
> 그 고양이가 여자**인지** 궁금해요.　　I'm curious if that cat is female.

PAST TENSE: ~았/었는지

If you wish to use ~(으)ㄴ/는지 in the past tense, attach ~았/었는지.

> 음식은 좋**았는지** 모르겠어요.　　I don't know if the food was good.
> 사람이 많**았는지** 궁금해요.　　I'm curious if there were a lot of people.
> 이 수업을 이해**했는지** 궁금해요.　　I'm curious if they understood the lesson.

> 이 어휘를 이해**했는지** 궁금했어요.   I was curious if they understood the vocabulary.
> 어제 날씨가 **추웠는지** 물어봤어요.   I asked if the weather was cold yesterday.

FUTURE TENSE: ~(으)ㄹ지

If you wish to use ~(으)ㄴ/는지 in the future tense, attach ~(으)ㄹ지.

> 이 문법을 이해**할지** 궁금해요.   I'm curious if you will understand this grammar form.
> 버스가 편리**할지** 궁금해요.   I'm curious if the bus will be convenient.
> 음식이 좋**을지** 모르겠어요.   I don't know if the food will be good.
> 잘 가르칠 수 있**을지** 모르겠어요.   I don't know if I'll be a good teacher.
> 사람이 많**을지** 궁금해요.   I'm curious if there will be a lot of people.

USAGE NOTE: QUESTION WORDS & "WHETHER"

In English, question words (e.g. "where," "when," "how," etc.) cannot really exist in the same sentences as "whether." But in Korean, question words ("어디," "언제," "어떻게," etc.) can co-exist with ~(으)ㄴ/는/~(으)ㄹ지. But depending on whether there is a question word in the sentence, the ~(으)ㄴ/는/~(으)ㄹ지 might emphasize different things. For example:

1 **어디에 가는지** 모르겠어요.   I don't know **where** we're going.
2 파티에 **언제 가는지** 모르겠어요.   I don't know **when** we're going to the party.
3 파티에 **어떻게 가는지** 모르겠어요.   I don't know **how** we're going to the party.
4 파티에 **왜 가는지** 모르겠어요.   I don't know **why** we're going to the party.
5 파티에 **누가 가는지** 모르겠어요.   I don't know **who** is going to the party.
6 **파티에 가는지** 모르겠어요.   I don't know **whether** we're going to the party.

Note: in the last sentence above, there is no question word used, so now the thing you "don't know" is whether you're going to the party or not.

All these sentences are grammatically correct, but notice how using ~(으)ㄴ/는/~(으)ㄹ지 highlights different things you "don't know" depending on the other words used in the sentence.

USED IN WCK   241 times

A/V ~ㄴ/는다면, N(이)라면
For hypothetical situations

10억이 있다면 집을 살 것 같아요.
If I had a million dollars, I think I'd buy a house.

This grammar form is used to hypothesize about a situation that has a **low likelihood** of occurring. This grammar form is used frequently in *Writing Conversational Korean* because of all the hypothetical questions like; "if X happened" or "if you could do Y," etc.

Grammar Form	Present Tense	Past Tense	Future Tense
Descriptive Verbs	~다면	~았/었다면	N/A
Action Verbs	~ㄴ/는다면	~았/었다면	N/A
Nouns	~(이)라면	~이었다면/였다면	N/A

DESCRIPTIVE VERBS

If attaching to a descriptive verb, attach ~다면.

있다	→	있**다면**	(If subj. has)
가능하다	→	가능하**다면**	(if it's possible)
불편하다	→	불편하**다면**	(if it's uncomfortable)

> 시간여행이 가능하**다면**, 미래로 가고 싶어요. If time travel was possible, I would want to go to the future.
> 10억이 있**다면** 집을 살 것 같아요. If I had a million dollars, I think I would buy a house.
> 재주가 있**다면** 좀비 세상에서 살아남을 수 있어요. If you have skills, you can survive the zombie apocalypse.
> 새로운 일을 시작할 수 있**다면** 행복할 것 같아요. I think I would be happy if I could start a new job.

ACTION VERBS

If attaching to an action verb, attach ~ㄴ/는다면.
If the action verb ends in a vowel sound, or ㄹ, attach **~ㄴ다면**.

하다	→	**한다면**	(if subj. does)
(!) 살다	→	**산다면**	(if subj. lives)

If the action verb ends on a consonant sound, attach **~는다면**.

마음먹다	→	마음먹**는다면**	(if subj. decides)
믿지 않다	→	믿지 않**는다면**	(if subj. doesn't believe)

> 다시 그 식당을 **간다면** 좋을 것 같아요.   It'd be nice if I could go to that restaurant again.
> 마음먹**는다면** 행복할 수 있어요.   I can be happy if I decide to be.
> 서로를 믿어 주지 않**는다면** 어려운 것 같아요.   I think it'd be difficult if you can't trust each other.

NOUNS

If attaching to a noun, attach ~(이)라면.
If the noun ends in a vowel sound, attach **~라면**.

부자	→	부자**라면**	(if subj. is a rich man)
첫 데이트	→	첫 데이트**라면**	(if it's a first date)

If the noun ends in a consonant sound, attach **~이라면**.

학생	→	학생**이라면**	(if subj. is a student)
선생님	→	선생님**이라면**	(if subj is a teacher)

> 저는 부자**라면** 세계 여행을 할 거예요.   If I was a rich man, I would travel the world.
> 첫 데이트**라면** 맛있는 음식점에 가고 싶어요.   If it's a first date, I would want to go to a good restaurant.
> 아직 학생**이라면** 결혼하지 않을 거예요.   I wouldn't get married if I was still a student.

WHAT'S THE DIFFERENCE?

~ㄴ/는다면	~(으)면
Involves situations that have a low likelihood of occurring (or are impossible).	Involves situations that have a medium or high likelihood of occurring.

REFERENCE PAGES

A/V~(으)면 - page 125

~ㄴ/는다면	~(으)면
O 시간여행을 할 수 있다면... If I could time travel... O 새로운 일을 시작할 수 있다면... If I could start a new job... (Implies that you're stuck in your current job and can't start a new one)	X 시간여행을 할 수 있으면... Awkward because time travel is not possible. O 새로운 일을 시작할 수 있으면... If/when I start a new job... (Implies that you're considering changing your job in the future)
Often has a wistful feel due to the implied low likelihood of occurrence.	*Does not have quite the same wistful feel as ~ㄴ/는다면.*
날씨가 좋**다면** 산책할 거예요. If only the weather was good, I'd go for a walk. 물고기 상태가 좋**다면** 내일 주문할게요. If perhaps the fish is in good condition tomorrow, I'll order some.	날씨가 좋**으면** 산책할 거예요. If the weather is good, I'll go for a walk. 물고기 상태가 좋**으면** 내일 주문할게요. If the fish is in good condition tomorrow, I'll order some.

PRACTICE EXERCISES

Given the following Korean sentences, write an equivalent English expression.

1. 10억이 생긴다면 나는 자동차 매장으로 달려갈 것이다.

2. 시간을 멈출 수 있다면 책을 더 많이 읽고 싶을 거예요.

3. 아무 노력없이 10억이 생긴다면 기부를 하고 싶어요.

4. 기회가 된다면 일본으로 가 보고 싶어요.

5. 전시회를 간다면 기억에 많이 남지 않을까요?

6. 부모님이 반대를 하신다면 그럴만한 이유가 있겠죠.

ANSWERS: 1. If I won a million dollars, I would run to the car dealership. 2. If by chance I could stop time, I would want to read more books. 3. If I happened to win a million dollars without any effort, I would want to donate it. 4. If I had the chance, I'd like to try going to Japan. 5. Wouldn't it be memorable if we went to an exhibition? 6. If my parents object, there's a good reason.

USED IN WCK   44 times

A/V~(으)ㄹ 정도(로)
Extents & degrees

비가 너무 많이 와서 앞이 잘 안 보일 정도예요.
It's raining so hard that I can't see in front of me.

The word "정도" in Korean literally means "degree" or "extent." It has two main usages:
   1 With descriptive verbs and action verbs to say that something happens to the degree or extent of something else. In English it's often translated to "something is so X that Y," or "something is X to the point of Y." Using 정도로 this way can make your sentence more expressive and emotive.
   2 With nouns (often time nouns) to mean: "about/approximately" that noun.

DESCRIPTIVE VERBS & ACTION VERBS

A/V~(으)ㄹ 정도(로) can be attached to action verbs and descriptive verbs.
If the verb ends in a vowel sound, attach **~ㄹ 정도로**
    불가능하다   →   불가능할 정도로   (to the extent of impossibility)
    귓가에 맴돌다* → 귓가에 맴돌 정도로   (to the point that it gets stuck in my head)
If the verb ends in a consonant sound, attach **~을 정도로**
    없다   →   없을 정도로   (to the extent of having nothing/none)
    죽다   →   죽을 정도로   (to the point of death)

> 죽을 정도로 공부했어요.   I studied to the point of death.
> 책상에 무릎이 아플 정도로 쿵 찧었어요.   I hit my knee on the desk so hard it hurt.
> 거부할 수 없을 정도로 서로에게 끌렸어요.   We were so drawn to each other that we couldn't deny it.
> 귓가에 맴돌 정도로 기억에 남아요.   It's so memorable to the point that it gets stuck in my head.
> 논평은 불편할 정도로 진실에 근접해 있었어요.   The remark was so close to the truth it was unnerving.

*귓가에 맴돌다 - lit. "to ring in one's ears," it means to have something (e.g. a song) stuck in your head.

NOUNS

정도 can be used after nouns to mean "about that noun." For example:

삼십분	→	삼십분 **정도(는)**	(about 30 minutes)
10개	→	10개 **정도(는)**	(about 10 pieces)
1시간 2시간	→	1시간 2시간 **정도(는)**	(about 1 or 2 hours)

> 예상한 시간보다 삼십분 **정도는** 더 자게 돼요.   I end up sleeping about 30 mins longer than I expect to.
> 10개 **정도** 만드는 것이 좋아요.   It's good to make about 10 pieces.
> 1시간 내지 2시간 **정도** 요가하는 걸 좋아해요.   I like doing yoga for about one or two hours.

COMMON USE: 어느 정도

A common use of 정도 is "어느 정도," which can be roughly translated to "somewhat," "to some extent," or "more or less."

> 첫 눈에 반한다는 게 **어느 정도**는 맞는 것 같아요.   I think love at first sight does exist to some extent.
> 28살 때 **어느 정도** 사회에서 자리를 잡기 시작할 수 있어요.   When you're 28 years old, you can start to establish yourself in society to some extent.
> 몇 마디 주고 받으면 이 사람과 대화가 잘 통할지 안 통할지 **어느 정도** 감이 오거든요.   After just exchanging a few words, I can get a sense of whether or not we click.

ENDING A SENTENCE: ~(으)ㄹ 정도예요.

You can end a sentence with this grammar form by attaching ~(으)ㄹ 정도예요. In past tense, this becomes ~(으)ㄹ 정도였어요.

> 비가 너무 많이 와서 앞이 잘 안 보일 **정도예요.**   It's raining so hard I can't see in front of me.
> 그 사람이 한국말을 아주 잘해서 한국 사람이라고 생각될 **정도예요.**   That person is so good at Korean that people think he is Korean.
> 민수 씨가 술을 많이 마셔서 정신도 못 차릴 **정도였어요.**   Minsu drank so much that he couldn't even regain consciousness.
> 이 시험은 아주 쉬워서 중학생도 모두 풀 **정도였어요.**   This test was so easy that even a middle schooler could have solved all of it.

V~(으)러 가다/오다

For going/coming for some purpose

한국어를 공부하러 카페에 가고 있어요.
I'm going to a cafe to study Korean.

If you want to say something like, "I'm going to a cafe to study" or "I came to the store to return something," you use this grammar form. This grammar is specifically used with the verbs "가다" (to go) and "오다" (to come), when you're coming or going somewhere for some reason or purpose.

Grammar Form	Present Tense	Past Tense	Future Tense
~(으)러 가다	~(으)러 가요	~(으)러 갔어요	~(으)러 갈 거예요
~(으)러 오다	~(으)러 와요	~(으)러 왔어요	~(으)러 올 거예요

ACTION VERBS

When the action verb ends in a vowel sound, or ㄹ, attach **~러 가다/오다**

공부하다	→	공부하**러 가다/오다**	(to go/come to study)
환전하다	→	환전하**러 가다/오다**	(to go/come to exchange money)
만들다	→	만들**러 가다/오다**	(to go/come to make)

When the action verb ends in a consonant sound, attach **~으러 가다/오다**

읽다	→	읽**으러 가다/오다**	(to go/come to read)
먹다	→	먹**으러 가다/오다**	(to go/come to eat)

> 한국어를 공부하**러** 카페에 **가요**.
> I go to a cafe to study Korean.
>
> 책을 읽**으러** 도서관에 **가고 있어요**.
> I'm going to the library to read a book.
>
> 환전하**러** 은행에 **왔어요**.
> I came to the bank to exchange money.
>
> 이 물건을 반품하**러 왔습니다**.
> I came to return this item.
>
> 말라탕을 먹**으러** 식당에 **가고 싶어요**.
> I want to go to a place to eat mallatang (soup).
>
> 공부를 하**러 가면서** 친구를 만나게 됐어요.
> While going to study I ended up meeting a friend.

5

WHAT'S THE DIFFERENCE?	
~(으)러 가다/오다	~(으)려고 하다
Used only with the verbs 가다 and 오다.	Used with 가다 and 오다 **and** other verbs.
X 한국어를 공부하러 책을 샀어요. This sentence is awkward because 사다 (to buy) is not 가다 or 오다. X 한국 칙구와 이야기하러 한국어를 배웠어. This sentence is awkward because 배우다 (to learn) is not 가다 or 오다.	O 한국어를 공부하려고 책을 샀어요. I bought a book to study Korean. O 한국 친구와 이야기하려고 한국어를 배웠어. I learned Korean in order to talk with my Korean friend.
Has essentially the same meaning as ~(으)려고 가다/오다.	When using with 가다 or 오다, it has the same meaning as ~(으)러 가다/오다.
한국어를 공부**하러** 카페에 가요. I'm going to a cafe to study Korean.	한국어를 공부**하려고** 카페에 가요. I'm going to a cafe to study Korean.

PRACTICE EXERCISES
Given the following English sentences, write an equivalent Korean expression.

1. I'm going to the library to study Korean.

2. I went to a cafe to buy some coffee.

3. I will go to Korea to practice Korean.

4. I came to Korea to learn Korean.

5. I came to the market to buy some veggies.

6. I went to Korea to go to a BTS concert.

7. I went to the mall to meet a friend.

8. Tomorrow I'll go to the gym to workout.

ANSWERS: 1. (저는) 한국어를 공부하러 도서관에 가고/가요 있어요. 2. (저는) 커피를 사러 카페에 갔어요. 3. (저는) 한국어를 연습하러 한국에 갈 거예요. 4. (저는) 한국어를 배우러 한국에 왔어요. 5. (저는) 야채/채소를 사러 시장에 왔어요. 6. (저는) 방탄소년단 콘서트에 가러 한국에 갔어요. 7. (저는) 친구를 만나러 쇼핑몰/백화점에 갔어요. 8. (저는) 내일 운동하러 헬스장에 갈 거예요.

REFERENCE PAGES

V~(으)려고 [하다] - page 177

A/V~기도 하다, N이기도 하다
"And also..."

스트레스를 많이 받기도 해요.
I also get really stressed.

~기도 하다 connects two clauses together with the feeling of; "**and also** this action/description." It's often used when listing actions or descriptions, or when adding on another action or description in addition to what was said before.

Grammar Form	Present Tense	Past Tense	Future Tense
Action & Desc. V	~기도 해요	~기도 했어요	~기도 할 거예요
Nouns	~이기도 해요	~이기도 했어요	~이기도 할 거예요

ACTION VERBS

Simply attach ~기도 하다 to the verb stem of the action verb, whether it's a vowel or a consonant.

스트레스를 받다	→	스트레스를 받**기도 하다**	(to also get stressed...)
보다	→	보**기도 하다**	(to also see...)
느껴지다	→	느껴지**기도 하다**	(to also feel...)
놀다	→	놀**기도 하다**	(to also play...)

> 거리감이 조금 느껴지**기도 합**니다. — I also feel a bit of distance.
> 스트레스를 많이 받**기도 해요**. — I also get a lot of stress.
> 본 것 같**기도 하**고 아닌 것 같**기도 해요**. — I kind of think I see it, and I kind of think I don't.
> 점심을 같이 먹고 같이 놀**기도 하**면서 친해졌어요. — We became friends while eating lunch and also hanging out.

DESCRIPTIVE VERBS

Simply attach ~기도 하다 to the verb stem of the descriptive verb.

길다	→	길**기도 하다**	(to also be long)
빠져들다	→	빠져들**기도 하다**	(to also get into it/absorbed by it/addicted)
싫다	→	싫**기도 하다**	(to also dislike)

> 연휴기간이 길**기도 해요**. — And the holiday period is also long, too.
> 시도하지 않은 운동을 경험해 보면 제가 그 운동에 빠져들**기도 해요**. — When I try an exercise I haven't tried before, I also get addicted to it.
> 심심해서 싫**기도 하고** 눈치 보여서 싫어요. — It's also boring and I don't like how people look at me.

NOUNS

To use this grammar form with a noun, attach ~이기도 하다.

축복	→	축복**이기도 하다**	(it's also a blessing)
버킷리스트	→	버킷리스트**이기도 하다**	(it's also on my bucket list)

> 축복**이기도 하**지만 부담이라고 좀 더 생각해요. — It's also a blessing, but I think it's a bit more of a burden.
> 파리에 가고 싶다 - PSG경기를 현지에서 보면서 식사하기. 버킷리스트**이기도 해요**! — I want to go to Paris - eating a meal while watching a local PSG match. It's also on my bucket list!
> 그건 단지 그들에 대한게 아니라, 우리들에 대한 것**이기도 해요**. — It's not just about them, it's about us, too.

WHAT'S THE DIFFERENCE?

~기도 하다	~도
Adds emphasis to the verb in the sentence.	Adds emphasis to the noun in the sentence.
그 여자가 예쁘**기도 해요**. That girl is **pretty**, too. (As well as being tall, smart, funny, etc.)	그 여자**도** 예뻐요. That **girl** is pretty, too. (As well as the other girls)
한국어를 읽**기도 해요**. I also **read** Korean. (As well as speaking, listening, etc.)	한국어**도** 읽어요. I also read **Korean**. (As well as reading other languages)

USED IN WCK   390 times

A/V~(으)ㄴ/는데
For providing background & context

한국에는 한우가 유명한데 좀 비싸요.
Hanwoo beef is famous in Korea... but it's a bit expensive.

~(으)ㄴ/는데 is a very common and conversational connective form. It is used to join two clauses together, where the first clause is giving some context or background information, and the second clause is describing some related result or situation. In English, ~(으)ㄴ/는데 can be translated to "and," "but," or "so," or even ."..."

Grammar Form	Present Tense	Past Tense	Future Tense
Descriptive Verbs	~(으)ㄴ데	~았/었는데	~(으)ㄹ 건데
Action Verbs	~는데	~았/었는데	~(으)ㄹ 건데
Nouns	~인데	~이었는데/였는데	~(이)ㄹ 건데

DESCRIPTIVE VERBS

If the descriptive verb ends on a consonant sound, attach ~은데
Note: verbs ending in ~있 or ~없 use ~는데.

| 좋다 | → | 좋은데 | (it's good, and/so/but...) |
| 많다 | → | 많은데 | (there're many, and/so/but...) |

If the descriptive verb ends on a vowel sound, attach ~ㄴ데

| 유명하다 | → | 유명한데 | (it's famous, and/so/but...) |
| 바쁘다 | → | 바쁜데 | (it's busy, and/so/but...) |

> 제주도는 다금바리라고 하는 생선이 유명한데 무척 비싸.
  Jeju island is famous for a fish dish called "dagumbari" but it's super expensive.

> 아직도 기억에 선명한데, 베프와 알고 지낸 시간이 10년이 넘었네요.
  I still remember it clearly, and I've known my best friend for over 10 years.

> 아 너무 많은데 지금 막 생각나는 건 없어요!
  Ah, there's so many but I can't think of one right now!

5

ACTION VERBS

If attaching to an action verb, attach ~는데 regardless of whether the verb ends on a vowel sound or a consonant sound.

공부하다	→	공부하**는데**	(subj. studies and/so/but...)
좋아하다	→	좋아하**는데**	(subj. likes and/so/but...)
먹다	→	먹**는데**	(subj. eats and/so/but...)
(!) 알다	→	아**는데**	(subj. knows and/so/but...)

> 저는 영어를 공부하**는데** 아직 잘 못 해요. — I study English but I'm still not very good.
> 오빠가 있**는데** 사이는 별로 안 좋아요. — I have an older brother but we don't get along very well.
> 밤 산책 하는 것을 좋아하**는데** 고양이는 산책 잘 안 해요. — I like walking at night, and cats don't go for walks very well.

NOUNS

If attaching to a noun, attach ~인데. It does not matter if the noun ends on a vowel sound or a consonant sound.

미국 사람	→	미국 사람**인데**	(subj. is American and/so/but...)
여자	→	여자**인데**	(subj. is a girl and/so/but...)

> 미국 사람**인데** 한국에 살아요. — I'm American but I live in Korea.
> 저는 아직 미혼**인데** 인생을 즐기고 있어요. — I'm still unmmaried and enjoying my life.
> 류승범이 나온 영화**인데** 제목도 기억이 안납니다. — It was a movie with Ryu Seungbum but I don't remember the title.

PAST TENSE: ~았/었는데

When talking about the past tense, you can add ~았/었는데 to the verb stem.

> 옛날엔 회를 되게 싫어**했는데** 지금은 좋아합니다. — When I was young I hated raw fish, but now I like it.
> 저번 여행에선 중국요리를 많이 먹**었는데** 담엔 동남아요리 도전해 보고 싶네요. — I ate a lot of Chinese food on my last trip, so next time I want to try South-East Asian food!
> 옛날엔 지구온난화가에 대한 말들이 많**았는데** 최근에는 별로 없어요. — In the past there was a lot of talk about global warming, but not so much these days.

STARTING A SENTENCE: "그런데" OR "근데"

If you wish to start a sentence with this grammar form, you can use "그런데" or "근데." "근데" is just an abbreviation of "그런데" and is more common in spoken language.

> **그런데** 왜 그런거 있잖아요?   But, do you know what?
> **그런데** 지금은 시대가 많이 변했어요.   But the times have changed a lot now.
> **근데** 내 베프도 영화를 좋아하거든요.   And my best friend likes movies too, you see.
> **근데** 한국에서는 군인이나 경찰이 아니면 총기를 가질 수 없어요.   And in Korea, you can't have a gun unless you're military or a police officer.

ENDING A SENTENCE: ~ㄴ/는데(요)

You can end a sentence using the ~ㄴ/는데 grammar form by attaching ~ㄴ/는데(요).

Note: if speaking casually, you can drop the -요.

This has four main usages:

1 To express a soft disagreement to something someone else says.

     A: 오늘은 날씨가 더워요.   The weather is hot today.
     B: 오늘 좀 **추운데요**.   Oh, actually I think it's kind of cold.

2 To express the expectation that someone is going to respond to what you said.

     환전하러 왔**는데요**.   I came to exchange some money.

You are expecting the other person to follow up with more questions.

3 To express surprise after experiencing something unexpected.

     와, 음식이 **좋은데요**!   Wow, the food is good, though!

Perhaps the restaurant looked really sketchy, so you're surprised that the food is so good.

4 To express that what you're saying is background information for some upcoming story.

     그 시절에 같은 반이었**는데요**.   We were in the same class in those days.

The person is establishing the background information, and is setting the scene to tell us more about it.

All of these four uses are commonly encountered in the wild. In "*Writing Conversational Korean*," it is most commonly used for 4.

5

WHAT'S THE DIFFERENCE?

~(으)ㄴ/는데	~지만
There might be some contrast between the two clauses, but the feeling is not as strong.	*Implies a strong contrast between clauses.*
열심히 공부했**는데** 시험을 잘 못 봤어요. I studied hard and I didn't do well on the test. (A slightly softer feeling sentence, the contrast is slightly vague)	열심히 공부했**지만** 시험을 잘 못 봤어요. I studied hard **but** I didn't do well on the test. (A stronger feeling sentence with more contrast)

WHAT'S THE DIFFERENCE?

~(으)ㄴ/는데	~고
Used to imply some contrast or give background information.	*Used to list actions or outcomes.*
서울에 **갔는데** 경복궁을 못 방문했어요. I went to Seoul but I couldn't go to Gyeongbokgung Palace. (The speaker went to Seoul, but they couldn't visit the palace, which was perhaps one of the reasons they went in the first place).	서울에 **가고** 경복궁을 방문하**고** 좋았어요. I went to Seoul and then I went to Gyeongbokgung Palace and it was good. (The speaker is just listing things they did in Seoul)

WHAT'S THE DIFFERENCE?

~(으)ㄴ/는데	~아/어서
Used to give background information.	*Used to give reasons for things.*
한국어를 배우**는데** 너무 재미있어요. I learn Korean and it's so much fun. (You're mentioning that you're learning Korean, and that it's fun)	한국어가 재미있**어서** 배워요. I learn Korean because it's fun. (You're talking about the reason you learn Korean, which is that it's fun)

{ Sometimes ~ㄴ/는데, ~지만, and ~고 are interchangeable and sometimes they are not. It depends on context. }

REFERENCE PAGES

A/V~지만, N~(이)지만 - page 112
A/V~고 N~(이)고 - page 108

A/V~아/어서 N(이)라서 - page 115

USED IN W.C. 51 times

V~던 N

For things you used to interact with

자주 가던 곳이에요.
It's a place I went to often.

This grammar form is used to recollect a past action or habit that **was repeated often or still continues**. It's often used to describe items that you've frequently interacted with in the past, and things you're currently using.

ACTION VERBS

Attach ~던 N to the verb stem of the action verb, whether it ends on a vowel or a consonant.

입다	→	입던 N	(the noun I used to wear...)
가다	→	가던 N	(the noun I used to go to...)

> 다니던 학교가 좋았어요. — The school I used to go to was good.
> 마시던 커피숍이 어디에요? — Where is the coffee shop I was drinking at?
> 고등학생 때 입던 옷이에요. — These are the clothes I used to wear in high school.
> 타지 않던 버스를 탔어요. — I rode a bus I don't usually take.
> 평소에 하던 행동들을 다 지키려고 해요. — I try to stick to all my usual behaviors.
> 어릴 때부터 자주 가던 곳이에요. — It's a place I went to often ever since I was young.
> 항상 원하던 목표를 달성했을 때가 가장 행복한 것 같아요. — I think I'm happiest when I achieve goals that I've always wanted to achieve.

WHAT'S THE DIFFERENCE?

V~던 N	V~(으)ㄴ N
Used for past behavior that was not continued, or was not completed.	V~(으)ㄴ is used for a past behavior (that may or may not have been repeated) that has been completed.

5

V~던 N	V~(으)ㄴ N
그 보던 영화가 좋았어요. That movie I didn't finish watching was good.	그 본 영화가 좋았어요. That movie I watched was good.
Used for actions that happened over a span over time (요즘, 항상, 자주, 올해, etc.)	Used for actions that happened at a specific time (지금, 어제, 지난 토요일, etc.)
요즘 마시던 커피가 맛있어요. The coffee I've been drinking lately is delicious. (The coffee you're referring to has been repeatedly drunk in the past)	어제 마신 커피가 맛있었어요. The coffee I drank yesterday was delicious. (You're specifically talking about that one coffee you drank yesterday)
Should not be used for actions that can only happen once.	Should be used for actions that can only happen once.
X 태어나던 도시가 좋았어요. (This sentence is awkward because "being born" is not an action that is repeated) 입던 옷이 좋았어요. The clothes I used to wear were nice. (Implies that you wore that item of clothing multiple times in the past)	O 태어난 도시가 좋았어요. The city I was born in was nice. (Simple past tense, completed action) 입은 옷이 좋았어요. The clothes I wore were nice. (Simple plain tense. It is not specified whether you wore those clothes multiple times or not)
Used for actions that you **recall** doing in the past.	Used to state a simple fact about the past. It does not have the same feeling of "recall" that ~던 has.

PRACTICE EXERCISES

Given the following Korean sentences, write an equivalent English expression.

1. 미국에서 살 때 같이 지내던 친구예요.

2. 대학 입시를 준비하던 기간에 '데미안' 읽었어요.

3. 기존에 있던 드라마 안 보면 전혀 이해할 수 없어요.

ANSWERS: 1. They're a friend I met when I lived in America. 2. I read 'Demian' when I was preparing for college entrance. 3. If you didn't watch the original drama, you won't understand it at all.

REFERENCE PAGES

V~(으)ㄴ N - page 145

A/V~았/었던 N

For something you recall experiencing once

마지막으로 여행했던 장소는 호주였어요.
The last place I traveled to was Australia.

This grammar form is used for **unique or one-off experiences** you recall having in the past, or for remembering how something used to be. It's used for nouns that were encountered just once, or at a specific time in the past.

DESCRIPTIVE VERBS & ACTION VERBS

If the verb (either descriptive or action) ends in ㅏ or ㅗ, attach **~았던** N

좋다	→	좋**았던** N	(the noun that used to be good...)
보다	→	**봤던** N	(the noun I saw one time...)
만나다	→	만**났던** N	(the noun I met one time...)

If the verb (either descriptive or action) ends in 하, it becomes **~했던** N

불편하다	→	불편**했던** N	(the noun that used to be uncomfortable...)
여행하다	→	여행**했던** N	(the noun I traveled to/in...)

If the verb (either descriptive or action) ends in something else, attach **~었던** N

하고 싶다	→	하고 싶**었던** N	(the noun I wanted to do...)
O 예쁘다	→	예뻤**던** N	(the noun that used to be pretty...)
(!) 아름답다	→	아름다**웠던** N	(the noun that used to be beautiful...)

> 마지막으로 여행**했던** 장소는 어디에요?   Where is the last place you traveled to?
> 마지막으로 여행**했던** 장소는 한국이었어요.   The last place I traveled to was Korea.
> 학교에서 가장 좋**았던** 날은 졸업식 날이었어요.   The best day at school was graduation day.
> 제가 살면서 가장 힘들**었던** 때가 있어요.   It was the most difficult time of my life.
> 제가 **봤던** 영화중 가장 최악이**었던** 영화는 설록: 유령신부입니다.   Out of all the movies I've seen, the worst one was Sherlock: The Abominable Bride.
> 제가 가장 행복**했던** 때는 친구들과 함께 처음으로 서울에 여행을 갔을 때예요.   The happiest time for me was the time when I went to Seoul with my friends for the first time.

5

WHAT'S THE DIFFERENCE?	
~았/었던 N	~던 N
Used for nouns that you've only interacted with once, or when talking about a discrete event that is not repeated in the past, nor continuous to the present.	Used for past behavior that was repeated in the past, or is yet incomplete.
어제 먹**었던** 과자가 맛있었어요. The snacks I ate yesterday were delicious. (You ate this snack for the first time yesterday and it was delicious)	내가 항상 먹**던** 과자가 맛었었어요. The snacks I always ate were delicious. (You're talking about a snack that you used to eat regularly in the past)
Used when talking about an action that happened at one specific time in the past.	Not used for actions that happened at one specific moment in the past.
O 마지막으로 여행했던 장소는 멕시코였어요. The last place I traveled to was Mexico.	X 마지막으로 여행하던 장소는 멕시코였어요. (This sentence is awkward because "the last place you traveled to" is a discrete event that is not repeated)
Used to recall situations in the past that have been **completed**.	Used to recall situations in the past that are yet **incomplete**, or are still ongoing.
남자가 쓰러**졌던** 여자를 세웠어요. The man stood up the woman who had fallen down. (The woman was lying on the ground and the man stood her up again) 어제 먹**었던** 과자를 오늘도 먹었어요. I ate the same snacks today that I finished eating yesterday. (Yesterday you finished eating all the snacks, so today you bought more of the same snacks and ate them, too)	남자가 쓰러지**던** 여자를 세웠어요. The man caught the woman as she was falling over. (The man caught the woman as she was falling and stopped her before she fell to the ground) 어제 먹**던** 과자를 오늘도 먹었어요. I continued eating the snacks I started eating yesterday. (Yesterday you started eating some snacks, but you didn't finish them all and today you ate some more)

Note: ~(으)ㄴ N is simple past tense with no added nuance of feeling. ~았/었던 N has the feeling of "recall" or "rememberance" of a unique, one-time event.

REFERENCE PAGES

V~던 V~던 N - page 259   V~(으)ㄴ N - page 145

A~구나, V~는구나, N~(이)구나

For when you learn something new

와, 한국어를 말할 수있구나!
Wow, you can speak Korean!

You can use this grammar form to express surprise when you learn some new information from your own experience or from someone else's experience. It's often used when talking out loud to yourself about something you just realized. In English, we usually do this by changing our tone of voice to express surprise. However in Korean, there is actually a grammar form for it.

Note: it is a very conversational grammar form and should be avoided in formal writing situations.

Grammar Form	Present Tense	Past Tense	Future Tense
Descriptive Verbs	~구나	~았/었구나	~겠구나
Action Verbs	~는구나	~았/었구나	~겠구나
Nouns	~(이)구나	~이었구나/였구나	~(이)겠구나

DESCRIPTIVE VERBS

Attach ~구나 to the verb stem of the action verb regardless of whether it ends on a vowel sound or a consonant sound.

비싸다 →	비싸**구나**	(oh, it's expensive!)
예쁘다 →	예쁘**구나**	(oh, it's pretty!)
똑똑하다 →	똑똑하**구나**	(oh, subj. is smart!)

> 아, 이 물은 좀 비싸**구나**! — Oh, this water is a bit expensive!
> 와, 그 여자가 예쁘**구나**! — Wow, that girl is pretty!
> 와, 똑똑하**구나**! — Wow, you're smart!
> 참 변함없이 살고 있**구나**... — Oh, you're living the same life...

ACTION VERBS (PRESENT TENSE)

Attach ~는구나 to the verb stem of action verbs, regardless of whether it ends on a vowel sound or a consonant sound.

모르다	→	모르**는구나**	(oh, subj. doesn't know)
! 알다	→	아**는구나**	(oh, subj. knows)

> 아, 이 단어를 모르**는구나**. — Oh, you don't know this word.
> 아, 이 단어를 아**는구나**. — Oh, you know this word.
> 와, 한국어를 말할 수 있**구나**. — Oh wow, you can speak Korean.

PAST TENSE

To express surprise about something that happened in the past, use ~았/었구나.

> 아, 그 영화 이미 봤**구나**! — Ah, so you've already seen that movie!
> 아, 콘서트 티켓이 비쌌**구나**! — Wow, those concert tickets were expensive!
> 아, 벌써 집에 돌아왔**구나**! — Oh, you already came back home!

FUTURE TENSE

To express surprise about something that will happen in the future, use ~겠구나.

> 아, 그 영화 곧 보겠**구나**! — Ah, so you're going to see that movie soon!
> 아, 콘서트 티켓이 비싸겠**구나**! — Ah, those concert tickets will be expensive!
> 아, 곧 집에 돌아오겠**구나**! — Ah, so you're going to be home soon!

NOUNS

To use with a noun, attach ~(이)구나

If the noun ends on a vowel sound, attach ~구나

미성년자	→	미성년자**구나**	(oh, subj. is underage)
남자	→	남자**구나**	(oh, subj. is a man)

If the noun ends on a consonant sound, attach ~이구나

학생	→	학생**이구나**	(oh, subj. is a student)
주말	→	주말**이구나**	(oh, it's the weekend)

> 아, 학생**이구나**. — Oh, you're a student.
> 와, 남자**구나**. — Wow, you're a man.
> 네 생일은 지난 주말**이었구나**! — Oh, it was your birthday last weekend!

COMMON USAGE: "그렇구나!"

You will frequently hear this grammar form being used in the expression: "그렇구나!" This is a combination of the verb "그렇다" (to be that way) and the ~구나 grammar form.
It is used to mean something like, "oh really!," "oh, cool," or, "oh, I didn't know/realize that."

    A: 다음주에 한국에 가요.   I'm going to Korea next week.
    B: 아, 그렇**구나**! 재미있겠네요.   Oh, cool! I didn't know that. That'll be fun.

Note: in formal language, it is also written as "그렇군요."

WHAT'S THE DIFFERENCE?

Both of these grammar forms are used when you learn/feel something after having an experience for the first time. But there are some small differences.

~구나	~네(요)
Used when you're speaking aloud to yourself.	*Used when you're speaking to others.*
어, 비가 오**는구나**! Oh, it's raining! (When talking aloud to yourself)	어, 비가 오**네요**! Oh, it's raining! (When talking to someone else)
*Can be used when you realize something because of your own experience **or someone else's experience**.*	*Can **only** be used when you realize something because of your own experience.*
어, 음식이 맵**구나**! Oh, I guess the food is spicy! (You take a bite, or someone else takes a bite and you realize it's spicy from their reaction)	어, 음식이 맵**네요**! Oh, wow, the food is spicy! (When **you** take a bit and realize that it's spicy)

WHAT'S THE DIFFERENCE?

~구나	~군요
Informal language (반말). Used in casual conversation and when talking out loud to oneself.	*Formal language (존댓말). Used when talking directly to someone in formal language.*
한국어를 말할 수 있**구나**! You can speak Korean! [casual] (Wow I didn't know that before)	한국어를 말할 수 있**군요**! You can speak Korean! [formal] (Wow I didn't know that before)

A~(으)ㄴ가요? V~나요?

To make questions less direct

미국에 왜 왔나요?
Why'd you come to America?

There are many ways to make sentences feel less direct in Korean. This grammar form is one that is specifically used for questions. You use this grammar form when you want to ask someone something, and want to make it feel softer and less direct.

Grammar Form	Present Tense	Past Tense	Future Tense
Descriptive Verbs	~(으)ㄴ가요?	~았/었나요?	~(으)ㄹ 건가요?
Action Verbs	~나요?	~았/었나요?	~(으)ㄹ 건가요?
Nouns	~인가요?	~이었나요?/~였나요?	~일 건가요?

DESCRIPTIVE VERBS

If the descriptive verb ends in a vowel sound, attach **~ㄴ가요?**

아프다	→	아픈가요?	(is subj. hurt?)
(!) 힘들다	→	힘든가요?	(is it hard?)
(!) 무섭다	→	무서운가요?	(is it scary?)

If the descriptive verb ends in a consonant sound, attach **~은가요?**

좋다	→	좋은가요?	(is it good?)
많다	→	많은가요?	(are there many?)
하고 싶다	→	하고 싶은가요?	(does subj. want to?)

If the descriptive verb ends in 있 or 없, attach **~나요?**

있다	→	있나요?	(does subj. have?)
맛없다	→	맛없나요?	(is the flavor bad? is it gross?)

> 혹시 팔이 아픈가요? — Is your arm hurt by chance?
> 이 영화가 무서운가요? — Is this movie scary?
> 이 음식은 맛없나요? — Does the food taste bad?

> 헤어졌던 애인과 다시 사겨 본 적이 있**나요**?   Have you ever got back together with an ex?

ACTION VERBS

Attach ~나요 to the verb stem of the action verb. It does not matter if it ends on a vowel sound or a consonant sound.

할 수 있다	→	할 수 있**나요?**	(can you do it?)
가다	→	가**나요?**	(are you going?)
(!) 만들다	→	만드**나요?**	(are you making?)

> 혹시 수영할 수 있**나요**?   By chance, can you swim?
> 혹시 이 주말에 파티에 가**나요**?   By chance, are you going to a party this weekend?
> 케이크를 만드**나요**?   Are you making a cake?

NOUNS

Attach ~인가요 to nouns.

대학생	→	대학생**인가요?**	(are you a university student?)
생일	→	생일**인가요?**	(is it your birthday?)

> 혹시 여자**인가요**?   By chance, are you a woman?
> 한국어를 공부하는 대학생**인가요**?   Are you a university student studying Korean?
> 오늘 생일**인가요**?   Is today your birthday?

PAST TENSE: ~았/었나요?

Attach ~았/었나요? regardless of whether it is an action verb or a descriptive verb.

> 누가 운전하는 법을 가르쳐 주**었나요**?   Who taught you how to drive? (just wondering)
> 진귀한 귀중품이 있**나요**?   Do you have a precious possession? (just curious)
> 어떻게 소유하게 됐**나요**?   How did you come into possession of it?

FUTURE TENSE: ~(으)ㄹ 건가요?

Attach ~(으)ㄹ 건가요? regardless of whether it is an action verb or a descriptive verb.

> 만약 내일 문신을 새겨야 한다면 어떤 문신을 새**길건가요**?   If you had to get a tattoo tomorrow, what tattoo would you get?
> 만약에 결혼한다면 상대방과 통장을 공유**할건가요**?   If perchance you get married, would you and your partner use a joint bank account?

> 아니면 별도로 사용**할건가요**?   Or would you have use separate accounts?

WHAT'S THE DIFFERENCE?

~(으)ㄴ가요? /나요?	~아/어요?
Has an additional level of softness/politeness.	Simple question without additional nuance.
미국에 왜 **왔나요**? Why'd you come to America? ("Oh, I'm just curious, but..." - more polite) 한국 사람**인가요**? Are you Korean? ("I'm just wondering, but..." - more polite)	미국에 왜 **왔어요**? Why'd you come to America? (Plain question, but could feel too direct) 한국 사람**이에요**? Are you Korean? (Plain question, but could feel too direct)

PRACTICE EXERCISES
Given the following English sentences, write a Korean expression using A~(으)ㄴ가요? V~나요?

1. Is the food too spicy?

2. Did you understand what I said?

3. Are you free this weekend?

4. Can you speak English, by chance?

5. By chance do you know Korean?

6. Are you a foreign-born Korean person?

7. Are you a BTS fan?

8. Did you go to the concert last week?

ANSWERS: 1. 음식이 너무 매운가요? 2. 제 말을 이해했(는)나요? 3. 이번 주말에(는) 시간이 있나요? 4. 혹시 영어를 (말)할 수 있나요? 5. 혹시 한국어를 좀 아는가요? 6. 교포인가요? 7. BTS 팬 인가요? 8. 지난 주에 콘서트에 갔나요?

A/V~(으)니까

Because / Therefore / So

더우니까 수영하러 가!
It's hot so let's go for a swim!

~(으)니까 is a connective form with two main usages:
1 To suggest cause and effect (similar to ~아/어서)
2 To express some realization after doing something

Grammar Form	Present Tense	Past Tense	Future Tense
Action & Desc. V	~(으)니까	~았/었으니까	N/A
Nouns	~(이)니까	~이었으니까/~였으니까	N/A

DESCRIPTIVE VERBS & ACTION VERBS

If the verb (either descriptive verb or action verb) ends on a vowel sound, attach **~니까**

일하다	→	일하**니까**	(because subj. works)
! 덥다	→	더우**니까**	(because it's hot)
! 힘들다	→	힘드**니까**	(because it's hard/difficult)

If the verb (either descriptive verb or action verb) ends on a consonant sound, attach **~으니까**

볼 수 있다	→	볼 수 있**으니까**	(because subj. can watch)
먹다	→	먹**으니까**	(because subj. eats)
좋다	→	좋**으니까**	(because it's good)

> 명절에는 가족들을 볼 수 있**으니까** 좋아.
On holidays I can see my family, so it's nice.

> 부모님께서 시간은 되돌릴 수 없**으니까** 최선을 다해요.
My parents tell me that you can't turn back time so do your best.

> 아끼는 사람들이 많**으니까** 좋아요.
There's lots of people I care about so it's nice.

> 이미 날씬한 상태에서 운동을 하**니까** 살이 쉽게 빠지지 않아요.
Because I'm already skinny, when I work out I don't lose weight.

> 아기를 돌봐야 하**니까** 음악회에 갈 수 없어요.
I can't go to the concert because I have to

REFERENCE PAGES

A/V~아/어서 N(이)라서 - page 115

> 설거지는 고무장갑 끼고 해도 축축해지**니까** 싫어용*.
> look after the baby.
> I don't like doing the dishes because I get wet even if I wear rubber gloves.

* "ㅇ" is sometimes added to the final syllable to make the sentence sound "cuter."

NOUNS

If the noun ends on a vowel sound, attach ~니까

| 새해 | → | 새해**니까** | (it's New Years, so...) |
| 힘든 시기 | → | 힘든 시기**니까** | (it's a hard time, so...) |

If the noun ends on a consonant sound, attach ~이니까

| 식당 | → | 식당**이니까** | (it's a restaurant, so...) |
| 운동 | → | 운동**이니까** | (it's exercise, so...) |

> 이제 새해**니까** 습관을 고쳐야 해요.
> It's the new year these days so I need to fix my habits.

> 지금은 좀 힘든 시기**니까** 혼자서 시간을 보내요.
> I'm having a bit of a hard time at the moment so I'm spending time by myself.

> 옛날 제주 흑돼지는 화장실 밑에서 키웠다고 해. 요즘은 사료를 먹이**니까** 괜찮아.
> It's said that in the past, Jeju pigs were raised under the outhouse. Nowadays they eat fodder so it's okay.

> 아무래도 어릴 때부터 "넌 언니**니까** 엄마 없으면 네가 엄마야."
> Nevertheless, ever since I was young I'd hear: "You're the oldest, so when I'm gone, you're the mom."

WHAT'S THE DIFFERENCE?

~(으)니까	~아/어서
Can be used in imperative sentences (when you make commands or requests).	Cannot be used in imperative sentences (when you make commands or requests).
O 추우니까 재킷을 입으세요. It's cold so please wear a jacket. O 더우니까 수영하러 가! It's hot so lets go for a swim! O 미끄러우니까 조심해. It's slippery so be careful.	X 추워서 재킷을 입으세요. Awkward sentence. X 더워서 수영하러 가! Awkward sentence. X 미끄러워서 조심해. Awkward sentence.

REFERENCE PAGES

V~(으)세요 - page 162

~(으)니까	~아/어서
Cannot be used for certain common greetings or sayings.	Can be used for certain common greetings or sayings.
X 만나니까 방가워요. This is awkward in Korean. X 늦게 왔으니까 미안해요. This sentence is awkward in Korean. X 선물을 보내 주시니까 감사합니다. This sentence is awkward in Korean.	O 만나서 방가워요. It's nice to meet you. O 늦게 와서 미안해요. I'm sorry for being late. O 선물을 보내 주셔서 감사합니다. Thanks for sending me that present.

PAST TENSE: ~았/었으니까

You can use this grammar form to talk about situations in the past tense by attaching ~았/었으니까 to the verb stem.

> 비가 **왔으니까** 길이 미끄러워요.   It rained so the streets are slippery.
> 준비를 잘 **했으니까** 문제없을 거예요.   As long as you've prepared well, it'll be fine.
> 운동을 병행 안 **했으니까** 건강하지 않은 방법이죠.   It's not a healthy method because I didn't work out at the same time.

USAGE NOTE: ~(으)니

You might come across "~(으)니" which is a short form of "~(으)니까" and means the same thing.

> 맨날 의자에 앉아 있**으니** 소화가 잘 안 돼요.   I was sitting in a chair all day so my digestion wasn't good.
> 그렇지만 그럴 수 없**으니** 평소에 건강검진을 자주 받아요.   But I can't do that, so I usually get a health check-up often.
> 자주 볼 수 없**으니** 문자 하나, 자주 전화해요.   I can't see them often, so I call frequently.

USAGE NOTE: "그러니까"

You can start a sentence with "그러니까." This is a combination of the verb "그렇다" (to be that way) and the ~(으)니까 grammar form. It is commonly translated to: "because," "so," "like I said," "I mean..." or even "that's what I'm saying."

> 그러니까!   I know, right! (That's what I was saying!)

> **그러니까** 소화가 잘 되고 피부가 깨끗해졌어요.
> So my digestion improved and my skin cleared.
> **그러니까** 투자로 돈을 늘리는 게 목표야.
> So my goal is to do more investing.
> **그러니까** 그런 능력이 있다면 마을의 중요한 힘이 될 거예요.
> So if you had those skills, it'd become an important strength for the village.

ENDING A SENTENCE: ~(으)니까(요)

This grammar form is commonly used to end a sentence. If speaking politely, use: ~(으)니까요 (note that this grammar form is a conversational grammar form and does not have an honorific ~(스)ㅂ니다 conjugation). If speaking casually, just say ~(으)니까.

This is similar to ending a sentence with ~아/어서(요) or ~거든(요) - see reference pages below.

> 괜찮아, 넌 이제 친구들 속에 있**으니까**.
> It's okay, you're among friends now.
> 걱정하지 않아요. 민수는 스스로를 돌볼 수 있**으니까요**.
> Don't worry, Minsu can take care of herself.
> 너무 심하게 하지마. 지금 정말 힘든 시기를 겪고 있**으니까**.
> Don't be too hard on them. They're having a hard time at the moment.

PRACTICE EXERCISES

Given the following Korean sentences, write an equivalent English expression.

1. 덥지도 춥지도 않고 옷도 예쁘니까 가을을 좋아해요.

2. 지구 온난화가 걱정되죠! 지구의 변화가 느껴지니까요.

3. 어렸을 때부터 본 사람이니까 영향을 받을 수 밖에 없어.

4. 부자가 되는 건 모두의 꿈이니까요.

5. 내 인생을 부모님이 대신 살아주시지는 못하니까요.

ANSWERS: 1. I like fall because it's not hot and not cold, and the clothes are pretty. 2. Of course I'm worried about global warming! Because I can feel the change in the Earth. 3. I've known him ever since I was young, so I have no choice but to be influenced. 4. Because being rich is everyone's dream. 5. Because my parents cannot live my life for me.

— REFERENCE PAGES —

A/V~아/어서 N(이)라서 - page 115   A/V~거든(요) - page 240

"N" ~(이)라는 N

For calling nouns by their names

어제는 다모라는 드라마를 봤어요.
Yesterday I watched a drama called Damo.

This grammar form is used to specify that something is called something else, for example; "a book called Harry Potter" or "a movie called Lord of the Rings." In Korean, the name of the thing comes **first** and the type of noun comes **second.** i.e. "Harry Potter-named-book" or "Lord of the Rings-named-movie."

NOUNS

If the first noun ends on a vowel sound, attach ~라는 N

해리 포터	→	해리 포터**라는 N**	(a N called Harry Potter)
인스타	→	인스타**라는 N**	(a N called Insta)
파파고	→	파파고**라는 N**	(a N called Papago)

If the first noun ends on a consonant sound, attach ~이라는 N

반지의 제왕	→	반지의 제왕**이라는 N**	(a N called Lord of the Rings)
방탄소년단	→	방탄소년단**이라는 N**	(a N called BTS)
구글	→	구글**이라는 N**	(a N called Google)

> 저는 어렸을 때 해리포터**라는** 책을 읽었어요.   When I was young I read a book called Harry Potter.

> 어제는 반지의 제왕**이라는** 영화를 봤어요.   Yesterday I watched a movie called The Lord of the Rings.

> 방탄소년단**이라는** 밴드를 들어 봤어요?   Have you heard of the band called BTS?

> 파파고**라는** 앱을 추천해요.   I recommend an app called Papago.

> 저는 어린왕자**라는** 책을 정말 좋아해요.   I really like a book called The Little Prince.

> 뉴욕에서 위키드**라는** 뮤지컬을 봤어요.   In New York I saw a musical called Wicked.

> 사샤**라는** 강아지를 키우고 있어요.   I am raising a dog called Sasha.

Appendix
Additional Information

The Appendix

What we will learn

The Topic & Subject Particles	276
Clausal Verb Tenses	280
Passive & Active Verbs	282
Small Numbers in Korean	284
Large Numbers in Korean	285
Korean Counters	286
Words for Times & Dates	287
Words for People	288
Honorific Vocabulary	290
Common Expressions	291
ㄷ Irregular	292
ㅅ Irregular	293
ㅇ Irregular	294
ㅂ Irregular	295
ㄹ Irregular	296

APPENDIX

The Topic & Subject Particles

Their similarities & differences

In this lesson, we are going to compare and contrast the ~은/는 topic particle and the ~이/가 subject particle. Confusion over these particles is one of the most common problems that English speakers encounter - even at intermediate and advanced language levels.

If you've ever puzzled over the ~은/는 and ~이/가 particles, and been unsure which one to use in your sentences, we hope to explain the main differences in this lesson.

WHAT'S THE DIFFERENCE?	
~은/는	~이/가
1 Denotes the **topic** of the sentence.	Denotes the **subject** of the sentence.
2 Places emphasis on the word(s) to the **right**.	Places emphasis on the word(s) to the **left**.
3 Used to refer to **established information**.	Used to introduce **new information**.
4 Used to talk about general truths and **facts**.	Used to talk about **descriptions**.
5 Used to imply **contrast** or comparisons.	Not used to talk about contrast or comparisons.
6 Can be attached to **any noun**.	Only attached to **sentence subjects**.

Now let's look at each of these points in more detail.

1 TOPIC VS SUBJECT

~은/는 introduces the **topic** of the sentence; the overarching main idea/theme in the sentence.
~이/가 introduces the **subject** of the sentence; who or what is performing some action or receiving some description.

> 메리는 먹어요.   Mary eats.   [Mary is the topic]
>
> In the sentence above, Mary is the main theme and topic in the sentence. This sentence is talking about Mary and what she is doing - in this case, she is eating.
>
> 메리가 먹어요.   Mary eats.   [Mary is the subject]
>
> In the sentence above, Mary is the subject of the sentence. The subject particle simply flags

her as being the person who is performing the action.

It is possible for a noun [like Mary above] to be either the topic or the subject in a sentence. In cases like this you can use one of the following 5 rules to help you decide which particle to use.

2 PLACING EMPHASIS
~은/는 places emphasis on the word(s) **to the right** of the particle.
~이/가 places emphasis on the word(s) **to the left** of the particle.

> 톰은 공부해요.   Tom studies.   [Tom is the topic]

In the sentence above, emphasis is placed on the word to the right : "공부해요" (studies). The emphasis is not so much on Tom himself - it's on what Tom is doing. In this case, he is studying.

> 톰이 공부해요.   Tom studies.   [Tom is the subject]

In the sentence above, emphasis is placed on the word to the left: "톰" (Tom). The emphasis is not so much on what he is doing, it's on who is doing the action. In this case, it is Tom.

Because of this feature, different particles are used to respond to different questions.
For example: If someone was to ask, "**what** is Tom doing?" you would reply: "톰은 공부해요" because you want to emphasize that Tom is **studying**. However, if someone was to ask, "**who** is studying?" you would reply: "톰이 공부해요" because you want to emphasize that **Tom** is studying.

3 ESTABLISHED VS NEW INFORMATION
~은/는 is used to refer to information that is already **established**.
~이/가 is used to introduce information for the **first time**.

> 소피가 운동해요.   Sophie exercises.   [Sophie is the subject]

Imagine someone asks you, "do your friends exercise?" you could reply, "소피가 운동해요" to establish Sophie as a new subject of conversation. You are using the ~이/가 particle to talk about Sophie for the first time.

> 소피는 조깅해요.   Sophie jogs.   [Sophie is the topic]

Suppose this same conversation continues and you want to keep talking about your friend, Sophie. You say "소피는 조깅해요" to talk more about the kind of exercise that she does (in this case, jogging). It's more natural to use ~은/는 now, because you've already established her as a subject. By using ~은/는, you are indicating to the listener that this is the same Sophie that

APPENDIX

> you mentioned before. You're just adding more information about the pre-established subject.

This pattern is frequently seen in Korean. When you first introduce a subject, you use ~이/가. But after that, when you talk about that subject again, you use ~은/는. This is similar to how in English, we first introduce a subject as "a(n) subject" and then when we refer back to it later, we can call it "the subject" because we've mentioned it before.

> > 강아지**가** 먹어요. 강아지**는** 고기를 먹어요.　　A dog eats. The dog eats meat.
> > 한 남자**가** 집에 살아요. 남자**는** 행복해요.　　A man lives in a house. The man is happy.
> > 나무**가** 밖에서 자라요. 나무**는** 커요.　　A tree grows outside. The tree is tall.

Note: this comparison with English is just to give you a better idea of how to approach new information versus established information. ~은/는 does not mean "the" and ~이/가 does not mean "a(n)."

4 TRUTHS VS DESCRIPTIONS

~은/는 is used to state general facts and truths.
~이/가 is used to describe specific things or situations.

> > 사과**는** 빨개요.　　Apples are red.　　[apples is the topic]
> In general, apples are red. A fact about apples is: they are red.
> > 사과**가** 갈색이에요.　　The apples are brown.　　[apples is the subject]
> These apples are being described as brown.

5 CONTRASTS & COMPARISONS

~은/는 is used when making contrasts and comparisons.
~이/가 is not used when making contrasts and comparisons.

> > 사라**는** 공부해요. 톰**은** 요리해요.　　Sara studies. Tom cooks.
> In the sentences above, we are contrasting two different people. Sara, is studying, but Tom is cooking. Because the actions of these two people are being contrasted, you should use ~은/는.
> > 사과**는** 좋아요. 빵**은** 안 좋아요.　　Apples are good. Bread is not good.
> Again, we are contrasting two different nouns (apples and bread). Therefore, you should use ~은/는 in these sentences.

> 한국어는 공부해요. 일본어는 공부 안 해요.   I study Korean. I don't study Japanese.

The sentence above would normally use the object particle ~을/를, but because these two nouns are being contrasted, it is more natural to replace the object particle with ~은/는.

6 NOUN USAGE

~은/는 can be attached to **any** noun. It can attach to subjects, objects, and topics.
~이/가 can **only** be attached to subjects. It cannot attach to objects or topics.
So while ~은/는 and ~이/가 can both attach to subjects, only ~은/는 can attach to objects or topics.

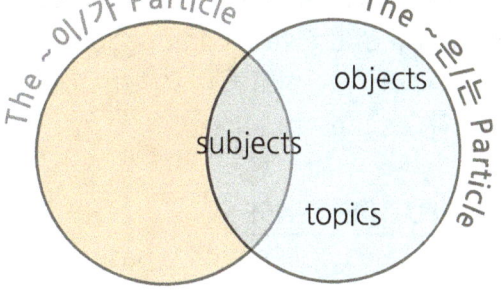

> 톰이 사과를 먹어요.   Tom eats an apple.   [Tom is the subject]
> 톰은 사과를 먹어요.   Tom eats an apple.   [Tom is the topic]
> 톰이 사과는 먹어요.   Tom eats an apple.   [Tom is the subject]

Apples are still the object, but the ~은/는 particle is being used to imply contrast with something.

> 톰은 사과가 먹어요.   An apple eats (Tom?)   [Tom is the topic, apples are subject]

Because the ~이/가 particles can only be used for subjects, the apple now has to be the subject who is connected to the action, "eating."

I'M STILL CONFUSED - IS THAT OKAY?

Yes! There is a **lot** of information in this lesson, and it will take time for it all to sink in. You can just refer back to this chapter whenever you have questions about ~은/는 and ~이/가.

DO NATIVE SPEAKERS KNOW ALL OF THESE RULES?

On an intuitive level, yes. However, if you ask a Korean person the difference between ~이/가 and ~은/는, they will probably say that they just "feel" it. While not encouraging to hear as a language learner, there is some element of truth to this. There is a difference in "feeling" between the two particles. And the longer you learn Korean, the more you will start to feel this difference, too.

Clausal Verb Tenses

An introduction to clausal verb tenses

WHAT IS A CLAUSAL VERB TENSE?
Sentences are made up of clauses. For example, take the sentence: 한국어를 공부하고 좋아요. (I study Korean and it's good). This sentence is made up of two clauses: 1 한국어를 공부해요 and 2 좋아요. The clausal verb tense is the tense of the verb conjugation that joins the two (or more) clauses together. In the sentence "한국어를 공부하고 좋아요," the clausal verb is "공부하다," and the tense of the clausal verb, (공부하다), is present tense.

CLAUSAL VERBS INVOLVING PAST & FUTURE TENSE
In English, the tenses of all the clauses have to align with what's going on in the sentence. E.g. if the situation happened in the past, you have to say "I **studied** Korean and it **was** good," and you cannot say: "I **study** Korean and it **was** good." Therefore, to an English-speaking brain, you might think that "한국어를 공부**하고** 좋았어요" is not correct, because the first verb is present tense while the second verb is past tense. However, this is a perfectly correct and natural sentence in Korean, because in general, the tenses of Korean sentences are **driven by the final verb in the sentence**.

CLAUSAL VERB TENSES USING ACTION VERBS
When you are making sentences using **action verbs** in Korean, you should generally try to keep your tense on the **final verb**.

> 피자를 먹고 잠을 **잤어요**.   I ate pizza and then slept.
> 공원에 가고 **좋았어요**.   I went to the park and it was nice.
> 음식을 먹고 학교에 **갈 거예요**.   I'll eat food and then go to school.

Note: You might come across sentences with a double past tense conjugation like: "한국어를 공부했고 재미있었어요." There is no significant difference in their meaning. Sentences like this are not inherently wrong, but, technically, "한국어를 공부하고 재이있었어요" is more correct, and probably sounds more natural to most native speakers. However, language is always changing and sentences with double past tense conjugations are becoming more commonly used.

APPENDIX

CLAUSAL VERB TENSES USING DESCRIPTIVE VERBS
Sentences with multiple clauses involving descriptive verbs are slightly different: in these sentences, the verb tenses of the clauses should generally **align with the final verb tense**.

> 서울은 더웠고 붐볐어요.	Seoul was hot and crowded.
> 한국어는 어려웠지만 좋았어요.	Korean was difficult but good.
> 저는 어렸을 때 기숙학교에 다녔어요.	When I was young I attended boarding school.

{ *If the clauses use action verbs, place the overall tense of the sentence on the final verb. If the clauses use descriptive verbs, conjugate all verbs into the same tense as the final verb.* }

Note: this is not a hard rule and in the real world, you will probably encounter sentences with all sorts of different verb tense combinations taking place. This is just a general rule of thumb for you to use when making your own sentences.

MIXED TENSES
When the two clauses are talking about **two different time periods**, it is logical to have sentences with mixed tenses. For example:

> 지금은 미국에 살지만 내년은 한국에 살 거예요.	Now I live in the US, but next year I will live in Korea.
> 어제는 추웠지만 내일은 더울 거예요.	Yesterday was cold but tomorrow will be hot.
> 작년에 여행했지만 올해는 못 해요.	I traveled last year, but I can't this year.

APPENDIX

Passive & Active Verbs

An introduction

Some verbs in Korean have two forms: a passive form (i.e. a descriptive verb form) and an active form (i.e. an action verb form). A common example is 좋다 (to be good, nice, liked) and 좋아하다 (to like). Other examples include: 무섭다 (to be scary) and 무서워하다 (to fear), and 슬프다 (to be sad) and 슬퍼하다 (to mourn/grieve).

So what's the difference? Essentially it comes down to two things:

1 PARTICLE USAGE

Passive forms like 좋다, 무섭다 and 슬프다, are descriptive verbs and **use subject particles.**
Active forms like 좋아하다, 무서워하다 and 슬퍼하다 are action verbs and use **both subject particles and object particles.**

Note: topic particles can be placed on objects and subjects of verbs so they are non-discriminant.

> 사과가 좋아요.   Apples are good/apples are nice/(I) like apples.

In this sentence, 좋다 is a descriptive verb that is used to describe apples as good/nice/likeable. It describes that the state that the noun is in.

> 제가 사과를 좋아해요.   I like apples/I love apples.

In this sentence, 좋아하다 is an action verb that is used to say you actively like apples. "Liking" apples is an action that you do. For this reason, 좋아하다 is often translated to "love" in English.*

> 바늘이 무서워요.   Needles are scary/(I) am scared of needles.

Here, 무섭다 is a descriptive verb used to describe the subject's feelings about needles.

> 제가 바늘을 무서워해요.   I fear needles/I am afraid of needles.

Whereas in this sentence, 무서워하다 is an action verb to explain your actions towards needles (i.e. your "fearful" actions).

> 제가 슬퍼요.   I am sad/I feel sad.

In this sentence, 슬프다 is used to describe your emotional state as being sad.

> 제가 아버지의 죽음을 스퍼해요.   I grieve the death of my father.

Whereas in this sentence, 슬퍼하다 is an action verb explaining your actions of sadness (i.e. mourning or grieving).

---

282   * The verb "사랑하다" (to love) is usually reserved for people or animals.

2 NARRATIVE

Passive forms like 좋다, 무섭다 and 슬프다 can **only** be used in the first-person.
Active forms like 좋아하다, 무서워하다 and 슬퍼하다 can be used in **either** first-person, second-person, or third-person narratives.

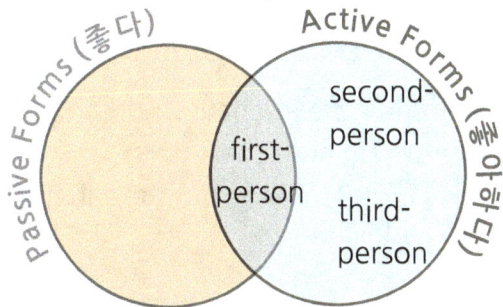

This means that, when talking in the first person (e.g. I/me/we), both forms can be used.

>	제가 좋아요.	I am good.
>	제가 사과를 좋아해요.	I like apples.
>	저는 바늘이 무서워요.	Needles are scary to me.
>	저는 바늘을 무서워해요.	I fear needles.
>	우리가 슬퍼요.	We are sad.
>	제 불행을 슬퍼해요.	I feel sorry for my misfortune.

However, when talking in the second or third person (you/they/he/she/it), you should active verbs. I.e. when talking about the feelings of someone else, it is incorrect to use the passive form of the verb.

>	사라는 빵을 좋아해요.	Sara likes bread.
>	사라는 빵이 좋아요.	Third-person narratives should use 좋아해요.
>	톰이 거미를 무서워해요.	Tom is scared of spiders.
>	톰이 거미가 무서워요.	Third-person narratives should use 무서워해요.
>	강아지가 슬퍼해요.	The puppy is sad.
>	강아지가 슬퍼요.	Third-person narratives should use 슬퍼해요.

APPENDIX

Small Numbers in Korean

Vocabulary list

There are actually two number systems in Korean - native Korean numbers (from traditional Korean) and sino-Korean numbers (from Chinese characters).
They are both written the same way, (1, 2, 3, ... etc.) but they are pronounced differently and used for different things.

NATIVE KOREAN NUMBERS		SINO-KOREAN NUMBERS	
NUMBER	PRONUNCIATION	NUMBER	PRONUNCIATION
1	하나	1	일
2	둘	2	이
3	셋	3	삼
4	넷	4	사
5	다섯	5	오
6	여섯	6	육
7	일곱	7	칠
8	여덟	8	팔
9	아홉	9	구
10	열	10	십
11	열하나	11	십일
12	열둘	12	십이
13	열셋	13	십삼
14	열넷	14	십사

Used for: ages, counting things in small quantities, and the time (in hours).

Used for: dates, money, the time (in minutes), addresses, phone numbers, and counting things in large quantities.

Note: "하나," "둘" "셋" and "넷" are written this way in their "dictionary form," but when used in a sentence to count things they become; "한," "두," "세" and "네" respectively.

Large Numbers in Korean

Vocabulary list

NATIVE KOREAN NUMBERS	
NUMBER	**LETTERS**
10	열
20	스물
30	서른
40	마흔
50	쉰
60	예순
70	일흔
80	여든
90	아흔
99	아흔 아홉

SINO-KOREAN NUMBERS	
NUMBER	**LETTERS**
10	십
20	이십
30	삼십
40	사십
50	오십
60	육십
70	칠십
80	팔십
90	구십
100	백
500	오백
560	오백육십
687	육백팔십칠
1,000	천
1,400	천사백
1,920	천구백이십
1,103	천백삼
10,000	만
50,740	오만 칠백사십
100,000	백만

Native Korean numbers aren't used above 99. For numbers above 99, use sino-Korean numbers.

The native Korean numbers shown above are most commonly used when talking about one's age.

For example:
Eighteen: 열 여덟 살
Twenty-one: 스물 한 살
Thirty-three: 서른 세 살

Note: "스물" becomes "스무" when it appears directly before a counter. E.g. "스무 살" 20 years old. But "스물 한 살" is 21 years old. "살" is the counter for age in Korean (see next page).

Korean Counters

Vocabulary list

Another important thing to know about Korean numbers is they use counters. These are similar to the English; "one **head** of lettuce" or "two **loaves** of bread." In Korean, these counters come after the noun. Here are some common counters:

COUNTER	USED FOR	EXAMPLE	MEANING
마리	animals	강아지 한 **마리**	one dog
개	things/objects	자동차 두 **개**	two cars
명	people	사람 세 **명**	three people
권	books	책 네 **권**	four books
병	bottles	물 다섯 **병**	five bottles of water
벌	clothing	바지 여섯 **벌**	six pairs of pants
켤레	pairs of things	신발 일곱 **켤레**	seven pairs of shoes
조각	slices/pieces	피자 여덟 **조각**	eight slices of pizza
시	time (hours)	아홉시	nine o'clock
살	age	열살	ten years old

When numbers are small (less than ten) it's common to use native Korean numbers.
Use sino-Korean numbers for large numbers.

NATURAL WORD ORDER
In English, the most natural word order is: number + counter + noun   e.g. three bottles of wine
In Korean, the most natural word order is: **noun + number + counter**   e.g. 와인 세 병

NUMBERS VERSUS LETTERS
The same as in English, numbers can be written with either words or numerals.

    강아지 한 마리   강아지 1 마리
    One dog   1 Dog

APPENDIX

Words for Times & Dates
Vocabulary list

Here we will give a quick overview of how to write times and dates in Korean.

NOUN	COUNTER	EXAMPLE	MEANING
Seconds	초	60초 [육십초]	60 seconds
Minutes	분	60분 [육십분]	60 minutes
Hours (o'clock)	시	5시 [다섯시]	5 o'clock
Hours (duration)	시간	3시간 [세시간]	3 hours
Days	일	7일 [칠일]	7 days
Months	개월	6개월 [육개월]	6 months
Years	년	2년 [이년]	two years

NUMBER+시	TIME (HOURS)
1시 [한시]	1 o'clock
2시 [두시]	2 o'clock
3시 [세시]	3 o'clock
4시 [네시]	4 o'clock
5시 [다섯시]	5 o'clock
6시 [여섯시]	6 o'clock
7시 [일곱시]	7 o'clock
8시 [여덟시]	8 o'clock
9시 [아홉시]	9 o'clock
10시 [열시]	10 o'clock
11시 [열하나시]	11 o'clock

NUMBER+시	TIME (HOURS)
12시 [열두시]	12 o'clock

DAY+요일	DAYS OF THE WEEK
일요일	Sunday
월요일	Monday
화요일	Tuesday
수요일	Wednesday
목요일	Thursday
금요일	Friday
토요일	Saturday

NUMBER+월	MONTH NAMES
일월	January
이월	February
삼월	March
사월	April
오월	May
유월	June
칠월	July
팔월	August
구월	September
시월	October
십일월	November
십이월	December

APPENDIX

Words for People
Vocabulary list

The culture around people's names is different in Korean. There are many ways to call people in Korean, without needing to say or know their name, or in place of "you." Here is a list of common terms:

CATEGORY	WORD	MEANING
General	아줌마	Middle-aged woman/"auntie"
General	아저씨	Middle-aged man/"uncle"
General	아가씨	Young lady
General	꼬마	Little kid/little boy
Familial	어머니 / 엄마	Mother / Mom
Familial	아버지 / 아빠	Father / Dad
Familial	동생	Younger sibling
Familial	여동생	Younger sister
Familial	남동생	Younger brother
Familial	언니	Older sister (for girls)
Familial	누나	Older sister (for boys)
Familial	오빠	Older brother (for girls)
Familial	형	Older brother (for boys)
Familial	고모/이모	Aunt (paternal/maternal)
Familial	삼촌	Uncle
Familial	할머니	Grandmother
Familial	할아버지	Grandfather
Familial	사촌	Cousin
Relationship	남자친구	Boyfriend
Relationship	여자친구	Girlfriend

APPENDIX

CATEGORY	WORD	MEANING
Relationship	남편	Husband
Relationship	아내	Wife
Relationship	연인	One's lover/significant other
Relationship	선배	One's senior (at school or work)
Relationship	후배	One's junior (at school or work)
Work/Occupation	회장님	CEO/Boss
Work/Occupation	사장님	Boss/owner
Work/Occupation	부장님	Team leader/manager

Note: this is not a complete list. There are many, many, many, Korean titles. Especially for family members. These are just some of the common ones to get you started. Check online if you wish to see more.

Honorific Vocabulary

Vocabulary list

REGULAR NOUN	HONORIFIC NOUN	MEANING
집	댁	house
이름	성함	name
나이	연세	age
생일	생신	birthday
우리	저희	we
밥	식사	rice/a meal

REGULAR VERB	HONORIFIC VERB	MEANING
보다	뵙다	to see/meet
말하다	말씀하다	to say/speak
먹다	드시다	to eat
마시다	드시다	to drink
물어보다	여쭈다	to ask
배가고프다	시장하시다	to be hungry
주다	드리다	to give
있다	계시다	to be somewhere/exist
죽다	돌아가시다	to die/pass on
자다	주무시다	to sleep
아프다	편찮으시다	to be hurt/in pain

Note: the tables above contain some common honorific vocabulary but it is not a complete list. Check online for more.

Common Expressions

Common sayings & expressions in Korean

EXPRESSION	MEANING	EXPRESSION	MEANING
안녕하세요	Hello	실례합니다	Excuse me. (Sorry for the inconvenience)
여보세요	Hello (on the phone)	좋은 아침이에요.	Good morning.
만나서 반가워요.	It's nice to meet you.	밥 먹었어요?	How are you?
안녕히가세요	Goodbye (when they are **leaving**)	잘 지냈어요?	How've you been?
안녕히계세요	Goodbye (when they are **staying**)	오랜만이에요.	It's been a while!
다음에 봐요!	See you next time!	화이팅!/파이팅!	You can do it!/Good luck!
감사합니다	Thank you	건배!/짠!	Cheers! (drinks)
아니에요.	Not at all/you're welcome.	잘 먹겠습니다	Enjoy the meal.
미안합니다.	I'm sorry.	잘 먹었습니다	Thank you for the meal.
몰라요.	I don't know.	좋은 하루 보내세요	Have a good day.
한국어 못 해요.	I don't speak Korean.	축하해요	Congratulations.
한국어를 조금만 해요.	I only speak a little bit of Korean.	걱정하지 마세요.	Don't worry.
천천히 말해 주세요.	Please speak slowly.	얼마예요?	How much is it?
뭐라고 했어요?	What did you say?	X 주세요.	Please give me X.
다시 말해 주세요	Please say it again.	괜찮아요	I'm okay.
적어 주세요.	Please write it down.	좋아요	It's good/I like it
잠시만요. 잠깐만요.	Just a moment.	아파요	I'm sick/hurt
		도와 주세요	Please help me
		배고파요	I'm hungry
저기요!	Excuse me. (Over here!)	이거 뭐예요?	What is this?

ㄷ Irregular

Irregular verb conjugations

Some verbs that end in "ㄷ" are irregular verbs. We will introduce some of these verbs and briefly explain how to conjugate them.

WHEN THIS CHANGE OCCURS
This change occurs for **some** verbs that end in a ㄷ final consonant. This means the verb has a ㄷ on the **bottom** of the syllable. For example: "듣다," and "걷다."
When adding a verb conjugation that starts with a vowel sound, the "ㄷ" turns in to a "ㄹ."
The rest of the conjugation follows as usual. For example:

    (!) 듣다 + ~아/어요   →   들어요   (subj. listens)
    (!) 걷다 + ~아/어요   →   걸어요   (subj. walks)
    (!) 묻다 + ~아/어요   →   물어요   (subj. asks)

WHEN THIS CHANGE DOES NOT OCCUR
1 If the verb conjugation you are adding starts with a consonant sound. For example:

    듣다 + ~는 것   →   듣는 것
    듣다 + ~(스)ㅂ니다   →   듣습니다

2 When it's not an irregular verb. Some verbs ending in "ㄷ" are not irregular verbs, and they conjugate the same as other verbs. For example:

    믿다 + ~아/어요   →   믿어요   (믿다, "to believe" is not an irregular verb)
    받다 + ~아/어요   →   받아요   (받다, "to receive" is not an irregular verb)

{ Verbs that undergo the ㄷ irregular conjugation will be marked with a (!) symbol in this book. }

ㅅ Irregular
Irregular verb conjugations

Some verbs that end in "ㅅ" are irregular verbs. We will introduce some of these verbs and briefly explain how to conjugate them.

WHEN THIS CHANGE OCCURS
This change occurs for **some** verbs that end in a ㅅ final consonant. This means the verb has a ㅅ on the **bottom** of the syllable. For example: "낫다," and "붓다."
When adding a verb conjugation that starts with a vowel sound, the "ㅅ" disappears. But the ~아/어/요 part is still added. For example:

    (!) **낫다** + ~아/어요   →   나아요   (subj. is better)
    (!) **붓다** + ~아/어요   →   부어요   (subj. is swollen)
    (!) **긋다** + ~아/어요   →   그어요   (subj draws)

Note: the ~아/어 part is always written on its own with ㅅ irregular verb conjugations. For example, 붓다 becomes 부어요 (not 붜요).

WHEN THIS CHANGE DOES NOT OCCUR
1 If the verb conjugation you are adding starts with a consonant sound. For example:
    낫다 + ~(스)ㅂ니다   →   낫습니다
    붓다 + ~는 것   →   붓는 것

2 When it's not an irregular verb. Some verbs ending in "ㅅ" are not irregular verbs, and they conjugate the same as other verbs. For example:
    씻 + ~아/어요   →   씻어요   (씻다, "to wash" is not an irregular verb)
    웃다 + ~아/어요   →   웃어요   (웃다, "to smile/laugh" is not an irregular verb)

Knowing which verbs are regular and irregular will come with time and practice!

으 Irregular

Irregular verb conjugations

Verbs that end in "으" are irregular verbs. We will introduce some of these verbs and briefly explain how to conjugate them.

WHEN THIS CHANGE OCCURS

This change occurs for verbs that end in the "으" vowel sound.
When adding a verb conjugation that starts with a vowel sound, the following changes occur:
1 The "으" disappears.
2 Add ~아/어요, but it is based on the vowel sound **from the second-to-last syllable.**

Note: if there is no second-to-last syllable because the verb is only one syllable long, then add ~어요.

(!) **쓰다** + ~아/어요 →	써요	(subj. uses/writes)
(!) **크다** + ~아/어요 →	커요	(subj. is tall)
(!) **아프다** + ~아/어요 →	아파요	(subj. is hurt)
(!) **바쁘다** + ~아/어요 →	바빠요	(subj. is busy)
(!) **슬프다** + ~아/어요 →	슬퍼요	(subj. is sad)

WHEN THIS CHANGE DOES NOT OCCUR

If the verb conjugation you are adding starts with a consonant sound. For example:

아프다 + ~(스)ㅂ니다 →	아픕니다
쓰다 + ~고 싶다 →	쓰고 싶다
쓰다 + ~는 것 →	쓰는 것
바쁘다 + ~(으)면 →	바쁘면

{ Verbs that undergo the 으 Irregular conjugation will be marked with a (!) symbol. }

ㄹ Irregular

Irregular verb conjugations

Verbs that end in "르" are irregular verbs. We will introduce some of these verbs and briefly explain how to conjugate them.

WHEN THIS CHANGE OCCURS
This change occurs for verbs that end in the "르" syllable.
When adding a verb conjugation that starts with a vowel sound, the following steps occur:
1 The "으" is dropped, leaving just ㄹ
2 Add a ㄹ to the bottom of the previous syllable
3 Add ~아/어요 depending on the vowel sound of the second-to-last syllable.

    (!) 다르다 + ~아/어요 →   달라요   (subj. is different)
    (!) 부르다 + ~아/어요 →   불러요   (subj. is called)
    (!) 고르다 + ~아/어요 →   골라요   (subj. chooses)
    (!) 모르다 + ~아/어요 →   몰라요   (subj. doesn't know)
    (!) 누르다 + ~아/어요 →   눌러요   (subj. presses)

WHEN THIS CHANGE DOES NOT OCCUR
If the verb conjugation you are adding starts with a consonant sound. For example:

    다르다 + ~(스)ㅂ니다   →   다릅니다
    누르다 + ~고 싶다   →   누르고 싶다
    고르다 + ~는 것   →   고르는 것

{ *Verbs that undergo the 르 irregular conjugation will be marked with a (!) symbol.* }

ㄹ Irregular

Irregular verb conjugations

Verbs that end in "ㄹ" are irregular verbs. We will introduce some of these verbs and briefly explain how to conjugate them.

WHEN THIS CHANGE OCCURS

This change occurs for verbs that end in the final consonant "ㄹ"
When adding a verb conjugation that starts with either "ㄴ," "ㅂ," or "ㅅ," the "ㄹ" disappears.

    (!) **살다** + ~는 것   →   사는 것
    (!) **알다** + ~는 것   →   아는 것
    (!) **만들다** + ~세요   →   만드세요
    (!) **울다** + ~(스)ㅂ니다   →   웁니다

WHEN THIS CHANGE DOES NOT OCCUR

If the verb conjugation you are adding starts with something other than "ㄴ," "ㅂ," or "ㅅ."

    살다 + ~아/어요   →   살아요
    만들다 + ~고 싶다   →   만들고 싶다
    알다 + ~아/어요   →   알아요

{ *Verbs that undergo the ㄹ irregular conjugation will be marked with a (!) symbol.* }

Thank you!

If you have time, **please review** our book on our website or on Amazon.
Your feedback means a lot to us!
And your review helps other Korean learners out there decide
if this book is a good fit for them.
감사합니다!

From Gooseapple Books

More Books
FROM GOOSEAPPLE BOOKS

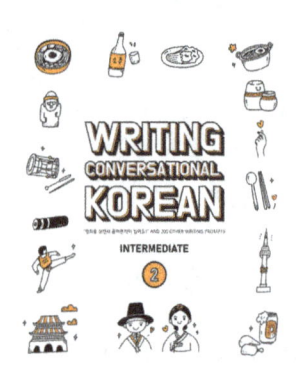

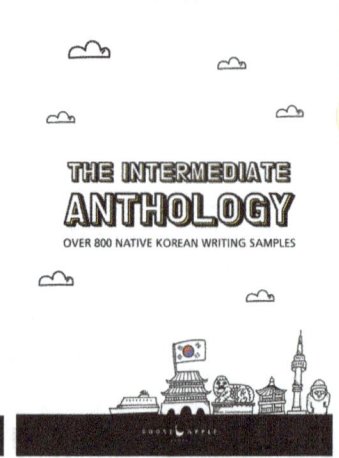

Writing Conversational Korean: Book One
" 코를 골아요?"
and 200 other writing prompts

Writing Conversational Korean: Book Two
"영화를 보면서 울어 본 적이 있어요?"
and 200 other writing prompts

1000 Korean Prompts
For Writing & Speaking

The Intermediate Anthology
Over 800 Native Korean Writing Samples

For more information, check out the books on our website: www.gooseapplebooks.com

www.ingramcontent.com/pod-product-compliance
Lightning Source LLC
Chambersburg PA
CBHW081707100526
44590CB00022B/3691